Translation and Religion

TOPICS IN TRANSLATION
Series Editors: Susan Bassnett, *University of Warwick, UK*
Edwin Gentzler, *University of Massachusetts, Amherst, USA*
Editor for Translation in the Commercial Environment:
Geoffrey Samuelsson-Brown, University of Surrey, UK

Other Books in the Series

Linguistic Auditing
Nigel Reeves and Colin Wright
Culture Bumps: An Empirical Approach to the Translation of Allusions
Ritva Leppihalme
Constructing Cultures: Essays on Literary Translation
Susan Bassnett and André Lefevere
The Pragmatics of Translation
Leo Hickey (ed.)
Practical Guide for Translators (3rd edition)
Geoffrey Samuelsson-Brown
Written in the Language of the Scottish Nation
John Corbett
'Behind Inverted Commas': Translation and Anglo-German Cultural Relations in the Nineteenth Century
Susanne Stark
The Rewriting of Njáls Saga: Translation, Ideology, and Icelandic Sagas
Jón Karl Helgason
Time Sharing on Stage: Drama Translation in Theatre and Society
Sirkku Aaltonen
Translation and Nation: A Cultural Politics of Englishness
Roger Ellis and Liz Oakley-Brown (eds)
The Interpreter's Resource
Mary Phelan
Annotated Texts for Translation: English–German
Christina Schäffner with Uwe Wiesemann
Contemporary Translation Theories (2nd edition)
Edwin Gentzler
Literary Translation: A Practical Guide
Clifford E. Landers
Translation-mediated Communication in a Digital World
Minako O'Hagan and David Ashworth
Frae Ither Tongues: Essays on Modern Translations into Scots
Bill Findlay (ed.)
Practical Guide for Translators (4th edition)
Geoffrey Samuelsson-Brown
Cultural Encounters in Translation from Arabic
Said Faiq (ed.)
Translation, Linguistics, Culture: A French-English Handbook
Nigel Armstrong

For more details of these or any other of our publications, please contact:
Multilingual Matters, Frankfurt Lodge, Clevedon Hall,
Victoria Road, Clevedon, BS21 7HH, England
http://www.multilingual-matters.com

TOPICS IN TRANSLATION 28
Series Editors: Susan Bassnett, *University of Warwick* and
Edwin Gentzler, *University of Massachusetts, Amherst*

Translation and Religion

Holy Untranslatable?

Edited by
Lynne Long

MULTILINGUAL MATTERS LTD
Clevedon • Buffalo • Toronto

Library of Congress Cataloging in Publication Data
Translation and Religion: Holy Untranslatable?/Edited by Lynne Long, 1st ed.
Topics in Translation: 28
Includes bibliographical references and index.
1. Translating and interpreting. 2. Language and languages–Religious aspects.
3. Language and culture. 4. Religion and culture. I. Long, Lynne. II. Series.
P306.2.T7364 2005
418'.02–dc22 2004022673
A catalog record for this book is available from the Library of Congress.

British Library Cataloguing in Publication Data
A catalogue entry for this book is available from the British Library.

ISBN 1-85359-817-8 (hbk)
ISBN 1-85359-816-X (pbk)
ISBN 1-85359-818-6 (electronic)

Multilingual Matters Ltd
UK: Frankfurt Lodge, Clevedon Hall, Victoria Road, Clevedon BS21 7HH.
USA: UTP, 2250 Military Road, Tonawanda, NY 14150, USA.
Canada: UTP, 5201 Dufferin Street, North York, Ontario M3H 5T8, Canada.

Typeset by Wordworks Ltd.
Printed and bound in Great Britain by the Cromwell Press Ltd.

Contents

Chapter 1

Introduction: Translating Holy Texts

LYNNE LONG

Motives for translating holy texts have been many and various, ranging from the evangelical to the curious, the subversive to the celebratory. But what exactly is it that defines a text as holy? And what is it about that holiness that makes translation difficult or even impossible? And when the impossible necessity of translation is forced on us, how do translators go about it?

In the 21st century it is politically and socially impossible to ignore holy texts from other cultures. The writings of postcolonial critics, such as Homi Bhabha and Tejaswini Niranjana, and of systems theorists, such as Itamar Even-Zohar and Gideon Toury, have been used as frameworks within which to discuss issues arising from the translation of holy texts. Postcolonial criticism has been one of the tools used for understanding the complexity of translating religious texts into colonised cultures. Bhabha, for example, has coined the term 'evangelical colonialism' (Bhabha, 1994: 34) to refer to processes of ideological and religious colonisation by imperial powers. Systems theory is particularly useful for understanding the position of translated holy texts in other cultures. Even-Zohar uses the term 'cultural interference' (Even-Zohar, 2001: section 1) to refer to the domestication and absorption by the target culture of parts of the source society's cultural repertoire. With the rise in migration and diasporas, holy texts are increasingly coming into contact with other cultures and becoming a means of introducing different religious ideas to new audiences. Bhabha's and Even-Zohar's conceptual terms give scholars a critical vocabulary with which to articulate such linguistic and cultural confrontations.

Any cultural contact, 'interference' or exchange requires translation, particularly in the area of what each culture holds as sacred or holy. But the holy resists translation, since the space it needs in the target language is often already occupied; available vocabulary is already culturally loaded with indigenous referents. The task of this book is to try to make sense of a cultural interface that requires translation, but at the same time defies it. The search for a new spirituality, the pursuit of truth or simply a dissatisfaction with organised religion have made alternative holy texts the subject of scrutiny over past centuries. Today the necessity to understand how other cultures work in order to live peacefully together makes them required reading and their sympathetic translation crucial.

Translated texts of all kinds, and particularly holy texts, have helped to shape cultures throughout history. The cultural heritage of Europe and the United States has been fashioned almost exclusively by the influence of Judeo-Christianity until the present century. As a consequence, translation theorists who work in this geographical area are used to regarding scripture as synonymous with the Bible. It is interesting that some of the most influential pieces of 20th-century writing about translation use as a metaphor for translation a story from the Old Testament of the Bible. The Book of Genesis Chapter 11:1-9 tells how the people of Earth originally belonged to one tribe and spoke one language. When they began to build a tower to consolidate their power, God confounded this activity by causing confusion, making them all speak different languages.

In *'Des Tours de Babel'* Jacques Derrida, French philosopher and deconstructor of philosophical texts, engages with the legacy of Babel. In Derrida's reading, the divine dismantling of both the tower and the single language implies the impossibility of reconstructing either (Derrida, 1985: 171). Conversely the creation of many languages makes translation necessary. As Derrida says, God 'at the same time imposes and forbids translation (Derrida, 1985: 170).' The confusion caused by the events at Babel reflects the confusions surrounding both the act and the processes of translation. The translator works to restore communication when God has decreed it should be destroyed, thereby working against God. There is confusion also in the plurality of languages making up God's text: confusion in the multiplicity of meanings and interpretations to be gathered from languages. Plurality is illustrated in the many possible readings of the French words of Derrida's essay title *'Des Tours de Babel'*, usually left untranslated and thereby validating many of his claims. Since the plural form of the definite article obscures the gender of the noun, *'des tours'* can mean 'some tricks', 'some turns' or 'some trips around' in addition to the primary meaning of 'of the towers', 'about towers' or 'some towers'. Then the sound of *'des tours'* is the same as *'détours'*, deviation from the path or even deconstruction of the tower. Is this why there is so much controversy about holy text translation? There are so many possible interpretations of the truth, so many possible versions of God's words. Is this why holy texts resist translation?

What is interesting about Derrida's perspective from the point of view of holy texts is his idea that God effectively resisted the imposition of a single power and a single language (and a single truth?). Babel therefore obliges us to confront a multiplicity of interpretations, to address languages and holy texts other than our own if we are to see a complete world picture: this collection of essays is an attempt to do that. We may still be confused as to whether Babel validates or even celebrates translation as an activity; what we do know is that there exists the possibility of multiple translations of God's text(s) and that these will be imperfect. We can rely only on Augustine's optimistic comment 'in fact this diversity has helped rather than impeded understanding, if readers would only be discerning' (Gavigan, 1966: 74).

In the same article, Derrida critiques Walter Benjamin's '*Die Aufgabe des Übersetzers*' ('The Task of the Translator') and challenges his idea that the translation of poetic or sacred texts is not always about communication with the reader. Benjamin sees translatability as one of the inherent qualities of a classic text, since translation ensures a text's afterlife and therefore its survival. A work that can be identified as a classic has within it the potential to be translated. Translation is crucial to the idea of the survival through time of any text, but becomes particularly important when the text relies for its status on its ancient authority, as most holy texts do. Benjamin identifies an unsettling characteristic of the translation process.'In its afterlife', he says,' ... the original undergoes a change' (Benjamin, 1968: 73). Holy text translators looking for divine guidance in the texts they translate do not want to enter into the idea of change through translation.

George Steiner, on the other hand, sees translation'as implicit in the most rudimentary communication' (Steiner, 1998: 496). Steiner's seminal work *After Babel* systematically explores translation as a process of interpreting and understanding against a background of complex linguistic interplay. The hermeneutic motion, the process of transferring meaning, the challenge of Babel, is exposed with all its complications and pitfalls. Steiner's view of Babel's legacy does not make easy reading for the holy text translator as it confirms the multiplicity of possible interpretations. What it does give is support for a contextual approach - linguistic analysis and cultural context combined. At the end of the book, Steiner reflects on what he calls the'internationalisation' of English, in other words English used synthetically as a language of communication but dislocated from its cultural base. The same kind of dislocation inevitably occurs with ancient holy texts when translated, since the language in which they were written is removed from its original setting and from all the accompanying referents and associations of memory and cultural context. Restoring the context is one of the most difficult things for a translator to do. Steiner is ambivalent about solutions to this particular translation problem. 'It would be ironic,' he says, 'if the answer to Babel were pidgin and not Pentecost' (Steiner, 1998: 495).

Derrida's philosophical ideas on language, Benjamin's notion of translation as afterlife and Steiner's conception of meaning and understanding in relation to translation, all directly or indirectly inform many of the articles in this volume. Their ideas have had considerable influence on the direction that translation studies as a discipline have taken, and have proved a useful framework against which to set investigations into translation processes.

In the 21st century, translation models can no longer be confined to Christian cultures: in these times of global travel and cultural exchange, most societies have experienced the cultural interference that exposes and converts them to other ways of living and by extension to other scriptures. This interface is essential for the growth of a society; Even-Zohar (2001: 3) writes,'no culture could manage without interference at one time or another during its history'. Migration, displacement and colonisation have combined to upset geographical models of religious distribution and to bring a greater variety of holy texts to the attention of a wider audience. The physical translation of a community from one place to another eventually requires the translation of the community's holy texts into the host target language as generations integrate into the host society. Equally the missionary/colonising dynamic has resulted in translation in the opposite direction: texts imposed on the host language from outside.

At the same time, translation studies as a discipline has also taken directions in addition to the familiar linguistic models. Using as a basis language studies such as that of Noam Chomsky (1957) and E.C. Catford (1965), Eugene Nida developed a contextualised approach to holy text translation, offering what he first described as'dynamic equivalence' as a possible alternative to the old paradigm of word-for-word faithfulness to the source text. The concept of dynamic or functional equivalence as it came to be called, gave Nida's holy text translators the possibility of different routes through the cultural maze (Nida, 1964). The status of the text made functional equivalence in the context of Bible translation a step too far for some theological commentators such as David Cloud (2001), who were concerned with *auctoritas* and with authenticity. Nevertheless, the expansion of translation from linguistics into the realms of philosophy and cultural theory opened up new and useful perspectives.

The'cultural turn' in translation studies (Bassnett & Lefevere, 1990) expressed the realisation that linguistic models were insufficient to account for translation processes and altered the way that the translation of literary texts was approached by giving the cultural context at least equal footing with the linguistic context. Mary Snell-Hornby was foremost in putting forward the concept of interdisciplinarity in translation theory (Snell-Hornby, 1994, 1995, 1997). Linguistic theories had not provided satisfactory strategies to cope with areas such as the translation of metaphor or ideologically layered texts - areas that abound in holy texts. If communication of meaning is a priority, cultural equivalence may sometimes offer the best solution. Layers of exegesis accumulate over time in any canonical literary work; these are theologically entrenched in scripture. The change implied in translation cannot easily be made if a shift in interpretation is likely to follow. Moreover holy texts are attended by culturally or liturgically specific terms; these linguistic spaces are often already occupied in the target language. How then does the translator proceed without implying a distance from or closeness to the target language terms already in place?

The 'cultural turn' generated interest not only in contextualising translations but also in putting the act of translation itself into a social and literary context. The ongoing development of polysystem research by Even-Zohar (1978, 2000, 2001) supported and refined by Gideon Toury (1997) examines translation as a socio-cultural activity, a means of promoting a language of limited diffusion or of building up a culture, or both. Toury cites the early 20th-century example of the Friesians in the Netherlands whose focus on the marketability and status of desirable texts led them to translate the Bible and modern classics of children's literature as a first step towards renewing and elevating Friesian culture. There are other, earlier examples. It can be no coincidence that both the Bible and Boethius' *Philosophiae Consolationis* (a high-status Latin text) were translated into Catalan (spoken in north-eastern Spain) between 1470 and 1480.

Scriptures are usually identified as central to their literary polysystem. Whether they are translations or not, they quickly assume the status of original. André Lefevere's early work on central texts and cultures (1992b: 71) and on patronage (1992a: 11) encouraged the closer investigation of issues such as the selection and marketing of texts, text ownership, publishers, authorship and copyright (Venuti, 1998a). Holy texts have the complication of institutional claims: the hierarchical structure supporting each religion expects to control the translation of its central text(s), at least in relation to their distribution among the faithful (Stine, 2004: 128–30). In 1963 during the Second Vatican Council when liturgy in the vernacular instead of Latin was approved for use in Catholic Churches, the International Commission on English in the Liturgy (ICEL) was formed. The members are appointed by the Vatican, which regularly issues documents advising on the manner of translating both the Scriptures and the Liturgy. Here is an extract from

Liturgicam Authenticam, a document on the use of the vernacular in the liturgy:

> ... it is to be kept in mind from the beginning that the translation of the liturgical texts of the Roman Liturgy is not so much a work of creative innovation as it is of rendering the original texts faithfully and accurately into the vernacular language. While it is permissible to arrange the wording, the syntax and the style in such a way as to prepare a flowing vernacular text suitable to the rhythm of popular prayer, the original text, in so far as possible, must be translated integrally and in the most exact manner, without omissions or additions in terms of their content, and without paraphrases or glosses. Any adaptation to the characteristics or the nature of the various vernacular languages is to be sober and discreet. (Vatican online; also on Adoremus, the website for the Society for the Renewal of the Sacred Liturgy)

The American Bible Society frequently engages with the theoretical and linguistic problems of translation, and is committed to 'providing translations of the Holy Scriptures that are faithful to the original wording of the original language Biblical texts' (American Bible Society online). The overriding concerns of both organisations are faithfulness to the original and doctrinal consistency. A new translation can be a serious means of challenging the orthodox readings of a holy text (Long, 2001: 141; Venuti, 1998a: 83) or the means of creating a new cultural identity through separation from the established traditions. Political correctness, racism, anti-establishment views, anti-feminism and many other areas of contention may be expressed through the choices available during the process of translation. Small wonder that hierarchies exert close control.

Not all holy texts come within institutional settings. Historically a proprietorial stance impeded both access and translation; in modern times this has in some cases been reduced and replaced by the vagaries of commerce and patronage in the shape of the publisher. The Internet has also to some extent militated against exclusivity. In many areas of religion, however, there remains the notion of an 'official' or 'authorised' version or translation of the relevant holy text. Approved or enthusiastic followers of the faith therefore perform translations for the faithful: academics perform them for their own research or as part of a programme initiated by a publisher ready to exploit a particular market.

Holy texts positioned on the periphery of a culture's literary polysystem tend to be treated with more latitude than those centrally placed, and receive correspondingly less attention in translation terms unless some specific reason arises. Political confrontation with nations of other religious beliefs or internal evangelisation might cause temporary interest in the translation and publication of relevant holy texts. The influx of refugees or migrants may be the future catalyst for the translation of formerly peripheral holy texts into the host language. The situation ebbs and flows through history as people migrate through the world. People have a tendency to be so closely bound up in what is happening in their small corner that they find it hard to relate to the shifts in other areas and it comes as something of a shock to confront different ideologies. The question of text ownership and authorship, its position in the source and target polysystem, the motive for translating, the translator's ideology, the way the text is marketed and its intended readership, all have a bearing on the way in which translation is approached.

Given the intricacies of the translation process, readers of holy texts need to be aware of the kinds of shifts and processes that may have taken place. Translation practitioners and theorists are in the unique position of being able to access the content of holy texts with some understanding of how translation procedure may have affected the interlingual transfer. All the contributors to this volume are involved in translation and in the study of holy texts as part or whole of their research programme. Their collected individual experiences provide insight into the complexities of holy text translation from which conclusions about the special nature of these texts and their translation strategies may be drawn.

This book is divided into two sections. The first part looks at broad issues and gives contextual framework to recurring themes. The second part takes specific case studies and develops more detailed argument against a background of shared practice.

Part 1: The Wider Picture

> Let the scriptures be your guide, therefore, in deciding what you must do and what you must abstain from. First learn the path of action, as the scriptures teach it. Then act accordingly. (Prabhavananda & Isherwood, 1944: 155)

Sri Krishna's advice to Arjuna in the above quotation from the Bhagavad Gītā would be considered equally pertinent to most other book-based religions. It underlines the idea that part of the exceptional nature of holy texts lies in their function as behaviour models for individuals, communities or whole cultures. As a result, their interpretation and by extension their translation is of serious consequence. Add to this the perception that scripture is divine revelation and we have the most compelling reasons for the translation process to be a serious and well-thought-out undertaking.

Given their unique combination of qualities, do we need to assign holy texts to a separate genre of their own? If the status of holiness is removed, all the familiar elements of literary texts remain exposed: narrative, history, poetry, proverb, dialogue, information. The overlay of divine authority makes translation more daring, and the overlay of exegesis makes it more difficult.

Christopher Shackle's long experience of texts sacred and secular moves from Greek through Arabic and Persian to Urdu and Punjabi. In his chapter 'From Gentleman's Outfitters to Hyperbazaar: A Personal Approach to Translating the Sacred', he reflects that he has come to align himself with the view 'that context rather than content makes the holy untranslatable'. This is to maintain that the intrinsic qualities of the text, whatever kind of text it is, remain the same, and what changes is the way in which it is received and employed by its readership. To take this argument one step further, the implication is that resistance to translation has more to do with control of interpretation than with any inherent textual untranslatability. Shackle continues the idea of context through the case study of the Adi Granth and the history of the approaches to its translation from the 19th century onwards.

If there is the possibility for translation in terms of the mechanisms necessary, the knowledge of all languages involved and a deep understanding of the text, the next question is whether translation of holy texts is permitted. Historically, translation has been used as a way to manipulate doctrine and shift exegesis (Lefevere, 1992b: 70, Long, 2001: 139), to reinterpret the text, or has been the means of rewriting the text for a different cultural context (Wright, 1990: 4). This latitude for change that becomes available through translation is not welcomed in a context where the aim is to discover and hold onto eternal truths. As a result translations of holy texts are often received with misgiving. The Qur'an, for example, is considered untranslatable from the original Arabic: vernacular versions are interpretations, representations, but are not the Qur'an itself (see Abdul-Raof's chapter in Section 2). The status of the divine word and fear of change or misinterpretation was for a long time a barrier to the translation of the Bible into the vernacular.

K. Onur Toker, whose background bridges philosophy and translation studies, argues very convincingly from a philosophical standpoint that translation, interpretation and speaking with tongues is not only permitted but is necessary for the building up of the house of God. In the second essay, 'Prophesy and Tongues: St Paul, Interpreting and Building the House', he uses the writings of Paul and the arguments of Derrida and Steiner to examine a theme that recurs in several other articles in this volume: that of the 'impossible necessity' of translation after Babel.

It is important for readers of holy texts to be aware that the words they are using as spiritual guidance and rules for living have undergone at least one and usually several translation processes. The Old Testament moved from Hebrew to Greek to Latin before it was transferred into other vernaculars: Buddhist texts moved from Sanskrit and Pāli, to Tibetan, Chinese and Japanese before being translated into other Asian and European languages. Moreover language change is not the only intervention that has taken place: selection of the canon, use of source text(s) and the process of editing have also been part of that transfer system.

Kate Crosby, expert in Sanskrit and Pāli Buddhist literature, reminds us in Chapter 4 'What Does Not Get Translated in Buddhist Studies', of the consequence of an incomplete canon and how the overall view of an emergent religion is shaped by the nature of material available. This might cause readers to reflect that editing and selection decisions made centuries ago when the Christian canon was newly gathered may have channelled reception in a particular direction. Access to forgotten or previously untranslated texts may require an adjustment to the overall perspective. Witness for example the impact of the discovery of the Gnostic manuscripts in the Egyptian desert in the 20th century (Pagels, 1979) or the finding of the Dead Sea Scrolls (Campbell, 1996, 2000). Crosby also points out the part that patronage and linguistic expertise play in the commissioning of translations, a subject briefly touched upon in some of the other papers and in the work of Lefevere (1992a: 11).

The texts of emergent or minority religions have peripheral status in the host literary polysystem for two reasons, because they are translated and because they serve a minority (Even-Zohar, 1978 in Venuti, 2000: 192). Sponsorship for the translation of these texts is difficult to obtain while they remain in a peripheral position, as publishers need to translate and print what they can reasonably expect to sell. Mainstream religious texts on the other hand have a central position in the social and literary polysystems of their own culture. This central position has several consequences: patronage is available, translations are carefully scrutinised, and the translated text is often given the status of an original in spite of its linguistic pedigree. Many people in Britain and the United States, for example, regard the 1611 King James Version of the Bible as an original in the sense of having best authority and authenticity, even though it was not the first rendering in English and there have been other translations since. The preface writer of the King James version appreciates the central position of the Bible in English culture and the sensitive nature of the translation process when he writes:

> ... whosoever attempteth any thing for the publike (specially if it appertaine to Religion, and to the opening and clearing of the word of God) the same setteth himselfe upon a stage to be glouted upon by every evil eye, yea, he casteth himselfe headlong upon pikes, to be gored by every sharpe tongue. For he that medleth with mens Religion in any part, medleth with their custome, nay, with their freehold; and though they finde no content in that which they have, yet they cannot abide to heare of altering. (Rhodes & Lupas, 1997: 11)

It would not be overstating the case to say that scriptural movement between cultures has been a major source of development in translation theory. Missionaries of every belief system were forced to address issues of linguistic transfer and to evolve strategies for bridging what Arthur Wright, referring to the domestication of Indian philosophy into Chinese society, calls 'the breadth of the cultural gulf to be overcome' (Wright, 1990: 7). These strategies are part of the history of translation and still inform contemporary debate. In the 4th century, Tao-an and his successor Kumarajiva were developing policies for translating the Sanskrit Buddhist texts into Chinese (Wright, 1990: 40) and in letters to his friends Jerome was confiding the problems he was having translating the Bible (Schaff & Wace, 1979: 113). In the 12th century, Robert Retenensis translated the Qur'an into Latin so that it could be studied by Christian theologians, and this version was printed in 1543 with a contribution to the commentary from Martin Luther and Philipp Melanchthon among others (Delisle & Woodsworth, 1995: 179). Luther's own translation strategies for 'Germanising' the Bible appeared in his *Sendbrief vom Dolmetschen* of 1530 (Luther, 1530/1940).

The next three chapters in this anthology set particular holy texts into historical translation contexts and show what effect this narrative has on the strategies employed. Holy texts belong to and are used by a much wider variety of people than other literary or historical texts. There is a far greater range of reader in terms of age, status, sophistication and nationality; there are questions of oral and written versions, of private and public use.

Leonard Greenspoon's chapter 'Perspectives on Jewish Translations of the Hebrew Bible' traces the history of Jewish translation of the Hebrew Bible into English by diasporic communities. He outlines the tension between translations that prioritise the source text and those in which the target text remains the most important. The theoretical ideas contextualising his argument are to be found in Schleiermacher's early 19th-century idea that the translator either moves the reader towards the writer or the writer towards the reader (Schleiermacher, 1813, reprinted in Schulte & Biguenet, 1992: 42). Venuti's development (Venuti, 1995) and extension of

Schleiermacher (Venuti, 1998) underpins a perennial dilemma for the translator: whether to domesticate or foreignise. Greenspoon also points out the different functions of the translations (see Vermeer, 1989) and their pivotal role in diasporic communities.

Will Johnson, in Chapter 6 'How Should We Translate Classical Hindu Texts?' continues the discussion about foreignisation and domestication as strategies, but this time in relation to classical Hindu texts, more particularly the Bhagavad Gītā. Some of the points made here about translating the classics echo Walter Benjamin's 1929 preface (already mentioned above) to his own translation of Baudelaire, *Die Aufgabe des Übersetzers* (reproduced in Venuti, 2000: 15) in which he talks about translatability as one of the inherent qualities of a work of art. Benjamin's premise is that the *Überleben* (the survival) and the *Fortleben* (the afterlife) of a classic depend on translation, whether interlingual or intralingual according to Jacobson's categories (Jacobson, 1959).

The public use of holy texts is taken up in Adriana Şerban's chapter, 'Archaising versus Modernising in English Translations of the Orthodox Liturgy'. She sets the diasporic Orthodox liturgy in a historical context and discusses the linguistic features that reflect current translation strategies. Her material covers the oral dimension of scripture in its active form and exposes the problems of translating for a wide community with differing expectations. The question of 'religious' language is a theme that runs through many of the chapters in different forms: here the discussion is about archaising in homage to the status of the text.

The final chapter in Part 1 addresses contemporary approaches to Bible translation from the point of view of translation theory. Peter Kirk's 'Holy Communicative: Current Approaches to Bible Translation Worldwide' gives a historical account of translation studies in a Biblical context and proceeds to describe and analyse the main threads of contemporary strategy including the formal versus functional equivalence debate and the problem of what is termed 'authenticity'. This chapter reflects the energy of debate currently taking place in the field of Bible translation today and is complemented by David Burke's chapter in Part 2.

Fierce argument about translating holy texts raged in 16th-century England (Bruce, 1961; Long, 2001; Robinson, 1954), much as it does in the modern-day United States. The difference between argument today and polemic in the 16th century is that modern technology has been the means of broadening discussion - many more people have something to say about the theory and practice of scripture translation. Much published work on translation now also appears on web sites and a search of the main bookshop sites for literature about translating the Bible turns up all kinds of relevant titles. There are aids for translators (Nida, 1959, 1974; Gutt, 2000a; Bible Society and SIL international publications), debates on gender-inclusive language (Carson, 1998; Polythress & Gruden, 2000; Strauss, 1998), hints on how to choose a translation, and issues of formal versus functional equivalence (Duthie, 1995; Ryken, 2002). There are numerous online resources for comparing different versions of the Bible, or for comparative translation analysis (see Realms of Faith). These web sites are being developed and refined, offering excellent points of departure for research. In the second part of this volume we take up some of these issues in more detail.

Part 2: Specific Studies

In few other areas of translation is the issue of language so important as in translating holy texts. The most immediate and pressing problem in view of the didactic function of many holy texts has always been to establish the hermeneutic content. Transfer between languages exposes the irreconcilable differences between linguistic systems: what can be expressed in one tongue cannot always be satisfactorily or meaningfully transferred into another. What is more worrying, the meaning of the source text in philosophical or theological writings may not always be apparent: early resistance to translation stemmed partly from uncertainty on this score. In this unpromising climate, the translation of holy texts often presents problems that may be resolved more easily by taking a holistic view of the source and looking at translation as first a process of understanding (Steiner, 1992: 1).

David Jasper covers exactly this context in the first chapter of this section, 'Settling Hoti's Business: The Impossible Necessity of Bible Translation'. Using a case study that has exercised the minds of linguists and theologians alike, he looks at strategies for solving hermeneutic puzzles presented in linguistic form. Different approaches to problem solving in these areas are very useful for the translator, since they often provide the catalyst needed to generate progress in translation techniques.

The second chapter, 'Sakya Paṇḍita on the Role of the Tibetan Scholar', continues the twin themes of linguistic difference and hermeneutic transfer. Jonathan Gold shows how the Tibetan teacher Sa-paṇ was keen to guide the interpreters of Buddhist holy texts around the pitfalls of linguistic errors of translation as early as the 13th century. The connection made by Sa-paṇ between translating and understanding is strong: he would have enjoyed reading George Steiner.

One of the things that keeps the translator in work is the changing nature of language. Language seems to regenerate and develop of its own volition despite efforts by institutions to curb its exuberance; linguistic and political fashions change and words fall in and out of favour. In Part 1, the contributors addressed the notion of archaic language; in Chapter 11, 'The Translation of the Hebrew Word 'ish in Genesis', David Burke gives us the background to a current language issue, that of 'inclusive' (Simon, 1996: 124) or 'gender neutral' language. He shows by detailed corpus analysis that perceptions of the ways translations are made are sometimes quite different from the reality. Applying linguistic methodology to an ideological problem in this way helps maintain a balanced and more scientific view of translation processes in what might otherwise be a more emotive context.

One of the common threads binding holy texts is that of their oral origin and their continued spoken use alongside the written form. Before literacy was widespread, narrative was relayed almost exclusively by word of mouth. Linguistic evidence of this phenomenon remains embedded in the early written texts of the Gospels. Preaching has long been used in many religions as a local means of communicating religious ideas. Buddhist scriptures were transmitted orally for the first 500 years and were written down only at the beginning of the Christian era (Conze, 1959: 11). The oral recitation and interpretation of Jewish scriptures has always been of major importance in the public liturgy. Islamic revelation took place orally; *al-qur'an* literally means a recitation (Dawood, 1966: 9).

Nile Green's case study, 'Oral Literature and the Suffis of Awrangabad', addresses precisely this dual aspect of holy texts. He investigates the power of the spoken word in the context of Sufi saints and relates the idea of recorded or remembered speech to the notion of faithfulness in texts. He reminds us that the movements of the sacred word from oral to written were also movements of translation. These observations might cause readers to reflect on the kind of faithfulness ascribed to what is considered to be divine utterance, if so many interventions have been made between ancient spoken word and modern listener.

Holy texts tend to be multifaceted, and function as literature, history, poetry, genealogy or philosophy as well as revelation. Their interpretation has a different perspective over time and varies according to the needs and cultural context of the interpreters. The function or *skopos* of their translation also varies according to the motive for translating. It may be simply for access or even as a language-learning tool, and as such translators may choose to proceed without reference to contemporary translation theories. For translations whose *skopos* includes use in a specifically religious context, there is always the requirement that, whatever language the text is converted to, the exegetical significance should remain constant.

The next chapter in this section, 'From Scriptorium to Internet: The Psalms of the St Alban's Psalter', details a very exact *skopos*, that of Internet presentation for use by both students and scholars of art history. Sue Niebrzydowski's brief was to translate the Latin of the Psalms for a modern audience in a way that made sense of the illuminations of the Albani text. The illuminators became for this purpose the interpreters of the text into another medium, which, as the translator outlines, had implications for the translation procedure.

The final two chapters are specifically related to cultural aspects of translation. This is not to say that culture and translation can ever be completely separated, only that these two chapters deal exclusively with the resistance of culture to translation. Chapter 15 is an essay by Hussein Abdul-Raof called 'Translating the Qur'an: Cultural Considerations'. Using examples from Arabic, he explains how cultural context impedes the transfer of metaphor, not only on a surface level where lexical equivalence is non-existent, but also at an exegetical level where religious concepts are explained by means of cultural referents.

Manuela Foiera's 'The Language of Soka Gakkai in Italy' approaches the same problem from the perspective of overlaying a new religion, Soka Gakkai Buddhism, on a culture where the linguistic space for expressing religious terms is already occupied by Catholicism. Technical language is exegetically specific in holy texts, but in this case even the basic religious items have already been appropriated by the incumbent religion. This is not a new problem for Buddhism, but this particular scenario also poses questions about national linguistic identity and religion and whether it is possible to be a first-generation Italian-speaking Buddhist, or English-speaking Muslim, and express religious ideas satisfactorily in one's native language.

Conclusion

What makes a text holy is how people use it, the status they give it and the significance it has for them. Different texts are holy to different cultures and central to different polysystems: translation shifts them into another set of systems, exposing them to another set of receivers. Understanding the function and status of a holy text in its source and target culture throws more light on the problems of translating it. The process does not always stop there, however, as the holy text may then be retranslated many times until one of its translations achieves the status of original.

The interdisciplinarity of translation studies is nowhere more evident than in the context of holy text translation. In this one volume the authors have addressed broad issues of historicity, linguistics, cultural theory, sociology, theology and philosophy as well as more specific cases of gender, art, metaphor, humour, status, editing, patronage and interpretation. Contributors have used a translation theory framework to bring together a variety of ideas and perspectives about translating holy texts in an attempt to decide whether translation of such complex literature is possible. Connections have been made between holy texts of different religions and similar problems identified in their translation. Although satisfactory solutions to these problems are not immediately apparent, the answer to the original question seems to be that holy text translation must be possible because it is happening. Whether it is permitted or not, it is necessary and difficult and will never be satisfactory to everyone.

Part 1

The Wider Picture

Chapter 2

From Gentlemen's Outfitters to Hyperbazaar: A Personal Approach to Translating the Sacred

CHRISTOPHER SHACKLE

The business of translating sacred texts is a serious one. Faith communities have always known this, and in the post-traditional circumstances in which most of us now find ourselves placed in one way or another, we can all recognise its great and continuing contribution to the development of one of the most important conditioning elements of contemporary consciousness. This is the diffused awareness on a hitherto unprecedented global scale of the manifold religious and spiritual heritage of the world's peoples, who in this postcolonial age also find themselves living in greater proximity to one another than ever before.

Sacred texts are rightly perceived to have a special character, defined on the one hand by their relationship to each other, on the other by their distinction from non-sacred texts (Ricoeur, 1995: 68–72). This distinction seemed so great to Cantwell Smith that, in his typically challenging *What is Scripture?*, he was led to suggest that scripture forms a distinguishable third literary mode alongside poetry and prose (Smith, 1993: 228, 362). We need not go quite as far as this in recognising the special position to which sacred texts are assigned by their inherent or ascribed claims to represent comprehensive systems of meaning on a scale unmatched by any other type of literary text. This comprehensive quality is recognised in the current fashion for paying attention to their non-textual character, in their oral, ritual and mantric dimensions. But since these elements are so much less susceptible to translation by conventional means, my emphasis in this chapter is upon sacred texts as written documents. Although it may be argued that a translation of a sacred text cannot hope to be successful without itself conveying something of the holy, there is after all a limit to the numbers of sign-systems that may be transferred by a single translation process.

When the strictly technical side of things is seen in this way, the difference between translating a sacred text and translating a secular text might be compared to singing oratorio rather than opera. Others who have shared my involvement in the translation of non-sacred as well as sacred texts will need little persuasion that both types need to be seen side by side. I will say more about this later in discussion of the translation of sacred texts from some non-Western languages. Fidelity versus freedom, the cultural contexts of originals and translations, the conditioned choices of formal as well as of linguistic reorganisation, especially the conditioned possibilities available to most academic translators whose literary sensibilities may not always match their linguistic and critical training – all these are issues to be faced by translators of sacred texts exactly as they are by all would-be translators of literary texts of any sort.

In the implications of their ambitions and in the scale and the intensity with which these are recognised, sacred texts are notably distinguished from other texts. I have come to align myself with the view that context rather than content makes the holy untranslatable. In reaching this recognition, I have been greatly helped by the development of modern translation studies, in particular the work done on post-colonial translation by writers such as Susan Bassnett and Harish Trivedi, Tejaswini Niranjana and Maria Tymoczko. The gift of the new discipline has been not so much assistance in the practicalities of translation as the enhancement of awareness of the processes involved, both at a systemic level and in terms of self-reflexivity of the context in which translators of the sacred operate. It is in this spirit that the present discussion is constructed around a series of personal reflections upon my own past and present experience of the business of translating sacred texts.

The Gentlemen's Outfitters

Let me begin by turning to the Biblical presence, since this must first require explicit and careful acknowledgement in any discussion of the translation of sacred texts in an English-dominated environment.

It is no part of my purpose to attempt an amateur recapitulation of the vast history of Biblical translation, although we should not overlook the unique power of each Testament individually or the Book as a whole to generate extreme fantasies of translation power. Take, for instance, the fabulous earthly reward said by the author of the *Letter of Aristeas* to have been bestowed by the King of Egypt on the first divinely-inspired translators, who turned the Hebrew Bible into the perfect rendering of the Septuagint: 'And he commanded that to each should be given three talents of silver and the slave who should hand it to him' (Thackeray, 1904: 51). Or in the case of the New Testament, large parts of which are the product of a multilingual environment, one might cite the persistent fantasy of reconstructive translation. This is a process by which an intensive study of the Gospels, coupled with an ample grasp of Syriac plus a good deal of inspiration, might hope to reconstruct the Aramaic originals of the *verba Jesu* that the evangelists record only in Greek, whether for scholarly purposes (see Black, 1998), or as inspirational Midrashic re-write (Douglas-Klotz, 1999). Or again, the miraculous power providentially bestowed on the 19th-century missionary Dr S.H. Kellogg, the future translator of the Bible into Hindi:

> On his first voyage to India, early in the sixties, just after leaving the American coast, the captain of the sailing vessel suddenly died. No other officer on board feeling competent for the responsible task, Dr Kellogg navigated the vessel to the mouth of the Hoogly with perfect success. And yet he had never specially studied navigation, but had devoted himself almost entirely to the elements of a clerical education. (Hooper, 1963: 56–7)

These, though, were wonders of which I knew nothing when I first encountered the phenomenon of the holy untranslatable. Let me take you metaphorically back to an old-fashioned gentlemen's outfitters, one of those establishments where young men were conservatively kitted out like their fathers and grandfathers, and describe to you my own initial experience of translating a sacred text. I can just find it in my heart today to be grateful for the some of the direct insights into tradition painfully gained at an English public school in the mid-1950s, when the Classical Upper Fifth's week began with the Monday morning Greek Testament class.

This class was quite divorced from the rest of our translation-intensive studies of non-sacred Greek and Latin literature (although I suppose the connection might have become apparent if I had followed some of my contemporaries into an Anglican theological college after an Oxbridge Classics degree). Our first text was the Epistle to the Hebrews, doubtless chosen because its Greek was less inferior to Attic standards than most of the New Testament. Preparing passages for oral translation and construing in class was very hard going, since our only permitted guide was the King James Version (KJV), which sounded so wonderful from the lectern in chapel, but which was far from helpful in parsing the Greek of such passages as Chapter 7, verses 15–18:

> *15* And it is yet far more evident: for that after the similitude of Melchisedec there ariseth another priest, *16* Who is made, not after the law of a carnal commandment, but after the power of an endless life.

17 For he testifieth, Thou art a priest for ever after the order of Melchisedec. *18* For there is verily a disannulling of the commandment going before for the weakness and unprofitableness thereof.

This, of course, is how scripture has so often been, quite as much sound as sense. But we had somehow to cope with the dry didacticism of the Greek neuter adjectives in that final verse's δια το αυτης ασθενες και ανωφλς (dia to autēs asthenes kai anōpheles). Had we been allowed such cribs, much more useful than the King James Version, which was itself cunningly tuned up from Tyndale's 'Then the commandment that went afore, is disannulled, because of her weakness and unprofitableness.' (Tyndale, 2000: 493), would have been the earnestly explicit post-war version by J.B. Phillips. With its one-man built-in mini-commentary this reads: 'Quite plainly, then, there is a definite cancellation of the previous commandment because of its ineffectiveness and uselessness' (Phillips, 1955: 194). And had we but known it, the 1960s were just round the corner with their real reach-out-by-translation committees to intelligibly plain speech in half as many syllables, whether in the New English Bible's: 'The earlier rules are cancelled as impotent and useless' or the Good News Bible's firmly unlatinate: 'The old rule then is set aside, because it was weak and useless.'

These and other recent versions (compared in Hargreaves, 1993: 103–6) marked major changes in the placement within the English religious and literary systems of the primary English sacred text. But they were still only on the horizon when at university I first moved from Classics into Oriental studies. Only in retrospect can I see quite how extraordinarily little shift of consciousness was at first required as we proceeded to the next counter, as it were, in order to be fitted for a light tropical suit in much the same cut as before, but of suitable weight for Middle Eastern wear. Much of the old philological kit was to come in handy, though the talk was now of archaic Arabic forms rather than use of the Greek aorist participles in the New Testament. School's advance preparation in the use of archaic English translations as the appropriate aids for scriptural study came in useful at Oxford in the early 1960s, when we were introduced to the study of the Qur'an. The recommended assistance was what in post-Saidian perspective now seems the bizarre choice of the English version by Sale, an early 18th-century production in sub-KJV style by a translator whose heart was perhaps more in his translation of the New Testament into Arabic.

Into the Hyperbazaar

I have spent a little time taking you back to the circumstances of my far-from-untypical early training in what I have called the 'gentlemen's outfitters' of a barely post-imperial Britain. The special place of scripture vis-à-vis all other kinds of literature ancient or modern was marked by a still-strong preference for translations in archaic English. I have done so in order to sharpen the contrast with the present, the postcolonial New Age of the English-based world. This world now embraces not just so much of America and Europe but also significant parts of the cities of Asia, not just the post-1960s generations but also a whole mélange of indigenous and diasporic faith communities. Postcolonial translation theory (Niranjana, 1992; Bassnett & Trivedi 1999; Tymoczko, 1999) is here certainly a necessary, if not a sufficient, guide.

Significantly fuelled itself by translations of the sacred, our postcolonial New Age has a varied and continuing demand for more. This is, in a word, the hybrid age of the hyperbazaar, which typically favours egalitarian over hierarchical, spiritual over religious, colloquial over formal, multicultural choice over national and ethnic canon and the bright eternity of the present over the venerated shadows of a carefully nuanced past.

Much might be said about the implications of these changes of context for our understanding of the immensely complex cultural phenomena associated with Biblical translation. Let me cite only the suggestive evidence of its many presences provided by three somewhat random book purchases made during the period of preparation for this chapter. The first was an Anglo-Irish barrister's edition of a small 18th-century Latin treatise seeking to prove that Greek rather than Aramaic was the language of Jesus and the apostles (Diodati, 1843). The second book was a commentary on the Greek Epistle to the Hebrews remaindered in tellingly mint condition from the library of Jews' College (Nairne, 1917). The third was a copy of the Bible in Albanian discovered on the shelves, but mysteriously missing from the stock records of the Warwick University bookshop (United Bible Societies, 1999), a truly Borgesian *trouvaille*.

I now want to explore some of the implications of the great general cultural shift that has taken place since the mid-20th century for the particular process of translating the holy. More in the spirit of suggesting lines of enquiry than in the ambition of achieving any systematic schema of approach, I again draw on some of my own experience, this time my experience as a professional academic who has worked in several linked fields in medieval and modern Asian Studies with an Indo-European linguistic emphasis. As an undergraduate I quickly moved from Arabic to Persian, that deceptively easy-looking language which promises such instant initial access to the cultural heritage of the eastern Islamic world. From there I moved somewhat further east to the New Indo-Aryan languages of Pakistan and Northwest India, specialising particularly in Urdu and Punjabi.

The sparseness of the academic presence allows Asianists a somewhat dangerous freedom to roam, which has the advantage of enforcing them to embrace a great variety of experiences through having to do so much themselves. Let me spell out some of the consequences of this rather peculiar situation. In the first place, we are called upon at one time or another to translate just about every kind of writing from a given source language into English. This gives a very wide perspective of the sheer textual and stylistic range of the source language, going well beyond the literary to encompass, for example, archival materials from different periods as well as contemporary official documents, private letters, and technical specifications. Within the narrower sphere of formal literature, we are again called on to attempt a great range of material varying considerably in period, style and genre and drawn from all sorts of different points along a spectrum of content and intent that spans the secular as well as the sacred. From this develops some sense of the particular place of the sacred within the source language and of the factors relevant to its translation. The comparative experience of working with more than one language or with more than one religious tradition must help further refine that perspective, if only through the undermining of any foolish confidence in the authority of our own expertise.

In case all this makes us seem pretty big fish in our exotic pools, it is salutary to turn from source to target language and to consider just what small players we are in the big pond of translations into English. The recent *Oxford Guide to Literature in English Translation* (France, 2000) devotes fewer than 30 of its 600 pages to Asian literatures, although it is telling that a much higher proportion of those pages is devoted to sacred literature than is true of the book as a whole. Western readers continue to look to Asia for spiritual reinforcement, and the best place to look for Asian literature in the hyperbazaar is not in the literature department but on the shelves labelled 'Mind Body Spirit'.

The translations of the sacred likely to be found there are of a fairly heterogeneous kind. Sadly, we must quickly give up hope of locating examples of Benjamin's fantasy ideal where 'the translation must be one with the original in the form of the interlinear version, in which literalness and freedom are united' (Schulte & Biguenet, 1992: 82). What we are more likely to find are free-standing English translations standing between their own covers, and there are not so very many of those to choose from. Translators are always liable to blame malign market forces for this sort of shortfall, but from a translation-studies perspective it is surely more a question of the difficulties of establishing the necessary systemic matches between source and target literary systems.

The canon of Islamic sacred literature is of course dominated by the

Qur'an, but a neutral discussion of Qur'anic translation is inhibited by the unique untranslatable status attributed to the scripture by Islamic orthodoxy (Abdul-Raof, 2001a: 19). Let us take instead the immense store of classical Persian art-poetry, which embraces centuries of great secular poetry alongside the greatest Sufi poetry of any Islamic literature. Yet it was Edward Fitzgerald's reworking of Umar Khayyam, a minor poet working in a minor genre, that slipped into English as one of the great translation success stories of all time. Its success was based as much on the spiritual appeal of its wistful fatalism to a significant section of the Victorian mind as on its prettily turned rhymes:

For some we loved, the loveliest and the best
That from his Vintage rolling Time hath prest ...

Quiller-Couch, 1919: 698

Fitzgerald has of course come in for harsh words of late (e.g. Bassnett & Trivedi, 1999: 6) but, as anyone who has tried knows, Persian poetry is unbelievably hard to translate into English so well as this. The compression of the language with its facility in forming condensed nominal chains, the elaborate self-referencing of a rhetorically complex system of imagery and the strict preference for heavily rhymed verses, themselves divided into carefully balanced hemistichs are just some of its difficult features. One can only regret that it was in the 19th century rather than in the 18th century that a serious start was made on translating Persian poetry into English.

Those interested in seeing the fate of Rumi, the greatest of all Persian Sufi poets, in English may consult the excellent study recently published by Franklin Lewis, whose enthusiasm I share for the 1794 version of the opening verses of the *Masnavi* by Sir William Jones:

Hear, how yon reed in sadly pleasing tales
Departed bliss and present woe bewails!

Lewis, 2000: 565

Lewis is particularly good on the mismatch between scholarship and translation in the case of Rumi's *Masnavi*, the great mystical epic that is commonly known and referred to as 'the Qur'an in the Persian language' or the 'second Qur'an' (Rumi, bibliographical data: online). The English version of Nicholson's massive edition (Nicholson, 1925–40) is virtually unreadable except as a crib to the Persian, and the popular translations of Rumi's lyrical poetry, published by Coleman Barks in the 1990s, bypass all that British scholarship. They are based instead on an English prose version produced by a Turk from Gölpinarlı's Turkish translations of Rumi. Thus conducted at three removes from the original, the style of Barks's translations is stripped down, with simple diction and contrived enjambements:

You've disappeared into the way?
Leave even that behind. Sit

With the essence inside love.
In that Chinese mirror you'll see

Hundreds of sword blades. Don't
Be afraid to use them. You've

Given up everything. You live
In absence. More is required.

Barks, 1999: 30

As Lewis says,

> The versions of Barks ... tend to present Rumi as a guru rather calmly dispensing words of wisdom capable of resolving, panacea-like, all our ontological ailments. This view of Rumi as a sage leads him to teleport the poems of Rumi out of their cultural and Islamic context into the inspirational discourse of non-parochial spirituality, all of which makes for a Rumi who shares the social assumptions of a modern American audience. (Lewis, 2000: 592)

This is, in a word, a highly reconstructive interpretation ideally suited to the New Age. It has had plenty of imitators, some even converting Hafiz into a Sufi master, as in Daniel Ladinsky's *The Gift*, not so much a paraphrase as a parody of the wondrously wrought style of the greatest master of Persian art-poetry:

You are
A royal fish
Trying to wear pants
In a country as foreign
As land.

Now there's a problem
Worth discussing.

Ladinsky, 1999: 168

Much more might be said about this hunger for translations of the spiritual, with their promises to their readers of infinite freedoms of insight. More might be said also about the ways in which this demand has been met by translators who feel that the spirit can only be properly conveyed by the exercise of a unique freedom in relation to the letter of the text. This freedom sometimes far exceeds even the imitation, let alone the paraphrase of Dryden's threefold spectrum (Schulte & Biguenet, 1992: 17), at whose other end lies literalistic metaphrase.

In the context of the translation of the sacred, it is certainly true that a narrow even literalistic metaphrase and a free paraphrase tend to be the strategies applied respectively to the translation of what might be termed 'religious' and 'spiritual' literature. Good examples would be the legalistic texts of Islamic *fiqh* or Hindu *dharmashāstra* on the one hand and Sufi lyrics and songs in praise of Krishna on the other. English mother tongue translators have also tended to take greater advantage of the linguistic freedom they enjoy in the target language, while members of faith communities have often had a keener consciousness of the need for fidelity to the source language. But nowadays in the circumstances of the hyperbazaar, it would certainly be misleading to make too much of any such neat distinction. When working on the Indian Ismaili hymns called *ginān,* my collaborator Zawahir Moir and I sought to achieve a prosaic clarity suitable for translations that are printed opposite original texts and attempt to convey their religious content:

> The Guide bears a bundle on his head, while the disciple carries a load. If you embark on a boat of iron, how can you get across? (Shackle & Moir, 2000: 79)

Taking explicit issue with this approach on the grounds that when translating religious lyrics 'straightforward' does not mean 'literal', an Ismaili translator makes full use of the New Age typographic layout to suggest the injection of the spirit:

> How will they cross ashore –
> The master
>   with a sack on his head,
> The pupil
>   with a load on his head.
> Both of them
>   seated in a metal boat?
>
> Esmail, 2002: 41

Translating the Adi Granth

This dichotomy between the religious and the spiritual (which is not only characteristic of contemporary Western consciousness but has also been manifested in different ways in many other cultures) is typically transcended in scripture. Scripture is itself a culturally-conditioned term. As uniquely valued vessels simultaneously containing both the religious and the spiritual, however, scriptures must be regarded as collectively constituting the test case for the theory and practice of the translation of the sacred and the holy. For while the spiritual may be the common property of humankind to translate as it will, scriptures have faith communities that look on any translation both eagerly for the evidence of the spirit and critically for evidence of a proper fidelity.

By way of a concluding example, let me therefore offer some observations on the translation of the Sikh scriptures, the Adi Granth or 'Original Book' – a large collection of the hymns of the Sikh Gurus and other holy men. It was compiled in the 17th century, first substantially translated into English in the later nineteenth century and retranslated many times since. It is after all a special quality of scripture that, just as it generates an exceptional quantity of exegesis and commentary, so too does it demand an exceptional frequency of translations in approximate reach to the impossible ideal of perfection.

The experience of translating a wide variety of South Asian religious and secular poetry from different periods (Shackle & Awde, 1999) shows that many of the issues to be faced in translating Sikh scripture are far from unique. Like other scriptures, the language is archaic, being a conservative mixture of Old Punjabi and Old Hindi, with a typically condensed syntax made possible by morphological distinctions that have subsequently been lost. As so often with scripture, this archaic quality makes its own technical demands for special study on translators, who neglect the exegetes at their peril. Then like much pre-modern South Asian religious literature, it is composed in verse for singing, being thus both technically very similar to, say, the Sufi poetry composed in South Asian languages for performance in *qawwali*, and intrinsically harder to translate than the non-scriptural Sikh hagiographic literature in prose. Rhetorically less sophisticated than the Persian poetry touched on earlier, many of the characteristics of this highly rhymed verse are intrinsically similar in their implications for translations into English (cf. Snell in Shaffer, 2000: 133–56). These notably include end-stopped lines and strong caesuras imposing very short syntactic units in paratactic relationship to one another, besides such awkward features as a strong presence of that relative–correlative construction 'Whoever perform virtue, they shall be rewarded' which is so difficult to bring off in contemporary English styles.

The stylistic choices made by different translators over the last century and a quarter have tended to favour either straight prose versions, which often manage to work in a considerable amount of commentary, or versions loosely reminiscent of the parallelist structures associated with English translations of the Psalms. These have been preferred to New Age renderings or to the model of the English metrical hymn, whose obvious closeness has its own inconvenient implications. Typical results of these four strategies may be briefly illustrated in reverse order by renderings of one verse by the first Guru Nanak (*jini kari upadēsu giāna-anjanu dīā, inī nētrī jagatu nihāliā* Asa ki Var 13:2; Adi Granth, 470).

Here the New Age version might be represented with a typical expansion of the 10 words of the original to 21 as:

He
  gave me
  his teaching
His wisdom
  gave my eyes
  the mascara
They need
  to see
  the world
As it is.

As a hymn, the same verse might be done in 12 words in the Long Metre (8.6.8.6) familiar from hymns such as 'All hail the power of Jesus' name, Let angels prostrate fall':

And with his teaching as their salve
These eyes survey the world.

Or again, the semicolon split characteristic of the psalm format might be followed, as in an older published version with 18 words:

> Who gave me the salve of divine instruction; with these eyes I then beheld God in the world.
>
> Macauliffe, 1963: 1, 236

Finally, the same verse may be rendered just as prose, in the following published version extended to 45 words with a commentary directed to 20th-century concerns:

> And who in the form of his teachings put the antimony of wisdom in my eyes and thus enabled me to see clearly with those eyes what the world really is, that is to say, it enabled me to see the anti-God in society.
>
> S. Singh, 1982: 92

Beside the intrinsic formal constraints that govern all translations from one language to another and the formal strategies variously employed, as suggested in the parallel versions just given, the translation of scripture involves a whole series of additional important considerations. The representation of the commentorial tradition either through incorporation (as in my last example) or else in footnotes is one such consideration. Another is that of one-to-one consistency in the rendering of key terms, perhaps a more obvious desideratum in a scriptural collection of hymns like the Adi Granth than when more impressionistically translating sets of Sufi poems for CD sleeve notes (see Navras, 2000). Scholars' versions can suggest the originals in italicised parenthesis, but such awkward glossing is hardly sustainable in versions intended to be free standing. Conversely, in the case of a multi-authored scripture such as the Adi Granth, there is the question, as yet hardly addressed, of the degree to which the attempt should be made to represent the rather different styles of the several Gurus and other contributors to the volume. Then there is the whole business of repackaging Asian scripture for the English book market. The sacred quality of the Adi Granth in the Gurmukhi script as the living Guru Granth Sahib of the Sikh community is no more readily transferable than that of the Arabic Qur'an into English. The Granth's huge size, comprising 1430 substantial pages in the standard printed editions, makes selective representation the norm, while its elaborate internal arrangement as a hymnal by musical *raga* and by poetic genre must be less meaningful in English than an arrangement by author or by theme would be.

Like all translations, the translations of the Sikh scriptures produced to date reflect not only the outcomes of consciously taken decisions on such fundamental technical and editorial issues but also the broader cultural and historical contexts in which they were produced. The Sikh scriptures were insufficiently classical for inclusion in such major 19th-century projects as the *Sacred Books of the East* series. The pioneering version by the German philologist Ernest Trumpp (Trumpp, 1877), commissioned by the India Office to help identify the position of Sikhism on the imperial map, remains remarkable for its combination of faithful prose renderings and extraordinary lack of empathy. Trumpp mechanically starts at the beginning and translates the first third of the contents straight through, after a disparaging introduction in the worst Victorian mode on the repetitiousness of the scriptures. The result is still usable but in a decidedly off-putting way.

Equally useful and decidedly more attractive is the selective early 20th-century presentation by Max Arthur Macauliffe. He worked closely with leading Sikh reformists, who were themselves defining the still-dominant exegetical tradition in modern Punjabi, to present the British with a more sympathetic picture of the religion as a socially progressive monotheism particularly deserving of imperial favour. He solved the intrinsic difficulty of presenting reams of religious verse in a prosaic, vaguely psalm-like translation (marked like Trumpp's with the usual archaic inflexions of the second person singular) by arranging his generous selections around a continuous prose narrative based on the non-scriptural hagiographic literature (Macauliffe, 1909,1963).

Complete English versions of the entire Adi Granth began to appear from within the English-educated elite of the Sikh community in India after independence and come tellingly stamped with different kinds of official postcolonial approval. The huge labour involved in the task is recognised in high-ranking endorsements from leading Sikhs and official figures prefixed to the pioneering one-man version by Dr Gopal Singh published in 1960. Its 'thees' and 'thous' were later removed in a somewhat modernised version (G. Singh, 1960, 1978). The eight-volume version by Manmohan Singh, first published by the senior body of the Sikh religious establishment in 1962 (M. Singh, 1962), is printed with the original and a translation into modern Punjabi in parallel columns. It is essentially a modernised adaptation of the traditional interlinear gloss rather than a free-standing translation. This tradition continues to dominate the diasporic market, most recently through the so-called Khalsa Consensus Translation, which has achieved huge currency through its inclusion in the major Sikh websites (www.sikhs.org; www.sikhnet.com), where its superiority to other versions is set out by its translator Singh Sahib Dr Sant Singh Khalsa.

With the establishment since 1947 of large Sikh communities in the English-speaking world outside India, the process of translating the Sikh scriptures is entering a third phase. The relative prominence of Sikhs in the South Asian diasporas encourages at second remove an academic market to meet the demands of courses in comparative religion. This is addressed by the selection in *Textual Sources for the Study of Sikhism* (McLeod, 1984), which has the great advantage of being the work of a native English speaker capable of properly reproducing English rhythmic patterns. Given the high value Sikhism places on the devout layman vis-à-vis the professional cleric, it is unsurprising that numerous partial translations of selected hymns should continue to be published in Britain and North America.

Often advertising as their express aim that of keeping the younger generation informed of their scriptural tradition, these versions tend to be stiffly close to the style of the Indian English translations. This restrictive mould was only really broken by Nikky Guninder Kaur Singh's selections published in The Sacred Literature Series as *The Name of My Beloved* (N. Singh, 1995), the first translation by a woman and the first consciously to attempt to produce a gender-neutral version suitable for the diaspora. I became involved with this exercise as a reader of her draft versions. Although we disagreed fundamentally about many issues, including linguistic bending away from the masculine (the language of the Adi Granth is more gender-specific than modern Punjabi in distinguishing masculine and feminine third person singular pronouns) my own awareness was enormously enriched by the experience of our extensive debate. It confirmed my belief that translation is essentially an iterative process. The bibliography will reveal my own preference for working in a two-person team as the best way to stay alert to serious errors of accuracy or judgement.

But as a firm believer in the ultimate untranslatability of the holy, I am hesitant to end in didactic mode. I hope during the free-ranging course of a necessarily summary treatment of a whole series of related topics to have covered some of the issues involved in the contemporary business of trying to translate sacred texts. If I have a single conclusion, it is to call for reflection on the process of setting up our translators' stalls in this new age of the hyperbazaar, on our motives for getting into the business – in a word, on the tricks of what is and what always must be a profoundly serious trade.

Chapter 3

Prophecy and Tongues: St Paul, Interpreting and Building the House

K. ONUR TOKER

In an attempt to justify the translation of the Bible into English, the 'Translators' Preface' to the King James Version (KJV) cites numerous passages from the Scriptures and the church fathers. Most of these passages are quoted in order to prove that the reading and the comprehension of the Scriptures form an indispensable and essential part of leading a Christian life. However, could one not argue – admittedly in a rather perversely elitist fashion – that such passages prove only that we should read and understand the Bible, not that we should translate it into English or, for that matter, any other vernacular language? After all, why should we risk fundamentally altering the sense and the form of Holy Writ when both are perfectly preserved in the original tongues of Hebrew and Greek? In order to counter such arguments, the translators cite another passage from the Scriptures that deals explicitly with the questions of interpretation and linguistic difference. In his first epistle to the Corinthians 14:11, St Paul writes 'Except I know the power of the voice [Therefore if I know not the meaning of the voice], I shall be to him that speaketh a barbarian, and he that speaketh shall be a barbarian to me' (Smith, 2001: 363). Of course, an inveterate elitist could still argue that St Paul's words only prove that we should learn the original languages of the Scriptures so that the Holy Spirit, who speaks in the Bible through the prophets, does not remain a barbarian to us. However, a little bit further on in the same chapter of the first epistle to the Corinthians 14:13, St Paul seems to argue that, rather than prophesying or preaching the gospel in foreign tongues which no one in the congregation can understand, one should interpret, that is to say, translate, such prophecies and the good news, i.e. the gospel, that they bear into a tongue that is understood by all: 'Wherefore let him that speaketh in an unknown tongue pray that he may interpret'. The Greek word used for 'interpret' is διερμηνεύῃ, a word that is cognate with our 'hermeneutics' and which can, as the Liddell and Scott *Greek–English Lexicon* testifies, also mean 'to translate' (the Greek New Testament used throughout this article is Douglas, 1990).

We should note that the Greek word for prophecy, προφητεία, whose various forms recur frequently in the first epistle to the Corinthians, means the 'gift of *interpreting* the will of the gods', and a προφήτης (prophet) is in fact 'an *interpreter* of the gods' (Liddell & Scott, 1951: 1539). Prophets are strange beings who are possessed by a spirit not their own – in the case of a Christian prophet, the Holy Spirit – and it is as if they merely translate the will of God from the divine language into the languages of human beings. According to St Paul, prophecy is one of the main spiritual gifts that men ought to desire over and above, say, the gift of speaking in foreign languages. Indeed, he argues, 'He that speaketh in an unknown tongue edifieth (οἰκοδομει, i.e. builds up) himself, but he that prophesieth (προφητεύων) edifieth the church' (I Corinthians 14:4). Here, St Paul's intention is not to denigrate the ability to speak in foreign languages; he himself seems to boast about being a proficient polyglot when he says 'I thank my God, I speak with tongues more than ye all' (I Corinthians 14:18). As the New Revised Standard Version (NRSV) translation puts it, Paul proclaims to the Corinthians: 'Now I would like all of you to speak in tongues, but even more to prophesy.' This is so because, according to Paul, one 'who prophesies is greater than one who speaks in tongues, *unless someone interprets* [διερμηνεύῃ], so that the church may be built up [οἰκοδομην]' (I Corinthians 14:5). A prophet is distinguished from someone who speaks in foreign languages not necessarily by virtue of the greater holiness of his subject matter, but by virtue of the hermeneutical task of translation and interpretation that he is engaged in. The ultimate end of this hermeneutical task is the building up or edification of God's church on Earth, which can be described, in somewhat Heideggerian terms, as the proper 'house of Being', the culture and tradition, in which good Christians ought to dwell. Indeed, Paul clearly states that he wants 'all things [to] be done for building up' or, as the KJV puts it, 'edification' (I Corinthians 14:26).

What exactly does the apostle Paul have in mind when he exhorts us all to build up or edify God's church through the hermeneutical task of prophecy? As J. J. Lias (1886: 95) points out, οἰκοδομει, the Greek word that is translated by building up or edification, 'introduces a metaphor taken from the gradual building of a house' and is applied primarily 'to the growth of the Christian Church.' The apostle Paul seems to argue that the gradual building of the Christian house of Being, the Church of God, should be achieved through interpretation and translation. One who speaks the word of God in a tongue unknown to his interlocutor should at the same time interpret or translate what he is saying into a language that they both understand so that his interlocutor may also be welcomed to the Christian house of Being. Thereby, one could say that the interlocutor is also, in a sense of the word that is perhaps more familiar to us, edified. The word 'edification', as it is ordinarily used in contemporary English, means 'instruction'; what the person who is edified by the word of God through interpretation or translation learns is a new set of concepts, a new tradition and culture, a new language in whose home he will henceforth dwell. The interpretation and translation of the word of God could be seen as a generous act of hospitality and openness to the other. The interpreter or the translator might have to speak or write in a language that is not his own: this is certainly the case with the apostle Paul, a Jew who preaches and writes in Greek. The interpreter or the translator of the Scriptures might even have to adopt the customs of his foreign interlocutors and thereby in a sense become a translated or mimic man himself. Indeed, St Paul declares that he has been 'made all things to all men': 'to them that are under the law, as under the law'; 'to them that are without law, as without law' (I Corinthians 9:20–21).

However, it is true that the person who is welcomed to the Christian house of Being through interpretation and translation must also in a sense be translated. After all, this house is nothing other than a new language, a new culture and tradition with its own set of signs such as the Scriptures, which the newcomer must adopt and make his own if he wishes to dwell there. Indeed, as Marc Hirshman (1996: 15), an Israeli Bible scholar, bemusedly notes, St Paul makes Gentile Christians adopt a Semitic genealogy by addressing them as the 'children of Abraham' (Galatians 3:7). St Paul makes a similar sort of claim in the first epistle to the Corinthians when he writes '*all our fathers* were under the cloud, and all passed through the sea, and were all baptized unto Moses in the cloud and in the sea' (10:1–2). Here, Paul is referring to certain episodes in the book of Exodus, which relates the history of the *Jewish* people, the Israelites. So how can he claim that all our fathers, including the fathers of the Corinthians, who must have been predominantly Gentile if not completely Greek, had the same historical experiences as the ancestors of the Jews? In his book *A Rivalry of Genius*, Marc Hirshman (1996: 14) argues that from the very moment of the inception of their faith 'Christians publicly stated that they were the true Israel, that only they could interpret Scripture adequately, and that Jews no longer had a share in it because they had refused to understand its true meaning.' The true Christian meaning or interpretation of the Old Testament is primarily, as Hirshman (1996: 11) indicates, that 'the prophets of Israel foretold the coming of Jesus'. By interpreting the Hebrew Scriptures correctly, Gentile and Jewish Christians *become* the true Israel; Paul argues that all the events that are related in the Old Testament 'happened unto them [all our fathers, i.e. the Israelites] for ensamples: and they are written for our admonition' (I Corinthians 10:11 KJV). The gist of St Paul's argument seems to be that we must interpret and translate the Scriptures correctly, not necessarily *verbum pro verbo* in the manner of an interlinear translation, but always taking the utmost care to preserve the kernel of sense, the true meaning, of Holy Writ, which is, according to Christianity, the coming of Jesus Christ.

The hermeneutic act of interpreting and translating the Scriptures 'correctly' is that which builds up the Christian house of Being, culture and tradition. If one's interpretation or translation manages to preserve the essential meaning of the Bible, then the house of Being in which one dwells is sound and one can confidently hope for salvation. If, on the other hand, one's interpretation or translation alters this essential meaning, then nothing awaits one but perdition. We should note that the gesture whereby Gentile Christians adopt a Jewish genealogy and history could be interpreted as a profound act of openness to the other: it is as if Gentiles are translated into Jews. However, we should also note that this very same act of hospitality and openness paradoxically brings with it, and perhaps produces, a profound gesture of hostility towards alterity: what Christianity holds to be the true meaning of the Bible must be preserved at all costs and all other interpretations that alter or differ from this true meaning must be interdicted. After all, as Antonio observes in *The Merchant of Venice* (Act I, 3:94), 'The devil can cite Scripture for his purpose.' The devil that Antonio is referring to is Shylock the Jew, but, as we see in Matthew 4:5, Satan himself can indeed cite scripture for his own purpose. There seems to be a strange logic that links hospitality and hostility towards the *hostis*, the other, in the fields of culture and hermeneutics. As we have seen, both the act of producing an interpretation or translation (which is meant to build a house of Being, a culture) and the act of receiving it involve profound gestures of hospitality and openness to the other. By the same token, yet paradoxically, both of these hermeneutical acts seem to involve hostile gestures of excluding alterity from one's culture and tradition, one's house of Being.

The hospitable aspect of the hermeneutic task of Pauline prophecy and edification manifests itself in the welcoming of the Corinthians (who were once as Paul notes (I Corinthians 12:2) 'Gentiles worshipping dumb idols') and other non-Jews into the house of Israel, so that one can address all Christians, Jewish and Gentile, as the children of Abraham. However, it seems that Jews who fail to recognize Jesus of Nazareth as the true messiah are somehow deprived of their birthright to dwell as hosts in the house of Israel and pride themselves on having Abraham as their ancestor. After all, according to John the Baptist, 'God is able from these stones to raise up children to Abraham' (Matthew 7:9), and this is exactly what Paul is trying to achieve through the hermeneutics of prophecy and edification. What is the rationale or motivation behind this apparently hostile act of dispossession and expulsion? According to Marc Hirshman, in the Christian framework non-Christian Jews lose their right to be called 'the true Israel' because they refuse to understand the true meaning of the Scriptures. Hence, their grave mistake, which leads to their expulsion not only from the house of Israel but also from the kingdom of heaven, is of a hermeneutical nature, primarily concerning the interpretation of the Hebrew Scriptures. In the gospel according to Matthew, Jesus clarifies his position in relation to the Hebrew Scriptures:

> Do not think that I have come to abolish the law [the Torah, i.e. the Hebrew Scriptures] or the prophets; I have come not to abolish but to fulfil. For truly I tell you, until heaven and earth pass away, not one letter, not one stroke of a letter, will pass from the law [the Torah] until all is accomplished. (Matthew 5:17)

Jesus effects this fulfilment by leading his entire life in accordance with the Scriptures. He is, after all, the word made flesh and many prophecies in the Old Testament find their full-blooded embodiment in his acts, which are often performed, as the evangelists untiringly remind us, so that the Hebrew Scriptures may be fulfilled.

However, it seems that the Christian fulfilment of the Hebrew Scriptures consists not so much in the meticulous preservation of their letter as in providing a bold new interpretation or translation of these ancient texts. When a Pharisee lawyer asks Jesus 'which commandment in the law [the Torah] is the greatest' in order to test him, Jesus quotes Deuteronomy 6:5: 'You shall love the Lord your God with all your heart, and with all your soul, and with all your mind.' After declaring this to be the greatest and first commandment, Jesus goes on to quote Leviticus 19:18: 'You shall love your neighbour as yourself.' 'On these two commandments', Jesus adds, 'hang all the law and the prophets' (Matthew 22:36–40). Jesus's claim that all the law and the prophets hang on these two commandments from Deuteronomy and Leviticus seems to suggest (although Jesus himself never clearly spells this out) that all the other commandments in the Torah, such as those concerning circumcision or the prohibition of pork, do not matter as much. Indeed, in the first epistle to the Corinthians (7:19) the apostle Paul declares that 'Circumcision is nothing and uncircumcision is nothing, but the keeping of the commandments of God.' St Paul takes up this issue again in his epistle to the Romans when he addresses the Jews: 'Circumcision is indeed of value if you [the Jews] obey the law; but if you break the law, your circumcision has become uncircumcision' (Romans 2:25). Then Paul goes on to make a distinction between spiritual and literal, i.e. physical, circumcision: 'those who are physically uncircumcised but keep the law [Gentile Christians] will condemn you that have the written code [the Torah] and circumcision but break the law.' 'For', Paul argues, 'a person is not a Jew who is one outwardly, nor is true circumcision something external and physical. Rather, a person is a Jew who is one inwardly, and real circumcision is a matter of the heart – it is spiritual and not literal' (Romans: 2:27–29). Or as the KJV puts it, 'circumcision is that of the heart, in the spirit, and not in the letter'. Non-Christian Jews such as Shakespeare's Shylock who live in strict conformity with the letter of the Mosaic law by being physically circumcised and not eating pork (Shylock cannot so much as stand the smell of pork) may very well be, Paul argues, taking the Scriptures too literally and missing their essential point, which is their spirit. After all, in the second epistle to the Corinthians, Paul writes, 'the letter [γράμμα] kills, but the Spirit [πνευμα] gives life' (II Corinthians 3:6).

St Paul's distinction between the spirit and the letter of the Scriptures is, of course, a hierarchical distinction between the signified and the signifier. As Derrida (1981: 20) points out, 'in the limits to which it is possible, or at least *appears* to be possible, translation practices the difference between signified and signifier.' If one can maintain, as Paul does, that the spirit (i.e. the signified) of the Bible is essentially separable from its letter (i.e. its signifier), just as the kernel of a fruit is distinct and separable from its shell, then one could argue that in translating the Old Testament it is possible to effect a transport of pure signifieds from Hebrew to Greek or any other language. Such a Pauline 'transport', if it were possible, would alter only the signifier or the letter of the Torah – which is, at any rate, deemed unessential – and it would preserve the signified, that is, the spirit, of Holy Writ in its pristine glory. Hence, in the Pauline framework, the Bible is (w)holy translatable and must be translated so that the Church may be built up. According to Paul, one who prophesies does not speak the word of God in unknown tongues or indulge in glossolalia, but translates the holy word from Hebrew or Aramaic into a language that is understood by all in his congregation. After all, 'one who prophesies is greater than one who speaks in tongues, *unless someone interprets*, so that the church may be built up' (I Corinthians 14:5, the NRSV translation). That is to say, the crucial difference between a prophet and one who speaks in tongues is that a prophet is, as the etymology of the Greek word suggests, primarily an interpreter.

The Christian house of Being is built not through speaking in tongues but through interpretation. As it is recorded in the second chapter of the

Acts, when the Apostles received the gift of speaking in tongues from the Holy Spirit at the Pentecost, 'Parthians, Medes, Elamites, and residents of Mesopotamia, Judea and Cappadocia, Pontus and Asia, Phyrigia and Pamphylia, Egypt and the parts of Libya belonging to Cyrene, and visitors from Rome ... Cretans and Arabs' all declared: 'in our languages we hear [the Apostles] speaking about God's deeds of power' (Acts 2:9–11). In other words, the gift of tongues allowed the Apostles to translate the word of God from Hebrew and Aramaic into all the languages of the world. They all spoke with different sounds or signifiers but they all proclaimed the same holy signified or spirit: 'God's deeds of power' – although many natives of Jerusalem sneered and thought the Apostles were, being 'filled with new wine' (Acts 2:13), merely indulging in glossolalia.

George Steiner (1998: 61) suggests that the gift of tongues that descended upon the Apostles at the Pentecost was a 'partial redemption' or reparation for the catastrophe of Babel. However, if, as Derrida (1985) argues in '*Des Tours de Babel*', the confusion of tongues at Babel was an act of divine punishment for the imperialist intentions of the Semites to 'make a name for themselves' and to impose their language on the universe, then the events of the Pentecost did nothing but compound and conclude the punishment at Babel. After the Pentecost, the Semitic tongues Hebrew and Aramaic completely lost their privileged status as sole bearers of the word of Jehovah. Henceforth, the spirit, the holy signified, of the Torah could be transported from the Semitic tongues to all the other languages of the world and the non-Christian Semites would be left with nothing but the worthless husks, the signifiers, of the holy word. As Steiner (1998: 252) indicates, the '*Megillath Ta'anith* (*Roll of Fasting*), which is assigned to the 1st century AD, records the [Judaic] belief that three days of utter darkness fell on the world when the Law was translated into Greek.' According to the Talmud, 'the omission or the addition of one letter [of the Torah] might mean the destruction of the whole world' (Steiner, 1998: 63); hence, the Hebrew Scriptures are (w)holy untranslatable because any translation of the Torah would inevitably alter its letter entirely. In this Judaic framework, the signified and the signifier, the spirit and the letter, of the Torah are totally inseparable and any attempt to extract and isolate the univocal spirit of the Law from its letter would in fact ruin it entirely. The letter of the Torah is Jehovah's own incision, inscription or mark: in Genesis 31:18, we read that on Mount Sinai Moses was given 'the two tablets of the covenant, tablets of stone, *written with the finger of God*.' Hence, it is gravely sacrilegious to alter the divine inscription, the mark, the letter of the Torah while pretending to preserve its spirit. A practising Jew must meticulously observe the letter of the Torah, therefore he cannot eat non-Kosher food and he must be literally, that is to say, physically, circumcised. On the other hand, according to St Paul, 'circumcision is nothing and uncircumcision is nothing'. Indeed, he argues that if one observes the spirit of the Law then one's (physical) uncircumcision is gloriously transformed into (spiritual) circumcision (Romans 2:26).

It is clear that in the Pauline and the Talmudic–Judaic frameworks we find two conflicting interpretations of (Biblical) interpretation. In the Pauline framework, the duty of the interpreter, who is at once translator and prophet, consists in preserving the univocal signified or spirit of the Bible in different, more common and intelligible, words or letters, that is to say, signifiers. The prophet or the interpreter reiterates and preserves what is essential in the Judeo–Christian tradition, the holy signified, the spirit of the Bible, while opening up this tradition, this house of Being, to newcomers by making it intelligible to them in words that they can easily comprehend. Hence, the task of the prophetic translator consists as much in building up the tradition as in preserving it; indeed, Paul calls himself 'the wise master-builder' (I Corinthians 3:10). The Pauline prophet-translator accepts the multiplicity of idioms, letters or signifiers in which the word of God finds expression; maintaining, however, that behind all this multiplicity there lies a univocal signified that is forever identically repeatable.

As we can see, in the Pauline interpretation of interpretation, the relation between the spirit and the letter, the signified and the signifier, the Truth and the actual words in which it finds expression, is, to a very large extent, arbitrary. However, this arbitrariness does not, as one might expect, render the representation of the spirit or the truth completely impossible. On the contrary, it is only because the spirit, the signified, the truth, is not tied to any specific signifier, letter or sound that one can represent and enunciate the same truth in different words and different tongues. However, the Pauline prophet is not only a translator of Scripture but also a translator of men; he not only represents the spirit of the Scriptures but also exhorts all men to represent or imitate this same spirit in their everyday lives. Indeed, the Pauline prophet-translator unveils the spirit of the Scriptures and presents 'the glory of the Lord as though reflected in a mirror' so that all Christians may be 'transformed into the same image from one degree of glory to another' (II Corinthians 3:28). This strange imitative metamorphosis is what builds up the Christian house of Being or community.

Chapter 4

What Does Not Get Translated in Buddhist Studies and The Impact on Teaching

KATE CROSBY

This chapter explores a range of issues affecting the kind of Buddhist texts that do *not* get translated and the impact that the resulting availability has on the teaching of Buddhism. The focus is on Theravada Buddhism, although some reference is made to other forms, particularly Tibetan Buddhism, by way of contrast. Theravada Buddhism is often referred to both by scholars and by its own apologists as 'early Buddhism' and treated as more true to original Buddhism than other forms. Although this attitude is gradually changing, it is my view that the current availability and continued patterns of translation prevent us from making a clear re-evaluation of Theravada. In this chapter I attempt to give a general overview, rather than a detailed survey, of the most influential factors, such as the range of languages involved and the difficulty of terminology and conclude with some examples of their impact.

The Nature of the Spread of Buddhism to the West

The spread of Buddhism to the West occurred through interest, movement and mission, i.e. interest on the part of Westerners, movement or the diaspora of Buddhist peoples to the West, and missionary activity, such as the *dhammadūta* (messenger of the Buddha's teaching) monks who serve both diaspora and convert Buddhists. On the whole, Buddhism first exerted an influence in the West through an interest in its ideas and texts, divorced from living Buddhism as practised by Buddhists. This changed relatively early in Hawaii and the United States, which received substantial numbers of Buddhist immigrants from East Asia from the second half of the 19th century. The influence of Buddhism on European religion and culture dates from much earlier: Buddhism in the form taken by early Christian monasticism for example, or the possible influence of the Korean printing methods used for the Buddhist canon on the development of the Gutenberg Press. But here I am talking about the interest in Buddhism per se. The accessing of Buddhism through texts isolated from a living tradition has continued as a significant feature of the Western approach to Buddhism both among interested lay people and within certain schools of scholars.

The nature of Westerners' interest in Buddhism from the 19th century onwards has had an impact on the type of texts selected for translation into Western languages. Aspects of Western interest include:

- 19th-century romanticism;
- the search for a single underlying religion;
- the Victorian emphasis on ethical and rational–scientific religion;
- mysticism and an interest in the Occult, particularly in the early 20th century;
- reaction against Christianity, both missionary forms as an aspect of European then United States imperialism, and, for Western converts, forms associated with 'the Establishment' and anti-liberal societal values from the 1950s to this day;
- interest in things Eastern as an aspect of the 'counter-cultural' revolution of the 1960s and 70s.

While all these themes arose in quite specific Western historical and cultural contexts, the attendant attitudes and resultant views regarding Buddhism continue to influence the perception of the religion. These attitudes, in as much as they often distort Buddhism and even turn it into a consumer commodity, might have been considerably moderated by now, were it not that they themselves continue to influence the selection of texts for translation. This in turn is significant since texts are still the primary means through which most Westerners access Buddhism, whether directly or through more general books based to some extent on primary sources in translation.

The attitudes outlined above have tended to emphasise the ethical and then either the mystical or the rational–scientific aspects of Buddhism, or both. This perspective has led translators to focus their attention on texts concerned with the ultimate goal of Enlightenment rather than on the broader aspects usually included under the term religion, such as ritual, authority, ecclesiastical hierarchies, daily practicalities or societal role. This emphasis in the portrayal of Buddhism is still so strong that students undertaking the study of Buddhism continue to be surprised and even disappointed that it values and serves these other dimensions of religion at all.

In general, the mystical aspects of Buddhism are more emphasised when looking at, for example, Tibetan or Zen Buddhism, while the rational–

scientific aspects of Buddhism are more emphasised when looking at Theravada Buddhism. Such a tendency in part reflects the context of early enquirers. For example, Tibetan Buddhism was early on often dismissed as a corrupt form of Buddhism on a par with the Protestant view of Catholicism. Early influential writing about Tibetan Buddhism either strenuously debunked or emphasised the mystical, (sometimes both) according to intended audience. Tibetan Buddhism was drawn on and used by the early Theosophists because of the mystery surrounding it. As a result, Tibetan Buddhism made relatively early mystical appearances in popular fiction such as in Arthur Conan Doyle's resurrection of Sherlock Holmes. Tibet's remoteness furthered its role as an object of projection (see Lopez, 1998).

Theravada, in contrast, was represented early on rather one-sidedly as a more rational religion free of 'magic' and 'superstition' in its true forms (see Hallisey, 1995). This representation partly reflects the ways in which Therevada presented itself, especially in reaction to colonial Christianity. Significant examples of such self-portrayal include the 'Panadura debate', which took place between Buddhists and Christians in Sri Lanka in 1873 and was published in English and attracted the interest of Theosophist Col. Henry Olcott (1832–1907). Another was the reform Buddhism of Anagarika Dharmapala (David Hewavitarne 1864–1933), who represented Buddhism alongside D.T. Suzuki (1870–1966) at the first World Parliament of Religions in Chicago in 1893. The centralisation and reform of Buddhism in 19th-century Thailand, in large part in order to create a European-style state as a defence against British and French colonial powers, played a major role in this self-projection. This portrayal of Theravada also reflects the attitudes of early significant Western presenters of it (such as T.W. Rhys Davids), and the much greater availability of canonical texts from the Pāli than from the Tibetan canon – in part thanks to the endeavours of Rhys Davids and the Pāli Text Society.

Where Theravada was represented through French scholars, as was more common in the case of Cambodia or Laos, the tendency to accept a broader range of the religious features of Buddhism as valid has been attributed to the general Catholic background of French scholars in contrast to the Protestant background of British colonial scholars working in Burma and Sri Lanka. Because of the decreased significance of French as an international language, and perhaps because of the interruption or change of scholarship reflecting both French and South-East Asian political developments, French scholarship in Theravada studies has not been as influential in recent decades as it once was. This in turn has allowed the rational–scientific portrayal of Theravada mainly based on relatively early classical Pāli sources to dominate the field.

We have, then, a contrast between the presentation of Tibetan Buddhism as mystical and involving the use of rituals and religious paraphernalia (such as prayer wheels, flags and the implements employed in tantric ritual) and the presentation of Theravada as more rational and involving self-transformation through meditations that work on psychological development. While this contrast in part reflects the way in which both forms of Buddhism were introduced to a Western audience, the contrast is strongly self-perpetuating. We find that those Westerners who are interested in Tibetan Buddhism are far more likely to accept and even emphasise the ritual and more cultural aspects of the religion than are those interested in Theravada. This attitude is perhaps further encouraged by the role that Buddhism has come to play in international attempts to protect Tibetan culture from the impact of Chinese occupation. Those interested in Theravada are much more likely to seek out Theravada monks or other teachers of Theravada purely for meditation and doctrinal guidance rather than to participate in or use the rituals, which might be the dominant aspect of the religious life of a Buddhist from a long-standing Theravadin background. Those interested in Tibetan Buddhism seem more likely to be interested in fairly well developed Buddhist philosophy, which fits in with the presentation of Tibet as the guardian of a higher, secret wisdom and also reflects patterns of translation. While many philosophical treatises from Tibetan have been translated, correspondingly few have come from Theravada philosophy, partly because of the emphasis within Theravada studies on its 'earliest' literature.

The Youth of Buddhist Studies

The relative youth of Buddhist Studies as an academic subject in the West, emerging only gradually from the Oriental philology of the mid-19th century, is also relevant to the limited availability of translated texts. In addition, the fact that it is a minority subject, with only a handful of scholars actively involved in producing translations of previously unavailable works, means that the production of new translations has been relatively slow. In Classics, the search for untouched material for research, especially for doctoral dissertations, has driven people into the less familiar territories of, for example, medieval and hybrid Latin, or relatively obscure contexts. In Buddhist textual studies almost any research into Buddhist primary sources is automatically innovative since there remain great swathes of untouched material. Some canonical literature and most commentaries are still untranslated: most medieval material, particularly that in hybrid or combined languages, has yet to be edited, let alone translated.

Difficulties Presented by Language Range

The diversity of languages required for someone to be considered a competent scholar in Buddhist textual studies is notoriously large. Since early Buddhism dismissed the notion of ritual purity and the sanctity of form over meaning or ethics, meaning (rather than the language of a statement or text) is crucial. This is not to deny that the concept of sacred language is present in some Buddhist traditions, but it tends to be of most relevance in ritual. As a result, texts were translated into many different languages as Buddhism spread throughout Asia and still continues to spread into Western languages. The result for aspiring Buddhologists is daunting, given that in the pre-modern world Buddhism stretched from Indonesia in the south, to the Danube in the west, from Mongolia and China in the north and to Japan in the east. As a minimum, textual scholars often aim to acquire Sanskrit, Pāli, Tibetan and Chinese – these being the main languages of the most accessible or the largest canons. Beyond this, scholars try to acquire Japanese, partly to access Japanese Buddhological scholarship. On top of this, some textual scholars try to gain access to regional Buddhism through, for example, central Asian languages such as Uighur and Sogdian, or Himalayan or South and South-East Asian languages, such as Newari, Khmer or Sinhala. Buddhologists often complain that, by the time they have learnt the pertinent languages to a sufficiently high degree, their brains are too worn out to produce useful work. Aspiring scholars should perhaps draw some solace from the recognition of the scarcity of both linguistic and intellectual talent in ancient China. The monk Kumarajiva (344–413), the creator of our smoothest translations into Chinese, was, so the story goes, held captive by the emperor to ensure productivity in translation both now and in the future. By day, Kumarajiva worked with a team of assistants at producing translations. By night, he worked with ten beautiful and intelligent princesses at producing the next generation of translators (Daishonin, 2000: 5).

The range of language skills is particularly relevant in the establishment of the base text from which translations are made, given that most extant Buddhist texts still exist only in manuscript form. Most printed texts are not critical editions. Often different versions of a text exist in different languages, and it is usual to compare these when making editorial decisions. The obstacles presented by the need to acquire such a range of languages affect the speed of translation as well as the type of texts translated. In the study of Theravada, its sacred classical language Pāli is far more commonly acquired than local medieval languages, such as the many Tai languages. As a result new translations are more commonly from Pāli texts, even though texts in local languages are more numerous and might reasonably be considered to reflect more closely the Buddhism of most Buddhists, only a minority of whom have ever had competence in Pāli.

An Undeveloped Technical Terminology in the Target Language

Related to the newness of Buddhist Studies and the difficulties of such a diversity of source languages is another problem that affects both what is translated and the quality of those translations. Buddhist texts contain a vast array of religious technical terms for which there are no equivalents in English. Often the Christian connotations of possible equivalents render them misleading or unacceptable. The desire to avoid Christian-derived terminology is heightened in the post-colonial attempt not to impose European values on to non-European traditions and by the stance of many Westerners who have converted to or are deeply interested in Buddhism in part as a rejection of a the Judeo–Christian tradition.

The first Tibetan and Chinese translators struggled with the issue of translating the technical terms at the heart of Buddhist teachings and eventually developed standardised vocabularies for Buddhist texts in their respective target languages. We are at the early, faltering stages of the same process for English. I was recently given a book to review (Brassard, 2000) that was entirely dedicated to establishing an English translation for the single Sanskrit term *bodhicitta*. *Bodhicitta* refers to the vow made to attain Buddhahood and bring others to Buddhahood, as well as to the attendant attitude and transformed psycho-intellectual identity it generates in the individual. Although discussing a concept central to much of Buddhist soteriology and broader religious practice, after an entire book devoted to no other subject, the author concluded by leaving the term untranslated. Progress in developing an English Buddhist vocabulary seems doomed to be slow, given the marginality of Buddhism in Western culture in contrast to its centrality in Tibet and China.

This paucity of a vocabulary in translation for Buddhist theological terms mostly affects the translation of non-*sūtra* texts. *Sūtra/Sutta* texts present Buddhist teachings in a narrative framework, often as a story about the Buddha giving a sermon in quite straightforward terms to a particular individual. Even here, however, when it comes to more technical, dry doctrine, as is particularly the case in larger Mahāyāna *sūtras*, translators are often at a loss to provide translations even on those occasions where we are reasonably certain of the meaning. *Sūtra* literature and its offshoots are probably better represented in translation than any other genre. Key genres that are less well represented include developed doctrinal or philosophical texts, monastic literature and ritual texts. The doctrinal text *Abhidhamma*, for example, is the systematisation and consideration of the key teachings of Buddhism, and how they function. The writings include philosophy, metaphysics, discussion of causality, psychology and cosmology. *Abhidhamma* forms one of the three main divisions of the Theravada canon, the others being the *Sutta* and *Vinaya* (monastic legal literature) collections. Throughout Theravadin history, an ongoing tradition of scholarship and living philosophy has added further *Abhidhamma* literature to this corpus. *Abhidhamma* literature tends to be very dry and is sometimes very succinct. In attempting to translate it, one often finds that less than one quarter of a sentence is made up with non-technical Pāli. The rest contains specific terms with no easy English equivalents. Texts concerning monastic law and ritual are also hard to translate for the same reasons. What are translators to do, for example, with the terms for the different parts of a monk's robe and the ways of sewing them that occupies a significant body of Buddhist literature? Yet to ignore this literature is to fail to reflect the great significance in Theravada of monastic dress and the main annual festival at which lay people formally donate robes to monks.

Unliterary Literature

On top of these factors, and on the whole adversely affecting the same under-represented genres listed above, is the desire of the translators and publishers to translate 'literature', in other words narrative or poetic literature. Richard Gombrich (1978), in making available the medieval *Account of the Kosala Statue*, a text of great use for our understanding of the development of Theravada religiosity, feels the need to apologise that it is 'devoid of literary merit.' The *Account of the Kosala Statue* is at least narrative. More challenging by far are ritual texts and manuals of instruction, which may, for example, repeat the same few words a thousand times in slightly differing order. Publishers are also wary of the length of a text for translation, and many Buddhist texts are extremely long, few are shorter than the Bible.

Texts Too Powerful for the Eyes of the (Philologically) Uninitiated

Sometimes translators have regarded parts of their texts as in some way inappropriate for the eyes of their audience. The dominant fear is that the reader may misconstrue the Buddhist tradition or misapply the understanding acquired from the text in question. With Victorian and early 20th-century translators, the problem often relates to material deemed obscene, for example the translation by I.B. Horner of the *Pāli Vinaya*, or monastic code. The first monastic rule is that a monk may not commit a sexual act. If he does, he may be disrobed. The 'may be' is important, for the tradition had to establish whether the monk should be disrobed, receive some lesser punishment or none at all. In order to do so the compilers rehearsed every possible combination, permutation and deviation of the sexual act in some detail, such as the use of open sores on corpses and proposed phenomenal feats of engagement with oneself, before pronouncing on exactly what level of punishment that particular act warranted. Horner, not wishing to impose the finer detail on a vulnerable audience, writes:

> It must be admitted that several early literatures have a coarse side ... Such lack of restraint as is found may be embarrassing to us, but it must be remembered that early peoples are not so much afraid of plain speech as we are. No stigma of indecency or obscenity should therefore be attached to such Vinaya passages as seem unnecessarily outspoken to us. For they were neither deliberately indecent nor deliberately obscene ... Nevertheless the differences in the outlook of an early society and a modern one may easily be forgotten and disregarded. I have therefore omitted some of the cruder ... passages, and have given abbreviated versions of others, while incorporating them in their unabridged state in Pāli in an Appendix. (Horner 1938: xxvi–xxvii)

Elsewhere, early translators such as W.D. Rouse (1895) felt it best to render scurrilous passages into Latin.

A modern parallel exists in the presentation of Tibetan texts, particularly texts relating to rituals that would require initiation in a traditional context. In such a case the Tibetan is provided, but a translation is not. The reasons differ slightly, although convey a similar sense of wishing to protect the tradition being presented. Rob Mayer gives his reasons for withholding a translation from the Tibetan of a Buddhist text as follows:

> To bring [this book of a Tibetan Buddhist text] down to a reasonable size for publication here, all of the translation ... had to be discarded ... There is an additional reason for not including any translation in this published version: a widely accepted ethical standard in Social Anthropology is that one should not betray the confidence of one's fieldwork informants. I see no reason why this minimum standard should not also be applied in philology. The PAN [Phur-pa bcu-gnyis] is a text that still plays an important part in the religious life of contemporary Tibetan Buddhism, and, like other esoteric tantric scriptures of its type, is tradi-

tionally governed by a code of secrecy that limits access to it to those with the necessary levels of initiation. From a traditional point of view, this makes it unsuitable for general publication and uncontrolled distribution in an English translation. In addition, Dilgo Khyentse Rinpoche specifically asked me not to publish for general consumption or inappropriately distribute the English translation. ... I accordingly gave K R my word of honour that the translation would not be distributed beyond the traditionally sanctioned recipients, and it shall not be. (Mayer 1996: 159–160)

While the main motive for not translating (sensitivity to those for whom the tradition under study is significant) is laudable, the fact remains that ability in a classical language qualifies the translator to translate or withhold the material. Somehow classical language training, be it in Pāli, Latin or Tibetan, acts an alternative initiation. As an aside, it is significant that a censoring approach, however laudatory, perpetuates the mystique and concomitant ignorance of Tibet. In the 1950s and 1960s credulity and ignorance allowed 'T. Lobsang Rampa', aka Cyril Henry Hoskin, the son of a Devonshire plumber who had never set foot in Tibet, to sell hundreds of thousands of copies of books about that country. *The Third Eye* (1956), *Wisdom of the Ancients* (1965) and *Chapters of Life* (1967) were largely informed from his own imaginings, but were presented as factual to an unsuspecting public, despite the protestations of Tibetologists at the time.

Specific Gaps in Theravada

I shall now turn specifically to the impact of these factors on the textual representation of Theravada, the dominant form of Buddhism in Sri Lanka and mainland South-East Asia, and the consequences for the study or teaching of the subject. Many of the factors outlined above have focused translation activity on Theravada literature in Pāli, in particular the relatively early *Sutta* texts containing narrative teachings of the Buddha. Such literature as is translated tends to be the medieval retelling of those stories, or perhaps of commentarial stories related to them. Medieval texts in general, as well as philosophy, developed doctrine, ritual and texts relating to other areas of religious life (such as healing or astrology) are rarely translated.

It may come as some surprise then that within Theravada, the most highly valued texts have often been, not those *Sutta* texts of the canon, but non-canonical ritual texts, particularly those dealing with ecclesiastical rites of passage. Their status is reflected for example in the costly ornamentation and special script with which Burmese ecclesiastical ritual manuscripts are prepared. Early European observers of Theravada witnessed the significance accorded these paracanonical ritual texts. As a result they were the very earliest Buddhist texts to be translated into European languages, from the late 18th century. Surprisingly, virtually no material of this kind was subsequently published until 1988 despite its presence in all collections of manuscripts.

The neglect of ritual texts and other categories reflects the emphasis on Buddhism as a rational–scientific religion by Victorian observers. The evaluation, found in both Victorian and reform Theravadin scholarship, of Theravada as 'early Buddhism', and the rejection of those practices not conforming to this view as 'corruptions', cannot be tested because on the whole only early literature and the rejected practices are accessible for observation. In its *Sutta* texts, Theravada is not particularly distinct from other forms of Buddhism. The non-canonical texts for *Vinaya* reflect the history of monastic lineages and hence paths of influence and development, while the historical developments of practices and beliefs are reflected in ritual texts and treatises. The history of the development of distinctive Theravada thought is reflected in *Abhidhamma* texts. Therefore the *Vinaya*, ritual and *Abhidhamma* traditions and medieval treatises are what make Theravada distinctive. All are virtually absent from Western shelves, which means that Theravada is not only misrepresented, it is actually unrepresented. It is virtually impossible to teach historical Theravada. Even if those scholars who are in the privileged position of being able access such texts, tell students about medieval Theravada, they can produce little published evidence in support of their claims.

I shall now offer briefly a couple of specific examples of the effect of the current situation regarding translated texts and will show how such 'censorship' through selection can transform our understanding of religious perspectives in Theravada. Then I shall turn to an example of how a change in emphasis might affect overall evaluations of Theravada Buddhism from a religious-studies perspective.

Example 1: Theravada is presented to the West as non-devotional. On the basis of sections of the Pāli canon, Theravada is represented as rejecting devotion to the Buddha, who is no longer present after his death, and as advocating only an-iconic forms of representation of the Buddha. The devotion to Buddha statues observed on the ground is usually attributed to a combination of, possibly modern, Hindu influence and corruption on the part of psychologically needy lay people. Texts such as the *Account of the Kosala Statue*, mentioned above, and more-recently published medieval ritual texts from throughout the Theravada world, indicate the mainstream

Theravada belief on the part of even scholarly monks that statues of Buddha are empowered by the Buddha.

Example 2: On the basis of the Pāli canon, Theravada is presented to the West as being unconcerned about ritual purity or blasphemy. This is in spite of uncomfortably problematic practices, such as the exclusion of non-high-caste males from ordination into the most powerful monastic lineages in Sri Lanka. A single medieval text found throughout the Theravada world, the 'Code of Discipline (*vinaya*) for Lay People', specifies horrible fates (such as aeons in terrible hells), for the monk or layperson who even so much as spits in temple precincts or speaks derisively about the Buddha.

The next example I wish to take affects our overall assessment of Theravada. I mentioned before the problem of ritual texts that might be lengthy and highly repetitive, and only slight variations on the same set of terms. There is an entire body of meditation texts of this kind found throughout the Theravada world referred to as representing the *yogavacara* tradition (see Crosby 2000: 141). The texts fall simultaneously into all of our problem categories outlined above. They are long (e.g. 4000 verses in abbreviated form, which would take about a year to read through fully and practice), repetitive, often use only technical terminology without definitions, are highly ritualised, contrary to our expectations of Theravada, of little 'literary merit', contain little narrative or explanation, and are preserved in hybrid Pāli often combined with a local language. The practices advocated use ritualised meditation for both soteriological and worldly ends, i.e. to gain Buddhahood or *nibbana* and to heal or be successful in battle. The practices are so removed from our understanding of Theravada meditation, an understanding that is based almost entirely on canonical texts (and a 5th-century compendium) and modern reform practice, that the *yogavacara* tradition has been treated as fake. Yet, increasingly, textual evidence suggests that it may have been the most widespread form of Theravada practice before the modern period. If this is the case, i.e. if *yogavacara* is the mainstream, then how does this affect our overall assessment of Theravada?

Buddhism as lived fulfils all the dimensions identified in other religions. The consequent spectrum of Buddhist practices has often been interpreted through analysing Buddhism into different spheres. If we take the example of Theravada and Tibetan Buddhism, we can see how this categorisation differs for the two and provides us with one of the most fundamental distinctions made between them. Spiro and Samuel provide excellent discussions of the two respective traditions and roughly parallel analyses. Spiro (1971: 11) offers the following three categories for Theravada Buddhism (I have noted the related practices in parentheses):

(1) nibbanic (ultimately self-transforming meditation);
(2) kammatic (merit-making, ethical action);
(3) apotropaic (amulets, ritual, etc.).

Spiro indicates that we move from religion at the nibbanic end to magic at the apotropaic end. Soteriology at the nibbanic end approximates most closely to our traditional emphasis in representing Theravada, which contrasts with apotropaic acts and rituals at the magical end, the types of Theravada dismissed by some writers as later corruptions, not truly Buddhist.

Samuel (1993: 31) offers three parallel categories for Tibetan Buddhism:

(1) bodhi-oriented (altruism and higher levels of tantric practice, using tantric ritual techniques);
(2) karma-oriented (merit-making);
(3) pragmatic (this-worldly concerns, interactions with spirits, using tantric ritual techniques).

Here magic and ritual are recognised at both ends of the spectrum. The use of ritual at the soteriological end distinguishes Tibetan Buddhism from Theravada in general and has occasioned the dismissal of Tibetan Buddhism as a later corruption, not truly Buddhist and less pure than Theravada.

Yet, suppose we accept the *yogavacara* tradition as mainstream Theravada. It employs tantric-style ritual practice at both the bodhi-oriented/nibbanic end and the apotropaic/pragmatic end. Thus, it is very similar to Tibetan Buddhism and fits Samuel's analysis more closely than Spiro's, removing the fundamental criterion for differentiation between the structure of these two religious traditions.

Conclusion

I hope to have shown that early representations of Theravada in the West, and the types of text valued in the process of representation, continue to influence the selection of texts for translation. In combination with other factors, texts selected for new translations tend to confirm rather than challenge that view of Theravada. The view that Theravada is early, rational–scientific and anti-ritual is so strong that it prevents evidence to the contrary from being revealed or taken on board. Theravada as a historical and developed religion is hardly represented at all and, in teaching pre-modern Theravada, scholars are forced to rely on canonical materials that serve only to confirm the view that Theravada is somehow earlier than other forms of Buddhism. Yet historical evidence indicates that Theravada may have been far more similar to Tibetan Buddhism, for example, than may be comfortable for us or for reform Theravadins to acknowledge, thus forcing scholars to rethink their most fundamental characterisations of Theravada Buddhism.

Chapter 5

Texts and Contexts: Perspectives on Jewish Translations of the Hebrew Bible

LEONARD GREENSPOON

As a group, Jewish translations of the Bible have not attracted as much attention as have similar phenomena among Christians. In part, this results from the far smaller number of Jews in comparison with major Christian denominations, to say nothing of Christianity as a whole. But there are other factors at play as well, arising for the most part because Jews have been and remain a minority in the societies where they have produced such versions. This minority status helps explain distinctive features of Jewish Bible translations, features that paradoxically pull in different directions.

The first, and by far more noticeable, direction leads to the retention of the original Semitic languages, Hebrew and Aramaic, in which the Bible (Hebrew Bible or Old Testament) was originally composed – even in a translation. This practice (or better, complex of practices) carries with it the set of characteristics most easily identifiable as Jewish, culminating in the insight that, in the Jewish tradition, Bible translations are intended to supplement, not supplant; complement, not replace, the original (Greenspoon, 2002a: 410; 2003a: 2006). At heart, this is a matter of language.

Pulling in another, not necessarily opposite, direction is a second linguistic issue: the use by Jews of Bible translations as a means to communicate information about the target, rather than the source, language. In some such instances, Jewish versions are aimed at immigrants, for whom proper diction and grammar may be judged as equally important as correct dogma and good deeds. In societies where Jews have been marginalised residents for several or even many generations, a Jewish version can bridge the cultural as well as the linguistic gaps separating them from wider acceptance and accommodation (Greenspoon, 1999).

In a sense, translations of both sorts aim to do more than promote and promulgate a 'Jewish' understanding of sacred texts that originated with them but have been appropriated by others – not that this all-important task is to be in anyway slighted. But these translations aspire to more, and I discuss this *more* below, a dimension that centres on language, but also extends to the full range of contexts in which Jewish translators, individually or in groups, find themselves.

In the quest for exemplars, we can do no better than to begin at the beginning; namely, with the Septuagint (LXX) or Old Greek (OG) version that originated in Alexandria, Egypt, during the first half of the 3rd century BCE. This is true at least for the Torah or Pentateuch, the origins of which form a central topic in the *Letter of Aristeas*, which provides one understanding of LXX beginnings from a perspective dated a century or so after the events narrated. For our purposes, it is sufficient to remark on the process of translation that the Letter attributes to the OG or LXX of the Torah (which in many ways became the standard by which later Greek translators and revisers worked): 72 individuals, revered for their blameless morality as well as their linguistic skills in Hebrew and Greek, worked in subcommittees to prepare a draft of each of the Five Books of Moses. Each draft was then submitted to the group constituted as a committee of the whole for discussion and approval (Greenspoon, 1993: 20–24, 2002a: 397–400, 2003a: 2006–2007).

The author of the Letter does not discuss the technique of these translators. However, modern studies, although casting serious doubt on the picture of a single group working at one time, reveal strong continuities between and among the OG versions of the Torah books, in the direction of sensible or comprehensible literalism. That is to say, the translators in general present in Greek what they read in the Hebrew, bending the rules of Greek grammar and style to accommodate the Hebrew on numerous occasions, but rarely ending up with what a moderately well-educated Greek speaker would have considered nonsense.

For the Jews of Alexandria and elsewhere in the Greek-speaking diaspora, the Torah was at the centre of liturgy and study, parallel to its central place in Jewish life to this very day. For that reason, the translators responsible for its rendering into Greek thought long and hard about the approach they were going to take to this novel undertaking. Sensible literalism allowed non-Hebrew speaking Jews to gain firsthand acquaintance with the original language and style of Sacred Writ, while at the same time having direct access (that is, in their own language) to the teachings of the Torah (necessarily refracted through the linguistic and theological/ideological lenses of the translators).

By stressing the literal or non-Greek aspects of LXX/OG Greek, we emphasise the degree to which non-Hebrew speakers of the early 3rd century would have found this text strange, even exotic – admittedly a judgement that not all specialists would support. Nonetheless, some recent studies such as that of Albert Pietersma (2002) have proposed the 'interlinear' model to describe the Greek Torah as an heuristic, if not literal, way of understanding both how the translators worked and how their original audience would have reacted.

Lacking any precedents for such an undertaking, these translators hit upon a procedure that some of their successors adopted, others adapted, while still others – both those responsible for the LXX and the revisers – rejected. We can also easily imagine that many striking or frequently-used expressions found their way from the LXX into the everyday parlance or literature of Hellenistic Jews and, more broadly, into the language of the general Hellenistic world.

One approach taken by revisers such as Aquila, whose work can be found in the Septuagint itself as well as in isolated quotations and marginal notations, was to jettison almost all features of the target language (in this case Greek) in favour of distinctive elements in the source languages, Hebrew and Aramaic (Fernández Marcos, 2000: 109–122; Jobes & Silva, 2000: 38–40, 305–306). For example, anyone who comes at the Septuagint of Ecclesiastes, widely understood to be a product of Aquila (or perhaps of his school) from a classical background, immediately and powerfully grasps how foreign-sounding this text is, to the point of incomprehensibility in many places. We may well wonder what Aquila had in mind with the production of such a text, which apparently extended throughout the Bible. Perhaps he sought thereby to teach Hebrew to Greek speakers by accommodating the Semitic language to the Indo-European as little as possible (and this in spite of the fact that Aquila was considerably more creative and less mechanical in fashioning his text than generally credited). Such a pedagogical goal must have resonated with a considerable number of readers, since Aquila's version was widely recognised in antiquity as superior.

Privileging the Semitic base or source over the target language has thus been a feature of Jewish translations from their beginnings. In the abstract, this privileging can be judged more or less extreme or even sensible, but such judgements are most appropriately delivered within the context of the audience targeted by the translators themselves – in which case the OG of the Pentateuch and Aquila's Ecclesiastes might both be judged successes (or failures), in spite of their obvious differences.

One modern reflex, as it were, of this approach, reminiscent of Aquila though decidedly more moderate, is the 20th-century German version produced by the philosophers Martin Buber and Franz Rosenzweig (Buber & Rosenzweig, 1994; Gilman, 2002: 105–114). Like Aquila, their first allegiance was to the Hebrew and Aramaic original. With that goal in mind, they stretched contemporary German – sometimes, it has been argued, taking it beyond the breaking point – to reflect the sounds and structure of that original. Native German-speakers, even those thoroughly immersed in Yiddish language and culture, would have repeatedly stopped to puzzle over what the 'German' text meant, or implied, or suggested. But, as Buber and Rosenzweig forcefully and repeatedly argued, this was exactly their point: the Hebrew Bible is a product of a society chronologically, geographically, and intellectually far removed from ours. Much of this separation revolves around its origins as a Jewish text. Moreover, the meaning of that ancient text is not always clear; it often exhibits an opaqueness that most modern translations manage to obscure in their commitment to clarity. In sum, Scripture can authentically speak to us today only when its distinctive cadences and characteristics are admitted, articulated and even celebrated.

Many of the same procedures, although with somewhat different results, have been followed by Everett Fox in the preparation of his Schocken Bible (Fox, 1995). Like his predecessors, Fox exhibits a keen interest in the sounds of the Hebrew language and in conveying word plays, a literary device notoriously difficult to translate from one context, to say nothing of one language, to another. Moreover, Fox alerts English readers of the Hebrew Bible to its numerous instances of 'leading words' through which the repetition of the same or related lexemes connects passages (within the same book or in different books) that have thematic or other sorts of links. Fox does this by using the same English word as a rendering in all relevant instances. Other translators typically avoid this practice; they prefer to vary renderings in accordance with our usage. Yet, as Fox points out, they do so at the cost of depriving their readers of the clues or keys to understanding that would have been available to the earliest readers or listeners of the text.

Admittedly, Fox is something of an exception in the world of Jewish Bible translating in that he has not worked within a communal context or with a committee. In these respects, he is also similar to Buber and Rosenzweig. On the other hand, his work has thus far been accorded a far wider and more positive reception than that of Buber and Rosenzweig, on whom, as he generously acknowledges, Fox is dependent – though at the same time he rightly insists on his independence. In addition to the intrinsic worth of his version, Fox has benefited from well-conceived marketing by his publisher and greater receptivity to his general approach on the part of the public (Greenspoon, 2002b: 119).

Be that as it may, Fox argues with considerable cogency that his approach, in addition to its other merits, is inherently, authentically and distinctively Jewish. His argument is carried even further in the writings of Edward Greenstein, who has produced a version of Esther that exemplifies the principles and procedures put into practice more extensively by Fox (Greenstein, 1989a, 1989b, 1990).

The insistence on maintaining distinctive features of Hebrew, even – or especially – in translation, goes hand in hand with a reliance on the Semitic text as transmitted by the Masoretes, that is, the Masoretic Text (or MT). Reliance on the MT as a source text has continued in the face of any possible deficiencies in it and the preservation of what many would term preferable readings in other ancient versions (or the possibility of 'creating' such readings by conjecture). This reliance on the MT is characteristic of Jewish translations on a wider scale, as we shall see below, and serves to highlight the prominence or, better, priority of this text in comparison with any translation. Jewish versions also reflect and maintain liturgical practices associated with the annual cycle of Torah reading.

In addition, Jewish translations, including but not limited to those already mentioned, of necessity grapple with Jewish exegetical traditions, some of which were already in place when the OG of the Torah was prepared. Because Jewish exegetes have been anything but unanimous, even Jewish versions that aim at being 'traditional' frequently differ in their rendering of passages, especially those passages of halachic or ritual significance (Greenspahn, 2002: 52–61, 2002a: 409–410, 2003a: 2015–2020; Margolis, 1917: 9–43, 51–63, 84–106; Orlinsky, 1992: 839–840).

We turn now to the second paradigm: namely, Jewish versions in which the target language assumes greater significance. I begin this discussion in the middle rather than in the beginning because the Jewish Publication Society (JPS) version of 1917 provides the most accessible means to introduce this phenomenon.

In 1908, Max L. Margolis, recently appointed as editor-in-chief for a new Bible translation under JPS auspices, faced a daunting challenge. For half a century, American Jews had possessed an English version of their own: the work of Isaac Leeser, an extraordinarily accomplished rabbi and communal leader (Sussman, 1985). Near the turn of the 20th century, efforts had been devised, but only haltingly carried out, to prepare a successor to Leeser's version. With the appointment of Margolis, JPS took over that challenge.

Leeser's version had been serviceable, but hardly a literary achievement of note. Only an organisation, in this case JPS, could bring to fruition the intended project, which was to unite non-Orthodox Jews in the work of translation. The board of editors appointed by JPS was carefully balanced among the most influential contemporary Jewish denominations and academic institutions. With well-connected rabbis predominating, Margolis was the only academically-trained linguist (in both Semitic and classical languages) and the only biblical scholar amongst its seven members (Greenspoon, 1988).

In spite of his impressive academic training and professorial experience, Margolis was in many ways an odd choice to edit an English-language version, not least because he was at that point still a fairly recent immigrant to the United States, having arrived at New York City in 1889. As it happened, Margolis's self-understanding as an immigrant was to play a major role in the direction that the JPS version, first published in 1917, was to take (Greenspoon 1987: 68–71). For Margolis, language was the key to successful integration into American society, not only for scholars such as himself. Every new American Jew needed to acquaint himself or herself with the best literary style and diction that the English language could offer. In Margolis's opinion, none other than the King James Version (KJV) offered precisely such a text. He was in no way deterred from his admiration for KJV by the fact that its language was more than 300 years old by Margolis' time, thus rendering many of its expressions antiquated, if not already obsolete. Of course, Margolis well understood that no translation is neutral; each is a product of its time, revealing the theological and ideological predilections of the translators themselves. Thus, he recognised that KJV was in need of theological remediation, even though it admirably performed its task as literary model.

The JPS leadership was not adverse to Margolis's proposals in this regard, although it was primarily moved by two other, more pragmatic, considerations. In the first instance, basing the project on an already existing text (that is, producing a revision rather than a fresh translation) was bound to be more efficient and less time-consuming. The earlier, abortive translation project mentioned above foundered on just this point: it was taking far too long. A centralised board of editors, presided over by a determined and dedicated editor-in-chief, would solve that problem, or so it was thought. Moreover, in early 20th-century America, KJV still reigned supreme (despite increasingly vocal criticisms), especially in the Protestant churches and homes with which JPS leaders were wont to compare themselves (Sarna 1989: 104–116).

The JPS version of 1917, in spite of its title and the thrust of all the publicity surrounding its launch, was in fact a revision of KJV. More precisely, it was a revision of the Revised Version of 1885, a product of the leading British Protestant denominations that, while accomplishing some updating and correcting (in addition to the introduction of what might fair-mindedly be termed a few steps backward), remained very much in the lineage of KJV. The text of the JPS version of 1917, like KJV itself, does not sound very much like Buber and Rosenzweig, or Fox, or similar Jewish efforts. Nonetheless, as Margolis and others would argue, the success of KJV owes a great deal to its ability to adapt into the English language some of the basic stylistic and even lexical features of the Semitic original (Bobrick, 2001: 240–243; McGrath, 2001: 230–235). Thus, the KJV translators, in their introduction, acknowledge their debt to and dependence on, among other sources, scholars (albeit non-Jewish) of the Hebrew language and the Old Testament (Rhodes & Lupas, 1997: 81–82). Moreover, the KJV translators were not unacquainted with or unaffected by medieval Jewish exegetes, in particular David Kimchi. Thus, this pre-eminently Protestant product, KJV, was more than a little influenced by Jews, even though no Jews served on the KJV committee (or that of the RV, for that matter), Jews being still officially banished from Great Britain in the early 1600s (Daiches, 1941: 183–208).

Only Jews could produce a Bible translation for Jews, Margolis insisted, although they could benefit from the best that non-Jewish versions had to offer. In making such arguments and following such a pattern, Margolis consciously and openly followed in the footsteps of an individual who was something of an example and hero for him; namely, the German Enlightenment leader, Moses Mendelssohn (Böckler, 2001; Greenspoon, 2003b).

Mendelssohn, active in the latter half of the 18th century, represented the Jew-in-progress of his time, much as Margolis or JPS leaders such as Judge Meyer Sulzberger reflected the socially, politically and intellectually up-and-coming Jewry of early 20th century America. Although not born into wealth or social prominence, Mendelssohn developed all the tools and talents, literary and intellectual, necessary to be a major player in the first generation or so of Jews liberated at last from the medieval constraints placed upon them by hostile Christian majorities. Christians, of course, remained in power, and many of them retained their animosity toward Jews. But, one by one, legal and social barriers fell against Jewish participation in the world at large.

Mendelssohn was a gifted speaker and writer on a wide variety of topics; not surprisingly, he was often embattled – and even embittered – by conflicts with Christian antagonists on religious and philosophical topics. His progressive views on many traditional Jewish beliefs, such as revelation, also brought him into combat with fellow Jews. Nonetheless, Mendelssohn remained convinced, in much the way that Margolis was some century and a half later, that there was no good reason why Jews should not partake of almost all the fruits of advanced societies such as the Prussia that Mendelssohn inhabited. Jews could be successful – and often were – in almost any endeavour at which Christians excelled. But there were distinctive features of Judaism about which Mendelssohn was unwilling to compromise.

One of the areas about which Mendelssohn felt most strongly was modern-language translation of the Hebrew Bible, in particular the Torah. He was unhappy, to say the least, with the Judaeo–German and other earlier versions prepared by German Jews during their centuries of living in German lands. Many of these translations used a simplified diction, perhaps appropriate to their intended audience – women and children – or were filled with Midrashic sorts of elaborations considered necessary for that same uneducated or undereducated audience (Billigheimer, 1968: 3–5; Gilman, 2002: 95–105).

Mendelssohn would have none of this. He believed that entry into middle- and upper-class German society would be unavailable to Jews until they improved their style of writing and speaking. For Mendelssohn, Luther's Old Testament version of the early 1500s, appropriately updated, formed a perfect basis for educating the German-speaking Jews of his day. At the same time, Mendelssohn balked at accepting many of Luther's theological phrases and expressions, which he correctly judged as antithetical to the Jewish interpretation of the biblical text. The text and accompanying commentary he prepared, made possible almost entirely from his own intellectual and financial resources, appeared in the late 1700s.

In many respects, Mendelssohn's translation functioned in the same way as did the version of Margolis, who, as noted above, willingly acknowledged the debt he owed to his predecessor. There were, however, differences beyond the different languages, German and English, into which the biblical texts were rendered. Firstly, Margolis worked with the institutional support of JPS. Not only did this help in providing the resources for the preparation and publication of the translation, but it also served to shield the version from at least some of the more vocal criticism of the sort that Mendelssohn encountered. Secondly Mendelssohn sought to educate a generation of German-speaking Jews who, by and large, descended from families long resident in those lands. Thirdly the earliest editions of Mendelssohn's Torah translation was printed in Hebrew letters, which was the way Yiddish and other Jewish German literature of his day was produced. Later editions, which appeared after Mendelssohn's death, presented the German in its usual script.

Even with these differences, the obvious similarities stand out and need not be repeated. Mendelssohn's version was not as influential for German-speaking Jews as the JPS version of 1917 was for English speakers. In fact, when Mendelssohn's grandchildren and other descendants looked at his text decades later, they did so as outsiders to Judaism, having converted to the Christian religion with which Moses Mendelssohn had fought so hard to find accommodation without capitulating.

Margolis's version was widely reprinted, in many different formats, through World War II and the 1950s. In the early 1960s, a new generation of JPS leaders determined that it was time for a new version, but were at first uncertain whether it would be a revision or new translation. It was because of the efforts of Harry M. Orlinsky that JPS embarked on a translation in a new style that, for Orlinsky, spoke more directly and meaningfully to the Jews of his day (Orlinsky 1974: 342–262, 396–417). As was the case with Mendelssohn and Margolis before him, Orlinsky was also influenced by developments within Christianity. Like his predecessors, he also proclaimed the inadequacy for Jews of any version of the Bible prepared under Christian auspices. But if the impulse was the same, the result was markedly different.

Orlinsky had studied briefly with Margolis during the final months of the latter's career as a professor at Dropsie College in Philadelphia. By the early 1960s, Orlinsky had gathered academic acclaim for his forays into textual criticism, biblical scholarship and archaeology, and had also demonstrated considerable interest and experience in Bible translation. JPS turned to him for advice in fashioning their new version.

Orlinsky was much taken by recent developments in translation theory that marked a shift from the more literal or formal approaches to the source text, in this case the Semitic tongues of the Hebrew Bible. As developed and promulgated by Eugene Nida of the American Bible Society (ABS), a new approach – at first named dynamic equivalence, later termed functional equivalence – was deemed better suited to the masses of Bible readers (and hearers) of the mid-20th century (De Waard & Nida, 1986). Advocates and adherents of functional equivalence translation ask that translators consider how the original text functioned and then determine how best to convey that function in the modern target language. Although it may be possible to retain the form of the ancient original in the process, this is not the highest priority. In contrast, formal equivalence translators emphasise the close, perhaps even inextricable link that unites form and meaning.

Functional equivalence is at the heart of two very popular Bibles prepared, published and widely disseminated by ABS: Today's English Version (TEV) or the Good News Bible (GNB) and the Contemporary English Version (CEV). It is also the decisive stylistic factor in the JPS Tanakh (1985), as the version overseen by Orlinsky came to be known. Among the most noticeable stylistic features of such versions are the jettisoning of the ubiquitous conjunction 'and' and the widespread use of subordinate clauses as opposed to the coordination found everywhere both in the Semitic original and in formal equivalence renderings (Orlinsky & Bratcher, 1991: 179–205).

Such features go beyond matters of text, as important as they are, to issues of formatting. Traditionally, printed English-language translations appear on two-columned pages, with verse and other markings prominently (and perhaps intrusively) inserted in the text itself wherever they fell. This has stood as the appropriate 'look' for English Bible over several centuries. TEV, GNB, CEV, and the Tanakh represent a break with this usual Bible formatting, much as they do with traditional Bible translating. In these versions, the text is spread across the page, as it would be in any other work of contemporary literature, and verse and other markings are placed more discreetly in the margins so as not to break up the reader's experience with the text.

For Orlinsky, all of this is perfectly compatible with an authentically Jewish Bible for today's Jewish communities. The Bible needs to be brought to them in terms of style and of format. It is serious reading, to be sure, but it should not be more formidable than any other serious English literature. It is also Jewish literature, and on this point Orlinsky has been as adamant as Margolis, Mendelssohn, or any other Jewish translator. Orlinsky was vigorously opposed to the inclusion of distinctively Christian renderings in a translation made for Jews, and he assiduously expunged them in favour of traditional Jewish understandings. To him, this was the hallmark of an authentically Jewish translation; that is, its reliance on Jewish exegetical sources (Hertz, 1961; Lieber *et al.*, 2001; Orlinsky, 1969, 1990; Plaut, 1981, 1996).

There is one other feature of the Tanakh that, for Orlinsky and his fellow editors, marked it as distinctively Jewish, and in this emphasis they were at one with far more literal translators such as Buber and Rosenzweig and Fox. Many pages of the Tanakh contain footnotes indicating that the meaning of the Hebrew (in this case, of course, the traditional Masoretic Text) cannot be determined. Christian translators (including those associated with the ABS), tend to use such notations sparingly, if at all, preferring to offer readers their interpretation of the text as the appropriate meaning. By contrast, Jewish translators, in general more attuned to the many ambiguities inherent in the Semitic original, are far more likely to acknowledge their uncertainty. In this respect, the Tanakh differs markedly from its Christian counterparts such as GNB and CEV.

Throughout its history Jewish translation of the Hebrew Bible has wrestled with a number of issues. In many respects, the problems Jewish translators faced, and the solutions they arrived at, were quite similar to those of Christian translators. But Jews operated in distinct environments and contexts; as a result, the circumstances of Bible translators in their communities differed from those of non-Jews. In particular, Jewish translators have always operated as a minority, which has major ramifications for both the process and result of their work, even in societies such as the United States, where Jews have in general found acceptance. Jews also have a commitment to the Hebrew language and to their own traditions of exegesis, both of which are bound to set them apart from others, even when such separation occurs in the friendliest of circumstances. Such circumstances can be viewed as obstacles to overcome (which, indeed, they sometimes were) or opportunities to be embraced – or at least creatively met. Thankfully, Jewish translators (as with Jews in general) have often productively adopted the latter approach, with the result that we are the beneficiaries of a rich and constantly-evolving tradition of Bible translation and commentary (Fisch, 1997; Greenspoon, 2002c; Herbert, 1968; Hertz, 1938; Hills, 1962; Kaplan, 1981; Sarna & Sarna, 1988; Singerman, 1990; *The Tanach*, 1996). This tradition prominently exhibits the 'plus' that I spoke of at the beginning of this article, not as a sign of the superiority of such versions (as has indeed been asserted on occasion), but as an indication of the distinctive features their readers find within. Such versions help to ensure not only the survival of Judaism, but also the vitality and vibrancy of a collection of words that still functions for many as the Word.

Chapter 6

Making Sanskritic or Making Strange? How Should We Translate Classical Hindu Texts?

W. J. JOHNSON

Although the title of this chapter sounds inclusive, not to say megalomaniac, my intention is not to discuss the translation of Hindu texts in general, but only the translation of one particular kind of text. Sanskritists – professional Indologists – are of course concerned about, if not always with, the huge number of classical Indian texts that have not yet been translated into modern languages, but that is not my business here. (Indeed, what *can* be said about such texts, other than that they need to be edited and translated?) For it seems to me that we can only begin to talk about 'translation' – i.e. how we *should* or might translate – in relation to specific examples, and in conformity to, or deviation from particular models.

So this chapter is concerned in general with texts that have been translated into English at least once, and in particular with those that have been subject to multiple translations. Among the latter the *Bhagavad Gītā* has the longest and most voluminous history. It was first translated into a modern European language (English) in 1785 by Charles Wilkins, and John Brockington (2001: 449) has estimated that more than 300 further translations into English had appeared by the end of the 20th century. A snap survey shows that there are currently nearly 200 versions in English offered for sale on Amazon's UK site, including one by me (Johnson: 1994) in the Oxford World's Classics series. A reasonable reaction to this might be 'enough is enough – for goodness' sake translate something else'. From one perspective, I sympathise: that was precisely how I felt when I was asked to do my own translation.

From another perspective, however (and this is where my prescriptive or polemical point comes in), there have still not been enough *Gītā* translations. Why not enough? Because the *Gītā* has not yet, in my view, become a classic for English-speaking culture in the way that, for instance, Homer has become a classic. By classic I mean a text that has come to be treated as part of the target tradition, whether literary, religious, cultural, or all these things, and in the process of assimilation, has to some extent redefined that tradition. Of course a little of the *Gītā*'s imagery has become familiar to some in the wider culture, perhaps most ambiguously in J. Robert Oppenheimer's assimilation of Krishna's theophany to the first thermonuclear explosion: 'I am become death, the destroyer of worlds', which is one way of translating *Gītā* 11:32. But, in spite of the number of times it has been translated, the *Gītā* has not yet, as a text, achieved the kind of cultural domestication that, for example, the *Iliad* has attained through the translations or versions of, for instance, Chapman, Pope, and Christopher Logue. One reason for this is that, so far, we have simply not had a sufficiently compelling version in English (and I include my own translation here). The *Gītā* has not yet met its Chapman or Logue. There are, of course, good reasons for this: wider cultural and political imperatives apply than simply the attention or inattention of talented poets. On the other hand, it does not take much imagination to suppose that in Britain, at least, with such confident Anglophone and Asian-derived cultural complexes to hand, the prerequisites for such a version have never been more obviously present. One might go even further and see this as part of a wider process through which in, Lorna Hardwick's words, 'cultures are actually created and defined by various kinds of translation'(Hardwick, 2000: 22.)

But whether or not the time for such an *avatāra* has really come, there are gains to be made from reflecting on the kinds of translations or re-translations we might attempt at this point in the *Gītā*'s Western history (the *Gītā* here being emblematic of a certain type of classical Hindu text, to which I shall return later). This means looking at some of the types of translations we already have and suggesting additions to or variations on these approaches.

In terms of language, if not sensibility, there are broadly two types of existing translations: those that domesticate the Sanskrit source and those that 'foreignise' it or make it strange, to use the terminology of Schleiermacher (Schulte & Biguenet 1992: 42). A more intricate distinction was made by the remarkable poet, translator and scholar A.K. Ramanujan (1999b: 156ff.) who referred to three intersecting types of translation: 'the iconic', 'the indexical', and the 'symbolic'. By 'iconic' Ramanujan meant a 'faithful' translation, i.e. a calque in so far as it preserves the characters, imagery, order of incidents and metre in another language and a different idiom. By 'indexical' he meant a translation that retains basic elements, such as plot, but fills the rest with local deities, folklore, poetic traditions and imagery.By 'symbolic' he meant a translation that uses plots and characters minimally, and uses them to say new things. In other words, a 'symbolic' translation maps a structure of relationships onto another plane and another symbolic system. It is often the aim of such a 'symbolic' translation to subvert a predecessor (the 'original') by producing a counter text (Ramanujan, 1999b: 157). Ramanujan points out that to some extent all translations (even so-called 'faithful' or 'iconic' ones) inevitably include all three kinds of elements. The question is therefore really one of what we read a translation for – i.e. their *skopos* as translations. Here I am arguing for a multiplicity of purposes, including the literary or poetic.

In the broadest sense, Ramanujan's types overlap in some places with the foreignising/domesticating distinction. However, it would take a much longer essay to draw out the full complexity and resonance of such divisions, so I restrict myself here to the simpler distinction, but, nevertheless, occasionally indicate the equivalent in Ramanujan's system of classification.

The domesticating translations of the *Gītā* form a large majority, but I shall look first at an example of what could be considered a foreignising translation. This is one made in 1944 by the American Sanskritist Franklin Edgerton in a volume containing a dual Sanskrit/English text. Edgerton himself (1994: vol. 1x) describes it as 'fairly literal' but not 'un-English'. He covers himself, however, by reprinting in the same volume Sir Edwin Arnold's poetic version of 1896, *The Song Celestial*, for those who cannot read Sanskrit. Students of translation are, I suspect, more interested now in Edgerton's literalness than in Arnold's late Victorian pseudo-Shakespearian version, although it is diverting to note that it was through Arnold's translation that Gandhi was introduced to the *Gītā*. The strangeness that Edgerton produces, however, is not of the self-conscious literary variety, but is essentially an aid for students, or anyone else wanting a word-for-word translation. In Ramanujan's terms, it is 'iconic'. To take an example from Chapter 2:

> But with desire-and-loathing-severed
>   Senses acting on the objects of sense,
>
> With (senses) self-controlled, he, governing his self,
>   Goes unto tranquillity.
>
> In tranquillity, of all griefs
>   Riddance is engendered for him;
> For of the tranquil-minded quickly
>   The mentality becomes stable.

Edgerton, 1994: vv. 64–65

Sanskrit is a heavily inflected language in which word order makes little or no difference to meaning, especially in verse. This version follows as closely as possible the Sanskrit word order, although it cannot follow it completely. 'Desire-and-loathing-severed' are connected by hyphens to indicate a Sanskrit compound; case endings are evoked at the expense of idiomatic English ('of all griefs' is a compound with a genitive plural ending); the passive constructions favoured by Sanskrit and abhorred by grammar-checkers are retained: 'Riddance is engendered for him'.

The question arises whether this method, or a version of it, could be adapted as a *literary* strategy in translating this text. While leaving that possibility open, although I am sceptical, I would at the same time want to reject any notion that this kind of translation is somehow more 'Sanskritic', in the sense of conveying more of the original, than other types of translation. This is not a claim that Edgerton makes – indeed, he rejects it implicitly by including Edwin Arnold's translation because it is capable, as he says (1994: vol. 2, 4), of giving 'a good idea of the living spirit of the poem'. He further states that 'the poetic inspiration found in many of the *Gītā's* lines can hardly be fully appreciated unless they are presented in a poetic form'.

Early in her career as a translator, Wendy Doniger O'Flaherty (1987: 124) argued otherwise, claiming that the literal rendition of compounds, and the element of puzzle-solving thereby presented to the reader, produced a language that was 'more easily intelligible than the widely accepted English verse of Ezra Pound, e. e. cummings and others'. This, however, avoids mentioning the real problem: that this Sanskritised English does not usually *sound* right in the way that Pound and cummings do. In fact, O'Flaherty herself, in the same paper modifies her earlier stance in favour of something more domesticating (O'Flaherty, 1987: 125).

There are two related reasons for rejecting any such claims, one general, one specific. The first and general reason is that, if in a translation we are attempting to create some kind of equivalent experience for the English reader, then strangeness of this kind is not something the Sanskrit reader would have experienced in the original. There are arguments about deliberately disorientating the English reader to preserve the 'otherness' of the other culture and so avoid orientalist appropriations. There is also the hope that you can inject interesting new idioms into English prosody by adopting this method. But, in all such cases, it seems to me that you end up with something more strange than Sanskritic. In fact, such strategies deny the possibility of equivalence and through their deliberate 'otherness' recommend departure from it. In which case it hardly seems to matter which particular text you depart from. I am not proposing that these strategies should be avoided or abandoned, I am simply arguing that it should not be claimed that they are inherently 'Sanskritic', or necessarily closer to the 'original' – an idea in itself problematic enough in the context of Indian epics.

The second, specific, reason for rejecting such claims is that there is a major difference between Sanskrit and modern English. Classical Sanskrit is an artificial language with an almost inexhaustible supply of true synonyms and truly synonymous constructions. Daniel Ingalls (2000: 81), for instance, points out that a simple English sentence such as 'You must fetch the horse' can be rendered into Sanskrit in at least 15 different ways with no loss, or addition, of social or emotional resonance – without the kind of shift in nuance and resonance that you get in English from saying, 'Fetch the filly!' rather than 'You ought to go and get the gee gee' or 'The nag should be brought here by you'.

While this characteristic of synonymity is, as Ingalls compellingly argues, most prominent in the classical Sanskrit of *kāvya* and *mahākāvya* (of lyrical and epic poetry), it seems to me that it is also very apparent in the pre-classical and perhaps more natural language of the *Gītā* and its 'nest' text, the *Mahābhārata*. In other words, what you have in the Sanskrit text could have been rendered with almost identical effect in a number of other ways. Therefore to follow the word order or compound construction in an English translation, in the belief that you are somehow being more Sanskritic or getting closer to the root meaning of the original, seems misguided. Making strange in this way would indeed be more strange than Sanskritic: the Sanskrit guest might hardly recognise the autistic part it was being asked to play; 'autistic' in the sense of being prevented from making a proper response to its environment. As Indologists know, the Indian tradition itself exemplifies this capacity for multiplicity – epic classics such as the *Mahābhārata* and the *Rāmāyaṇa* have, in Ramanujan's words (1999a: 118), 'multiple existences' in many languages, in oral and written forms, classical and folk modes, television, comics, songs and Bollywood movies.

Edgerton is perhaps an extreme example, but the 'translationese' of many versions by professional Sanskritists is a close cousin to his 'literal' version. Writing in 1937 in the introduction to his co-translation of some of the *Upanishads*, the poet W.B. Yeats declared that the versions of 'the most eminent scholars' left him incredulous:

> Could latinised words, hyphenated words, could polyglot phrases, sedentary distortions of unnatural English – 'However many Gods in Thee All-knower, adversely slay desires of a person' – could muddles, muddied by Lo! Verily! and Forsooth, represent what grass farmers sang thousands of years ago, what their descendants sing today? (Purohit Swāmi & Yeats, 1970: 7–8)

What then of the domesticating translations which, as I have indicated, are in the majority? The most immediately striking thing about them, in contrast to the kaleidescopic variety of Indian versions, is their uniformity and their blandness in English. In other words, what we have in English is multiplication without multiplicity (cf. Ramanujan 1999b: 156ff). One reason for their similarity is that there are relatively few complete Sanskrit/English dictionaries. The most comprehensive, to date, and the one favoured by most Anglophone translators, was compiled by Monier Williams at the end of the 19th century. Indeed, when I was beginning my own translation of the *Gītā*, I was told by a far more eminent Sanskrit scholar than myself that I would know when I was getting it wrong because it would start to deviate from other translations.

Within the general type of domesticating translations, however, there are some versions that do indeed deviate significantly from their rivals. These include the most widely available and, if unreformed student habits are anything to go by, the most popular version by Juan Mascaró (1962) in Penguin Classics.

Is it amongst this group that we should be looking for a classic, culture-defining, or culture-redefining translation? Unfortunately, the chances of such a discovery are not high. When we examine these idiosyncratic versions closely, we realise that their deviation from the norm is not so much in terms of language or, perhaps more exactly, idiom, but in terms of theology. The use of language in itself is unexceptional, and too often imprecision is value-added to blandness. Indeed, Mascaró's Penguin version comes close to being a kind of New Age all-purpose *Gītā* for the Western world, imposing uniformity through the language of international mysticism, and courting universality through theological homogenisation. Compare, for instance, Edgerton's very literal translation of *Bhagavad Gītā* 4:24:

> The (sacrificial) presentation is Brahman; Brahman is the oblation;
> In the (sacrificial) fire of Brahman it is poured by Brahman;
> Just to Brahman must he go,
> Being concentrated upon the (sacrificial) action that is Brahman.
>
> Edgerton, 1994

with Mascaró's version:

> Who in all his work sees God, he in truth goes unto God: God is his worship, God is his offering, offered by God in the fire of God.
>
> Mascaró, 1962

I do not think that Mascaró's strategy is necessarily illegitimate in itself; indeed, I argue for a variation on it below. I should, however, prefer something with more linguistic vitality. The localised problem for those teaching Indian religions is that non Sanskrit-reading students do not recognise that this is an indexical or even a symbolic translation, not a literal, faithful or iconic one, to use Ramanujan's terminology.

An analogous, although very different, case of deviation by theology from the translational norm is that presented by the well-known version, the *Bhagavad Gītā As It Is* by Swami Prabhupāda of the International Society for Krishna Consciousness, popularly known as the Hare Krishnas (Bhaktivedanta Swami Prabhupāda, 1968). This is a sectarian Vaishnavite reading of the text, in which a particular theological position turns the 'translation' into exegesis and commentary in a standard and traditional way although to the uninformed this may not be immediately apparent. The '*As It Is*' makes all the difference. Again the use of English is unexceptional, and the deviation from the norm is in terms of content rather than intensity or variety of expression. Swami Prabhupāda's version of *Bhagavad Gītā* 4.24 goes as follows:

> A person who is fully absorbed in Krishna consciousness is sure to attain the spiritual kingdom through his full contribution to spiritual activities, for the consummation is absolute and the things offered are also of the same spiritual nature.

It *is* the same verse as that translated by Edgerton and Mascaró. In other contexts I would argue that if the *Gītā*'s theology is strange to us, we have a better chance of discovering possible universals by immersing ourselves in its cultural specificity than we do by obscuring it. (My own, more literal translation reads:

> The offering is Brahman, the oblation is Brahman, poured by Brahman into the fire that is Brahman. Brahman is to be attained by the man who concentrates intensely on the action that is Brahman. (Johnson, 1994)

This is close to Edgerton, but instead of his parenthesis I employ an endnote: 'Brahman: here the supreme being and the totality of the sacrifice.')

To summarise, I am equally dissatisfied with linguistically strange and linguistically uniform translations, including the subtype of translations that are theologically, but not linguistically, singular. What then am I hoping for? And what are the possible models?

The comparison I made at the beginning between the *Gītā* and the *Iliad* was more tendentious than random. It is now recognised in the West, although perhaps not as widely as it should be, that the *Gītā* too is a part (in terms of length, a very small part) of a comparable Indo-European epic, the *Mahābhārata*. However, the epic nature of the *Bhagavad Gītā* has not yet produced an epic-style translation, although van Buitenen (1981) has embedded it theologically and narratively in his uniform prose translation of parts of the rest of the *Mahābhārata*. The difficulty, it seems to me, is to find an epic style and range of expression that, at the same time, or sequentially, can deal with the didactic, theological and philosophical portions of a 'live' religious text. I have myself experimented with and published different styles of epic translation for other parts of the *Mahābhārata*, but this has been mostly translation of narrative material. The search for such a style or range of styles should begin, although not necessarily end, with the best translations of comparable epics such as the *Iliad* and the *Odyssey*. There are other models as well, but one that should definitely be avoided, in my opinion, is that provided by non-Hindu religious texts, notably the Christian Bible. The King James Version, for instance, has a style that, for those who know it, forever resonates with its content. Many translations of the *Gītā* – particularly, and perhaps inevitably, in the 19th century – have taken the neo-Biblical route, with all the inappropriate echoing that entails. In short, the epic model whether Greek, Latin or other may be a good place to start, precisely because it is drawn from an idiom, which is *not* associated with a *live* religious content. Indeed, the *Gītā* has plenty of such content itself without needing what amounts to a layer of further commentary contained in the idiom of the translation itself.

This merely emphasises what we all already know – that, whether we like it or not, the language we use in a translation shapes our understanding of its content. What I am arguing here is that, at this point in its English-language history, we would benefit from an epic and poetic, even a dramatic translation, i.e. reading, of the content of the *Gītā*. Peter Brook in his controversial staged, and subsequently filmed version of the *Mahābhārata* included a summary dramatised version.

One characteristic of the *Gītā*, and of the *Mahābhārata* in general, that I have not mentioned so far is that the original is composed in a very flexible and content-accommodating syllabic verse, probably devised and honed in the process of oral recitation. Again Homeric and epic analogies suggest themselves. Recent translators from the Sanskrit have too often ducked the verse question, sometimes claiming, somewhat disingenuously, that plain or even clunky English prose is necessarily a better solution than potentially sub-standard verse. I am not, however, recommending imitation of the Sanskrit metrical patterns, a strategy almost certain to produce the same kind of inorganic strangeness that is generated by following the Sanskrit word order.

Verse in the hands of English poets, of course, might take us somewhere else. Given that there have been so many domesticating translations (more than 300), why have no obvious classic versions appeared in English? Why, for instance, has no major English poet tackled the *Gītā?* Yeats may have come closest when, as already mentioned, in 1937 he produced with Shree Purohit Swāmi a version of ten principal *Upanishads*. Disappointingly, perhaps because Yeats was interested in the mystical, his version seems to suffer from an over-reverential approach. It is also in prose. Possibly the best chance so far of a really compelling English version of the *Gītā* died when T.S. Eliot assimilated his reading of it into *The Dry Salvages* (1979).

In general, however, this neglect, when compared with the poetic attention given to Homer, Virgil, and Ovid, obviously reflects educational patterns, and the weight of Greek and Latin classicism in English literary culture. With a few exceptions (Gustav Holst springs to mind), only specialist scholars learn Sanskrit in the West. But in this respect at least, Greek and Latin are quickly catching up. One unexpected but positive result of this is that some of the best recent versions of, for instance, Homer in English have been produced by poets who have little or no Greek, but work from literal translations. Their very lack of knowledge of the original language often appears to be an advantage, in that they do not have the scholar's inhibition about detaching themselves from the left-hand page in search of imaginative equivalence and communicative energy. Perhaps, above all, they are not, either in the personal or academic sense, theologically interested parties.

This is not to say they produce that mythical beast the neutral or value-free translation. What they impose, and what I am commending to translators from the Sanskrit, is a *different* kind of value system. In Ramanujan's terms, these are 'symbolic' translations.

It may be that professional Sanskritists, and their publishers, need to be less jealous of their texts and encourage – indeed, commission – the poets to take their turn, including, perhaps, Anglophone poets immersed in Hindu religious culture, who may not be Sanskrit readers themselves. These poets may produce 'indexical' translations in Ramanujam's term, whereas non-Hindu related poets might produce something more symbolic. In other words, perhaps at this point we should aim for collaborative or two-tier translations again – a return of a kind to the Edgerton/Edwin Arnold pattern. This may produce a new strangeness in English, but one that could be strangely familiar to growing sections of the British and American populations.

The general plea is for new purposes in the translation of the *Gītā*. New audiences require new and different kinds of translation, and there is of course a symbiotic relationship between audiences – real or imagined – and the ways in which translators translate. At the same time I would want to avoid the linguistic inhibitions of an over-reverential approach. While the theology is to some extent carried in the language used, the *Gītā* would, in my view, benefit from being de-theologised and re-established as epic. In English the literal rendition of content is not enough: we also need linguistic vitality. That is to say, we need a literary as well as a religious classic. Indeed, can there be a 'religious classic' on its own without the literary dimension? Those less theologically involved might be better placed to achieve this literary dimension. Better perhaps, at this stage, to have the translator hesitantly imagining or re-imagining the meaning, rather than those convinced they know it in advance, or who look through the language rather than with it.

Chapter 7

Archaising versus Modernising in English Translations of the Orthodox Liturgy: St John Crysostomos in the 20th Century

ADRIANA ŞERBAN

The Orthodox Liturgy

The word 'liturgy' comes from Ancient Greek (Λειτουργία) and literally means 'the work of the people' or 'public service', and in the Orthodox Church it refers to the celebration of the Eucharist. The Orthodox Church is composed of a number of autonomous Orthodox Churches, most (though by no means all) of them being national churches such as the Serbian Orthodox Church, the Romanian Orthodox Church, the Greek Orthodox Church. The customary liturgy used almost daily throughout the year by most Orthodox Churches is that of St John Crysostomos (Golden-Mouth), although other forms of Eucharistic celebration do exist. On ten occasions during the year the liturgy of St Basil is used, and during weekdays in the Lent the liturgy of St John Crysostomos is replaced by the liturgy of the Presanctified Gifts. Some Orthodox Churches in the Middle East use the liturgies of St James, St Gregory, and of St Cyril.

While 'liturgy' primarily designates the celebration itself, which includes an array of verbal and non-verbal components considered together (most notably the persons involved in the celebration, the words that are either recited or chanted, the icons, candles, incense, the special attires of priests and deacons, and the actions that are performed), 'liturgy' also refers to the *text* itself in its written form that is read or chanted. It is also frequent for the word 'liturgy' to be used in connection with parts of the text. Thus, many editions of the liturgy that target the laity do not include in full the part of text usually chanted or read by priests and deacons, especially the prayers recited in a low voice.

St John Crysostomos or Golden-Mouth, so named on account of his eloquence, wrote his liturgy in Greek in the 4th century CE. As Christianity spread, the Greek text of the liturgy was translated (alongside the Bible itself and other religious works) into a variety of languages. Old Church Slavonic is an important example. The liturgy was translated by the saints Cyril and Methodios after 866 and subsequently acquired the status of a source text in itself, in much the same way as the Greek Septuagint and the Latin Bible translated by St Jerome had become authoritative texts and 'the basis of the new religion to be expounded and assimilated' (Long, 2001: 3). Such is the status of early translations into Old Church Slavonic that this language is still used in the Orthodox Churches of Slavic countries, although modern Russian and Serbian, for example, are so different from the old liturgical tongue as to render comprehension impossible. Old Church Slavonic had also been the liturgical language of Romanians until late in the 17th and in the 18th century, when translations into Romanian started being used instead. The Romanian text of the liturgy used at present is, undoubtedly, archaising; it is nonetheless easily intelligible to a contemporary audience. The Orthodox Church of Greece, on the other hand, still uses the original version of St John Crysostomos's text, which dates back almost 2000 years. Needless to say, the language is hardly accessible to speakers of Modern Greek, a situation paralleled by that of the Old Church Slavonic text used by the Orthodox Churches of Slavic countries.

English Translations of the Orthodox Liturgy

In the British Isles, Orthodox Christianity has never been as widespread as Catholicism and then Protestantism have been, and English translations of the Orthodox liturgy were, for a long time, unnecessary. The first Greek Orthodox community was established in London as late as the 1670s. After this date immigrants, mostly Greeks and Russians, but also from other European Orthodox countries and from the Middle East, continued to increase the number of Orthodox Christians in Britain.

In most cases Orthodox immigrants to non-Orthodox countries still belong to their national or home Orthodox Church. In the United Kingdom, for example, this has led to the emergence of several Orthodox Churches, most notably the Greek Church (the Archdiocese of Thyateira and Great Britain) and the Russian Church (the Diocese of Sourozh, which is under the jurisdiction of the Russian Patriarchate of Moscow). In the United States the situation is even more complex, as virtually all the national Orthodox Churches are represented. While most churches tend to be rather ethnic and celebrate the liturgy in their own language, the number of heterogeneous congregations is on the increase. In those places where Greeks,

Russians, Romanians and other Orthodox worship together, celebrating religious services in a language with which only part of the congregation is familiar and then in terms of tradition rather than linguistic familiarity, is perceived to be an exclusive practice (Gregorios of Thyateira, 1995: xii). A further argument that has been brought in favour of an English translation is that the young generation of Greeks, Russians, and other Orthodox who have been brought up in the United Kingdom no longer feel bound by tradition to maintain a text that they do not understand fully (Gregorios of Thyateira, 1995: xi). Finally, translations are needed by British converts to Orthodoxy.

An impressive number of English translations of the liturgy appeared in the 20th century, mainly because many Orthodox dioceses wanted to produce their own version and did not agree with previous translations published by other dioceses. The Archdiocese of Thyateira and Great Britain produced three translations, the first of which appeared in 1932 and went through a number of reprints until the middle of the century. In 1979 a new translation by Archbishop Athenagoras Kokkinakis was published. This was issued in two formats: the smaller for the convenience of the congregation and the larger for use by the clergy. Finally, in 1995 yet another translation of the liturgy was commissioned by Archbishop Athenagoras's successor, Gregorios of Thyateira. This translation was the work of a committee that included several native speakers of English, and the text obtained the approval of the Ecumenical Patriarch.

A number of translations from the Old Church Slavonic, rather than from Greek, were also published in the United Kingdom in the 20th century. In 1939 The Fellowship of St Alban and St Sergius produced a translation which 'follows the use of the Russian Church, and is made from the Old Slavonic version of the Greek service-books which that Church employs' (*The Divine Liturgy*, 1939: vii), as the translators' preface states. However, the prayers and ceremonies according to the Russian rite differ very little from those of the Greek Church, as the translators hasten to point out. The 1939 translation went through a number of reprints and in 1982 a new translation was published, primarily for use by the Stavropegic Monastery of St John the Baptist in Essex. This new version is based primarily on Old Church Slavonic service books in consultation with the Greek texts, and the English language used is modelled upon pre-Reformation primers, the King James Bible and the Book of Common Prayer, which the translators considered to be 'liturgical English at its noblest' (*The Orthodox Liturgy*, 1982: vi). It is then particularly interesting to note how, in the absence of an Orthodox tradition in Britain that new translations could take as a reference point, a number of 20th-century translations (though by no means all of them) preferred to look back to the language of Catholic and Protestant models, rather than to start afresh, using contemporary English. In a sense, then, the process of translating the Orthodox liturgy into English is one of colonising the past.

In conclusion, rather than there being a single English translation of the liturgy used in all, or at least in the majority of, English-speaking Orthodox dioceses, there is a multitude of translations being used simultaneously. This is hardly surprising, however, given that the assimilation of other Christian texts into new environments, including the assimilation of the Bible itself, has usually tended to follow a similar progression from an initial diversity of translations to the emergence of a fixed, authoritative text (Long, 2001: 3). English translations of the liturgy (either from Greek or from Old Church Slavonic) have also been published in the United States and in Australia, but the present chapter focuses on 20th-century translations published in the United Kingdom only.

The Liturgy as Central Text

Undoubtedly, the single most important text in Christianity is the Bible itself. So central is the Scripture to Western culture as a whole that scarcely any account of the latter can afford to overlook the importance and impact of the Scripture. Admittedly, the liturgy is not, in the Orthodox Church, on equal footing with the Bible. On the other hand, however, the importance of the liturgy in Eastern Christianity is difficult to overestimate. Part of the focus that in a religion such as Protestantism, for example, is placed on reading the Bible, in the Orthodox Church is shifted to the daily celebration of the liturgy. The subtle difference in emphasis here is between reading and comprehending, on the one hand, and praying, on the other.

In the Orthodox Church the liturgy has traditionally been regarded as *the* act of worship. It gives a foretaste of the kingdom of heavens while drawing people together for the common task of celebrating: 'the holy Liturgy is not simply one of the activities of a parish, it is the reason for its existence' (Gregorios of Thyateira, 1995: ix). The liturgy is considered to be the ultimate expression of belief in action, combining as it does the *lex credenti*, or 'the way of believing', with the *lex orandi* or 'the way of praying' (Ciobotea, 1990: 25). It is also a re-enactment of the life of Christ. Consequently, it is a document of immense theological implications and authority.

The status of the liturgy as central text is, to a large extent, derived from the Bible itself. The liturgy is a deeply biblical text in terms of both content and style (i.e. the type of language used). In a sense, it is a patchwork of quotations from the Bible reworked as prayers. According to Ciobotea (1990: 25) there are 98 references to the Old Testament and 124 references to the New Testament in the liturgy, a fact of which the translators of the 1982 English version were well aware. They write in their preface that 'in constructing their liturgies the Early Fathers sought to formulate their prayers and exhortations in the words of the Scriptures' (*The Orthodox Liturgy*, 1982: vi). Furthermore, the 1982 translation includes a large number of footnotes indicating the verses in the Bible that are referred to by particular instances in the liturgy. It then becomes obvious that one of the most important translation tools a translator of the liturgy into a new language needs is a good version of the Bible in that language. At this point it is useful to mention that so far there has been no official Orthodox translation of the Bible into English, and that the King James Version is normally used.

The authority that the liturgy derives from its association with the Bible is reinforced by its own long tradition. The liturgy has existed for almost as long as Christianity and the books of the New Testament. Therefore many of the issues raised by its translation would be also true of the Bible or, indeed, of 'any document having a long history and involving the deep personal attachment of many people and the vast, vested interest of numerous institutions' (Nida, 1964: 26). It has been repeatedly pointed out that no one who translates into a language with a tradition is completely free to do what he or she likes, 'because the historical background always tends to dictate the extent to which receptors will accept a particular translation as 'faithful', 'accurate' or 'effective'' (Nida, 1964: 179). As Nida goes on to observe, Scripture translation perhaps elicits the most acute form of all the possible pressures on a translator *because* of the very nature of religious belief in historical revelation as expressed in the Bible and, we would add here, reflected (and enacted) in the liturgy. Indeed,

> if a text is considered to embody the core values of a culture, if it functions as that culture's [religion's] central text, translations of it will be scrutinised with the greatest of care, since 'unacceptable' translations may well seem to subvert the basis of the culture [religion] itself. (Lefevere, 1992b: 70, my additions)

Translations of such texts were, for a long time, predominantly source-text oriented, a situation that has to an extent changed with the advent of target-oriented approaches advocating dynamic, rather than formal, equivalence.

The fact that, in many countries, Ancient Greek and Old Church Slavonic texts of the liturgy have not been replaced by versions in contemporary idiom, is very telling. The difficulties and potential for controversy inherent in such a task have combined with the conservatism of the Church, leading to the maintenance of the existing texts. In this context, the decision to translate into another language, English, must be seen as the answer of an otherwise extremely tradition-oriented Church to the increasing pressure of contemporary realities.

The Liturgy as Text

It would be impossible to make sense of the processes involved in translating the liturgy without recognising its status as central text, and it would be equally unhelpful to overlook the fact that, after all, the liturgy is also a *text*. As such it should be amenable to analysis in much the same way as other texts are, in terms of the particular genre, discourse, and text-types involved, the function it fulfils, and the conventions at work within the specific genre. In other words, the danger of 'getting caught in the trap of [...] sacredness' (Stamps, 1993: 38) must be avoided to a certain extent if one is ever going to dare say anything at all about liturgy translation, let alone to translate the liturgy.

We can begin our discussion of the liturgy as text with the notion of genre. Following Kress (1985), Hatim and Mason (1990: 69) define genre as 'conventionalised forms of texts which reflect the functions and goals involved in a particular social occasion as well as the purposes of the participants in them'. Furthermore, the participants in the social events reflected in genres are involved in attitudinally-determined expression characteristic of such events. Various modes of expression are possible, including evaluative or committed (Hatim & Mason, 1990: 70). Following Foucault (1972), these have been referred to (e.g. by Kress, 1985; Hatim & Mason, 1990) as 'discourses'. Finally, the site where there are attempts to solve particular discourse problems is called a 'text' (Kress, 1985: 12); depending on the particular text-type classification adopted, texts can be argumentative, narrative, expository or instructional.

The Eucharistic liturgy is a particularly complex genre, incorporating as it does a variety of genres including the genre of spoken and of silent prayers, chants, sermons and unison speech. Moreover, several discourses are present, e.g. of exhortation, of praise and of thanksgiving. Finally, narration and argumentation are some of the text-types included. The central idea behind this classification is to emphasise the presence of the human actors involved, the fact that various aims and purposes are involved each time the liturgy is celebrated, its dependence on the particular context in which it is used, and the importance of conventions.

According to Crystal (1995: 371), the religious genre (to which liturgy belongs) is a particularly distinctive and well-established genre, with a number of special characteristics that include lexical, grammatical, and discourse-related features. The language used is deliberately retrospective, always looking back to a previous model and to earlier periods in the history of English (or of other languages). The language is also consciously prescriptive, concerned as it is with issues of orthodoxy and identity, both with respect to texts and with respect to rituals. This special type of in-group language together with conventions associated with it are often fiercely defended by those who regard it as inextricably linked to their identity. But some people will always be more prepared than others to accept, or even to welcome, changes. As has been frequently pointed out (e.g. Brenneis, 1986; Goodwin, 1986; Leenhardt, 1980), audiences can be extremely heterogeneous, and relate to one and the same text in a variety of ways.

Of particular importance to the perspective on translation taken here is Alan Bell's (1984) model of audience design. Bell (1984, 2001) argues convincingly that style is always a matter of the communicators' response to their audience, and that communicators adapt to their perceived audience at all levels of linguistic choice. The communicators may be aware of and designing for an audience, or their design may be non-deliberate. Starting from Erving Goffman's (1981) notion of 'participation framework', Bell provides a taxonomy of categories of receivers that includes:

- addressees (who are known to the speaker, are ratified participants in the speech event, and are directly addressed);
- auditors (known to the speaker and ratified, but not directly addressed);
- overhearers (known to the speaker, but not ratified and not directly addressed);
- eavesdroppers (of whom the speaker is not even aware).

According to Bell (1981) each receiver group exerts a different degree of influence on the text produced by a communicator; the addressees are, usually, the most influent, and are followed by the auditors.

It is not my aim here to offer a full account of Bell's (1984) audience design model, which also includes referee design, and distinguishes between initiative and responsive design. Rather, my aim has been to emphasise the importance of the human participants involved whenever language is used, including in translation, and to point to the fact that not everybody can be taken into account all the time. A further insight from Bell (1984), from Goffman (1981) and from studies in accommodation theory (e.g. Giles *et al.*, 1991) is that communicators do not always operate on the basis of warranted assumptions about their audience. Mass communicators in particular can even be unaware of who has joined the audience, and so simplification and stereotypical assumptions are frequently involved.

The final dimension needed for the perspective on translation adopted here comes from functionalism (Nord, 1997) and *skopos* theory (Vermeer, 1996). Both are target-oriented approaches, in that they move away from the view upholding the primacy of the source text above all other considerations; they focus on the function of the translated text within the target culture, and in view of target addressees. Hans Vermeer starts from the assumption that all human actions presuppose a point of departure and a purpose that gives the direction; *skopos* theory holds that translating is a purposeful activity, and that translation strategies are determined by the *skopos* (aim, purpose) to be reached.

These are then some of the considerations that inform my analysis of archaising and modernising below. The central status of the liturgy is crucial in accounting for some of the issues involved in translating it. However, the perspective taken in this study is based on the assumption that the liturgy is, essentially, a translated text that can be approached from the perspective of genre conventions, context, the participants involved (commissioner, translators, receivers) and the specific aims and purposes that shape it. Following Bell (1984, 2001) it is assumed here that audience design of some kind always takes place when language is used, and therefore takes place in translations of the liturgy. Since, according to Bell (1984: 161), audience design is manifest at all levels of linguistic choice, archaising and/or modernising features in translations of the liturgy may well reveal the particular audience design involved.

Archaising versus Modernising in Translation

According to David Crystal an archaism is basically 'a feature of an older state of the language which continues to be used while retaining the aura of its past' (Crystal, 1995: 185). Archaisms appear in a diverse range of contexts, most obviously in historical plays and novels (such as those by Sir Walter Scott), in poetry, sometimes in children's stories and in fairy tales. In religious and legal settings, where tradition is very important, archaisms are particularly frequent.

The process of 'archaising' usually refers to the deliberate use of archaisms in order to convey 'remoteness of time and place through the use of a mock antique language' (Bassnett, 1991: 72). It is not restricted to translation; thus, Tolkien, for example, makes frequent use of archaisms in order to suggest the legendary status of the narrated events. The purpose of using an archaising strategy instead of contemporary (i.e. modern) language will be discussed later in this chapter. Let us just add for the moment that archaising as a strategy for literary translation was very fashionable in the Victorian period and that, although at times pedantic, it was nonetheless based on some justifiable theoretical principles. Most notably, it introduces an alternate existence, a 'might have been' which enhances the text. According to Bassnett (1991: 72–73) 'the archaising principle [...] can be compared to an attempt to "colonise" the past'. A modernising strategy, on the other hand, involves the use of contemporary language; of course, 'contemporary' refers to different stages of the language depending upon what the centre of reference is taken to be.

It is important at this stage to make a distinction between 'archaic' and 'archaising', 'modern' and 'modernising'. A text written by Spenser, for instance, sounds archaic to a 21st-century reader, but it is not archaising; it simply is written in the English language used in Spenser's period. 'Translating' it into contemporary English would be 'modernising' the text. In the case of translating Spenser into a foreign language, on the other hand, one of the first decisions to be taken would be whether to use the modern idiom, or a previous stage of that particular language (and if so, which stage), or else the modern idiom combined with some archaisms. This is, of course, the very issue involved in translating the Orthodox liturgy (a text that dates back to the 4th-century CE) into English, in the 20th century.

The most frequently-encountered types of archaisms include nouns (*damsel, sire*), adjectives (*undefiled*), verbs (*wot, quoth, succour*), adverbs (*ere*), prepositions (*unto*). Some archaic grammatical features are present-tense verb endings (*-est, -eth*) and their irregular forms (*wilt, shouldst*), past tenses (*spake*), contracted forms (*'tis, 'gainst*), pronouns (*thou, ye*), and vocative constructions beginning with *O*. These are obvious archaisms, but there are less salient ones linked to differing conventions (sentence length, text strategy). In the context of the current tendency towards inclusive language, gendered language (using *he* or *man* when both genders are involved) is gradually becoming archaic, too.

'Archaising' and 'modernising' are obviously strategies of style; hence the temptation to dismiss them with the explanation that they are or are not used in a particular (translated) text because of 'stylistic reasons'. Of course, this far from settles the issue; the question that immediately follows is, what reasons? There has been an increasing tendency in stylistics to move away from a formal perspective to a pragmatics-oriented approach, as can be seen in the volume entitled *The Pragmatics of Style*, edited by Leo Hickey (1989). Language is studied in relation to its users, in an endeavour to ascertain not only what happens in a (translated) text, but why it happens, and what are the issues involved. In conclusion, it is important to talk about what style (and archaising) does before we can begin to understand anything about it.

As has been pointed out above, a main convention of the religious genre is the particular language used, often called 'religious language', 'liturgical language' or 'the language of reverence'. Tradition and convention are obviously involved in the maintenance of a particular style. Thus, according to Nida, '[...] strong traditionalists often prefer archaisms, which seem not only to strengthen historic associations, but also to heighten the mystery of religious expression' (Nida, 1964: 179). The main point about Nida's comment is that, besides convention and identity preservation, there has to be a number of other reasons involved in any linguistic choice. Thus, archaisms usually create a certain distancing, which is perceived to be appropriate when dealing with the divine; they may therefore be employed to signal reverence. However, the assumption that greater respect is indicated by using an archaising style is linked to a particular ideology about the religious genre in general, rather than being an objective observation. Indeed, some may choose to believe that contemporary language is entirely appropriate as a means of conveying a spiritual message. Finally, both archaising and modernising may be the result of reasons other than the translator's own assumptions; issues of accommodation to the demands of the commissioner or concerns about the acceptability of the translation can also be involved, as are considerations of the aims to be achieved. Nida's pursuit of an 'equivalent effect' for example, is an obvious instance of *skopos* oriented strategy.

Archaising versus Modernising in English Translations of the Liturgy

I now turn to examples from English translations of the liturgy, and discuss the archaising and/or modernising strategies used. Only the target texts are investigated here, as the aim is not to compare source texts and translations, but to compare different translations of the same text in terms of degrees of archaising or modernising. Samples from three English versions of the liturgy were scrutinised for evidence of archaising features, or for their absence, using the classification of archaisms presented above. It was initially envisaged that the entire text of the liturgy would be thus investigated, but it soon became obvious that the patterns that can be observed in one section of the liturgy (e.g. a particular litany or prayer) are repeated throughout the translation. In other words, a particular word or expression is systematically translated in the same way.

Our first example gives, in parallel, a section of the 1979 translation by

Archbishop Athenagoras Kokkinakis, and the corresponding section in the 1995 translation carried out under the direction of Archbishop Gregorios of Thyateira and Great Britain. Archaisms are underlined, as are instances of modern English in the 1995 version that correspond to archaisms in the 1979 translation.

Example 1:

> *[Greek original]* Only-begotten Son and Logos of God, who being immortal yet didst condescend for our salvation to be incarnate through the most holy Theotokos and ever-virgin Mary and without change didst become man; who wast crucified, subduing death by death. Christ our God, who art one of the Holy Trinity, glorified with the Father and the Holy Spirit, save us. (Kokkinakis, 1979: 92)

> *[Greek original]* Only-begotten Son and Word of God, who, being immortal, accepted for our salvation to take flesh from the holy Mother of God and Ever-Virgin Mary, and without change became man; you were crucified, Christ God, by death trampling on death, being one of the Holy Trinity, glorified with the Father and the Holy Spirit: save us! (Gregorios of Thyateira, 1995: 8–9)

It is obvious, in Example 1, that the two translations differ significantly in terms of the strategy adopted. The 1979 version employs a number of archaisms (*yet didst condescend, didst become, wast crucified*) but also several Greek words such as *Logos* (word) and *Theotokos* (mother of God). Further differences between the two translations are the use of more specialised terms (e.g. *incarnate*) in the 1979 translation, as well as of literary terms (e.g. *subdue*, which is replaced by *trample* in the other translation). By comparison, then, the 1995 translation appears to be systematically and significantly more modern. Archbishop Athenagora's 1979 version, on the other hand, gives the impression of a more conservative approach, but also presents a contradiction. The English archaisms used would appear to target an audience that is familiar with such terms, at least to an extent, and can recognise them as part of the conventions of the religious genre in English. This would suggest a native English audience, or persons who have studied literature. The Greek terms used, on the other hand, point to a totally different direction, namely Greek migrants, and perhaps suggest that the translation is intended primarily for them rather than for all Orthodox Christians in the United Kingdom.

Our next example presents three English translations of the prayer of the second antiphon (a section of the liturgy). To the 1979 and 1995 translations, we now add a sample from the 1982 English version of the liturgy; the abbreviation OCS indicates that this particular translation was based on Old Church Slavonic manuscripts.

Example 2

[Greek original] Lord, our God, save thy people and bless thine inheritance; preserve the fullness of thy Church, sanctify those who love the beauty of thy house, glorify them by thy divine power and forsake us not who hope in thee. (Kokkinakis, 1979: 90)

[Old Church Slavonic original] O Lord our God, save thy people, and bless thine inheritance. Preserve the fullness of thy Church. Sanctify them that love the habitation of thy house. Do thou by thy divine power exalt them unto glory; and forsake us not who put our trust in thee. (The Orthodox Liturgy, 1982: 38)

[Greek original] Lord our God, save your people and bless your inheritance; protect the fullness of your Church, sanctify those who love the beauty of your house, glorify them in return by your divine power, and do not forsake us who hope in you. (Gregorios of Thyateira, 1995: 7)

As far as the 1979 and the 1995 translations are concerned, the same pattern can be observed as that in Example 1, which points to a significantly stronger degree of archaising in the 1979 text than in the 1995 one. The most archaising of the three appears to be the 1982 version, which is clearly based on a very different approach with respect to style compared to the 1995 text.

Finally, Example 3 illustrates the different way in which each translation deals with references to gender; in the texts below, these are presented in bold.

Example 3

[Greek original] Holy God [...], who has brought all things out of nothing into being and hast made **man** according to thine image and likeness, endowing **him** with all thy gifts and giving **him** wisdom and understanding; who has not rejected the sinner but granted **him** repentance for salvation [...]. (Kokkinakis, 1979: 96)

[Old Church Slavonic original] O Holy God [...]; Who didst bring into being all that exists; Who didst create **man** in thine own image and likeness, and didst adorn **him** with thine every gift; Who givest wisdom and understanding to **him** that asketh, and art not wroth with the sinner, but dost grant repentance to salvation [...]. (The Orthodox Liturgy, 1982: 44)

[Greek original] Holy God [...], out of non-existence you brought the universe into being and created **male and female** according to your

image and likeness, adorning **them** with every gift of your grace. You give wisdom and understanding to **those** who ask, and do not reject the sinner but for **our** salvation you have established repentance. (Gregorios of Thyateira, 1995: 12)

The 1979 and 1982 translations use the form *he* and *man* when referring to both genders.The situation is very different in the 1995 version, which uses *them, those,* and *male and female* instead. In conclusion, the latter translation shows awareness of gender issues, and uses inclusive language.

What can the examples above tell us about some of the processes involved in translating the liturgy into English? It is perhaps tempting to assume that the 1995 translation uses contemporary English *because* it is the most recent translation of the three, and ideologies may have changed since Archbishop Athenagoras's 1979 translation. The pressure to use inclusive language certainly was stronger in the 1990s than in the 1970s. Also, the increasing pressure of modern life on the Church may have contributed to the decision not to use archaisms. However, the assumption that, the more recent a translation is, the more modernising its strategy, is contradicted by the fact that the 1982 version is more archaising than the 1979 one. Other reasons, besides year of publication, must therefore be sought to account for the different strategies adopted.

The 1982 translation was intended to be used at St John the Baptist Monastery, Essex, while the other translations target the laity. The systematic search for archaic forms modelled upon the language of the Authorised Version and the Book of Common Prayer, in the 1982 translation, are then likely to be due to the monastic audience targeted. The 1995 translation, on the other hand, has a broader group of receivers in mind; as stated in the preface, the intention is to '[...] bring this tradition of ours closer to the new generation and to our people in general' (Gregorios of Thyateira, 1995: xii).

Two members of the 1995 committee, the Reverend Archimandrite John Maitland Moir and Professor Andrew Louth, who were contacted during this research, confirmed the importance, for this translation, of reaching people. The issue of style (i.e. archaising versus modernising) was discussed at the first plenary session of the committee; at that point, some members of the committee were in favour of an archaising translation, while others supported the opposite view. The argument that it is important to provide a translation that should not be as great an obstacle to understanding as the original language itself finally won. Significantly, the decision was based on an awareness of who the receivers are and what their needs are. Using an archaising language would have provided a comforting familiarity for Anglican or Catholic English converts to Orthodoxy, who would have recognised echoes of the King James Bible and the Book of Common Prayer, but the young generation of Orthodox migrants (Greeks and others) would have felt estranged. In a sense, then, this translation is based on the deliberate decision (i.e. *skopos*) to address as large an audience as possible: a heterogeneous audience with, at times, conflicting needs. The 1982 translation, on the other hand, addresses a relatively compact, more conservative, receiver group, and this is reflected in the archaising strategy adopted.

Conclusions

The three translations discussed here differ in terms of their degree of archaising and/or modernising. This difference cannot be accounted for solely by the shift in ideology and the relaxation of conventions that may be assumed to have taken place, within the Church, between the publication in 1979 of Archbishop Athenagoras's translation and the1995 translation of the liturgy. Translation strategy is governed, to a large extent, by the intended purpose of the translation (*skopos*) and by the translators' assumptions about who their audience will be – in other words, by the translators' audience design.

Chapter 8

Holy Communicative? Current Approaches to Bible Translation Worldwide

PETER KIRK

Historical Introduction

From the day that the Christian Church was founded, the day of Pentecost, the proclamation of the Christian message has been directed to speakers of many languages from 'every nation under heaven' (Acts 2:5, New Revised Standard Version). Within a few decades, the words of Jesus Christ, originally spoken in Aramaic or Hebrew, had been translated into Greek, the *lingua franca* of the Mediterranean world, and published in the familiar Gospel form. The four major Gospels and the other early Christian writings that were later collected with them to form the New Testament also contain many quotations from the Hebrew Bible translated into Greek. The Christians were not the first to translate the Hebrew Scriptures; the Greek and Aramaic translations date from well before the time of Christ. But it was in Christianity, and from its very start, that the principle was clearly established that the Holy Scriptures, even the words of God and of Christ, could and should be translated. For the early Christian vision was of a perfected community consisting of 'a great multitude that no one could count, from every nation, from all tribes and peoples and languages' (Revelation 7:9, NRSV) and Scripture translation was soon seen as a means towards making this vision a reality. As early as the 2nd century CE, the New Testament was being translated into other major languages of the time: Latin, Syriac and Coptic. Ever since then Bible translation has been a continuing effort of the Christian community. The pace was modest during the Middle Ages; it is estimated that portions had been translated into 35 languages by 1500. Translation accelerated rapidly during the Reformation period and afterwards, so that by 1800 parts of the Bible had been translated into 68 languages, and by 1900 into 522 languages. During the 20th century there was further acceleration: by the end of 2001, the full Bible was available in 392 languages, and the New Testament had been published in a further 1012 languages. Portions had been published in an additional 883 languages, so the total number of languages represented was 2287 (United Bible Societies, 2002a, 2002b, 2002c, and Noss, 2001, supplemented by some unpublished historical statistics from Wycliffe Bible Translators).

But, of the 6809 living languages listed (in 2000) by the Ethnologue (Grimes, 2000: online) there remain well over 4000 into which no part of the Bible has been translated. According to estimates released in July 2001 by SIL International (formerly known as the Summer Institute of Linguistics) and Wycliffe Bible Translators, there is a need for Bible translation in about 3000 more languages spoken by 250 million people. This is in addition to about 1500 languages, spoken by 130 million people, in which translation work is in progress. Thus the work of Bible translation continues.

From the start, the purpose of Bible translation has been to communicate the Christian message to the widest possible audience. Christians have never considered it sufficient to translate only for the academic elite of a country. In the 2nd century CE, the educated people of Egypt would have understood the original Greek text. However, the Church wanted to communicate with the common people and so translated the text into the various dialects of their Coptic language, even though it had to adapt the previously little-used Coptic alphabet in order to do so (see Takla, 1996: section IV); and the Coptic church still exists. Similarly, agencies (such as SIL International) involved in Bible translation today often have to develop alphabets for unwritten minority languages in the developing world before translating the Bible into them. If they did not, the message could not be brought to the many groups who have not learned the national language and received education in it.

Furthermore, even in early Christian times it was realised that a good Bible translation need not necessarily be a literal one. Jerome, the translator of the definitive Latin version, the Vulgate, pioneered a middle road between literalism and uncontrolled freedom, insisting that 'the sense should have priority over the form' (Nida, 1998: 23; see also Jerome, 395: online, paragraph 5; Robinson, 1998a: 88–89, 1998b: 125–126). Martin Luther aimed to:

> express the Word of God, as codified in the Bible, in the language of the common people ... [this] means translating 'freely'... However, when essential theological 'truths' were concerned, Luther would sacrifice this principle of intelligibility and revert, for doctrinal reasons, to word-for-word translation. (Kittel & Poltermann, 1998: 421; see also Luther, 1530: online; Nida 1964: 14–15)

The great translations of the Reformation era, including the English King James or Authorised Version (KJV/AV), used a similar approach. But Western churches gradually became preoccupied with fine doctrinal distinctions dependent on certain literal renderings, and so Bible translation, where it was done, came to be more dominated by literalism or formal correspondence.

Dynamic Equivalence

In the second half of the 20th century, Jerome's tradition of sense-for-sense translation was rediscovered and extended. Pioneering work such as J.B. Phillips' New Testament translation (1959) was followed up by *Today's English Version* (the New Testament in 1966 called *Good News for Modern Man*, and the complete Bible in 1976, both published by the American Bible Society) and others. Eugene Nida and Charles Taber (Nida, 1964; Nida & Taber, 1969) laid the theoretical foundations of this 'new concept of translating', which they called dynamic equivalence. These ideas gained rapid acceptance in the Bible-translation community: essentially the same principles are taught by John Beekman and John Callow (1974), Mildred Larson (1984), Katharine Barnwell (1986, 1987), and Jan de Waard and Eugene Nida (1986). By 1985, Don Carson (1985: 1) could write that 'dynamic equivalence has won the day'; however, some, especially in more conservative churches, remained strongly opposed to this innovative approach. In order to avoid certain misunderstandings, de Waard and Nida (1986: 7, 36) later replaced the term 'dynamic equivalence' with 'functional equivalence', but they stated clearly that 'The substitution of "functional equivalence" is not intended to suggest anything essentially different from "dynamic equivalence"'. The same general approach is also known as idiomatic translation or meaning-based translation (Beekman & Callow, 1974: 20, note 3; Larson, 1984: 15–18). Despite increasing criticism since the 1990s, it continues to be the basis for most new Bible translation work, especially work in lesser-known languages.

The foundation of dynamic equivalence is the conviction that a translation should be communicative. Nida and Taber (1969: 1) begin their discussion with the premise that 'what one must determine is the response of the receptor to the translated message ... Correctness must be determined by the extent to which the average reader for which a translation is intended will be likely to understand it correctly'. The original authors intended to communicate a message to their audiences, and the aim of a translation, according to this approach, is to communicate the same message to a modern audience, in a different language, and a different cultural context.

Communication of the message is given priority over resemblance of the translation to the original text; stylistic considerations are not ignored, but they are secondary.

Barnwell, in her widely used introductory course in Bible translation (1986; see also 1987), summarises the dynamic equivalence method in terms of three 'essential qualities' (1987: 40–41): accuracy, clarity and naturalness. According to Barnwell (1986: 23), a good translation should be:

- *Accurate:* the translator must re-express the meaning of the original message as exactly as possible in the language into which he [sic] is translating.
- *Clear:* the translation should be clear and understandable. The translator aims to communicate the message in a way that people can readily understand.
- *Natural:* a translation should not sound 'foreign'. It should not sound like a translation at all, but like someone speaking in the natural, everyday way.

As accuracy is defined not in terms of formal features but as accurate re-expression of meaning, it cannot be separated from clarity. More recent work (Larsen, 2001; Andersen, 1998) has suggested a fourth essential quality, 'perceived authenticity' or acceptability to the target audience.

The quality of naturalness is perhaps the most controversial of these three. But it is central to the dynamic equivalence programme, as seen in Nida and Taber's (1969: 12) definition, 'Translating consists in reproducing in the receptor language the closest natural equivalent of the source-language message, first in terms of meaning and secondly in terms of style'. However, naturalness has its limits set by the requirement of accuracy, which, for example, rules out historical adaptation. Nida and Taber (1969:12–13) continue:

> The best translation does not sound like a translation. Quite naturally one cannot and should not make the Bible sound as if it happened in the next town ten years ago, for the historical context of the Scriptures is important ... In other words, a good translation of the Bible must not be a 'cultural translation.' Rather, it is a 'linguistic translation.' Nevertheless, this does not mean that it should exhibit in its grammatical and stylistic forms any trace of awkwardness or strangeness. (Nida & Taber, 1969: 12–13)

In evaluating this, the anticipated target audience must be clearly understood. Barnwell (1987: 43) has in mind minority groups with little or no formal education, and expects that 'We are translating not only for the educated, but also for the ordinary, less-educated people ... not only for Christians ... for all kinds of people in the community'. For less-well-educated people, the foreignness of a text, if this is reflected in a translation, will not be appreciated but will simply be confusing. It is widely recognised that in languages with a long literary tradition and a large educated readership, there is a place for formal correspondence translations alongside dynamic equivalence ones. De Waard and Nida (1986: 42) concede that 'All of these varieties of translating and adapting', including literal translation, 'have a certain legitimacy for particular audiences and special circumstances'. However, in most such languages formal correspondence translations already exist, although they may be in need of revision. But there are probably no living languages in which every speaker has the level of education to read a formal correspondence translation with full understanding. So, it may be argued, there is always a need for dynamic equivalence translation, which will at least be understood rather better, although it will never be perfectly communicative to all.

The dynamic equivalence approach has always had its critics (Marlowe, 2004: online; Fitton, 1998: online), the most vocal of them in the more conservative churches, and specific translations have been criticised with lists of alleged exegetical and theological errors. Perhaps the real fault found is that the translation is different from the traditionally accepted one, normally the KJV/AV for English speakers. We must also appreciate the difficulties that many less-well-educated people, even in Western countries, find in understanding the more literal translations, especially if these are also in old-fashioned language. More careful theological critics, such as Carson (1985), have cautiously accepted Nida's general principles of dynamic equivalence while warning against excesses that others have proposed or practised.

Foreignising and Domestication

The goal of making Bible translations that communicate the message to a wide audience is also often in tension with the aspirations of some scholars to produce translations they consider academically acceptable. The key issue to recognise is that different audiences are best suited by translations of completely different types. An edition prepared for teenagers or for newly-literate adults will not be suitable for high level scholarly study, and vice versa. Unfortunately this issue is often obscured by marketing claims such as those in the promotional material for the English Standard Version (ESV, 2002) that this new version is 'one Bible for all of life ... suitable for any situation'. Moreover, scholars often judge Bible translation methods according to the criteria they use for literary translation, without clearly recognising that most readers of the Bible read it, not as literature, but as an authoritative religious text and as a practical guide to life.

Critics of dynamic equivalence appeal to Friedrich Schleiermacher's much-quoted argument (taken here from Venuti, 1998b: 242) 'On the Different Methods of Translating', that 'there are only two. Either the translator leaves the author in peace, as much as possible, and moves the reader towards him. Or he leaves the reader in peace, as much as possible, and moves the author towards him'. Schleiermacher preferred the former strategy (foreignising) to the latter (domestication), for according to Peter Fawcett (1998: 111) he 'imagined readers so attuned to cultural diversity that they would develop an ear for translations from different languages'. But, unlike Schleiermacher's imagined audience, the real audiences for most Bible translations, especially into minority languages, mostly do not have this level of sophistication, and so are likely only to be confused by foreign features in their Bibles. In some circumstances explanatory footnotes and glossaries may be helpful. In other cases, especially with newly-literate audiences, they may add to the confusion.

Many scholars today claim to follow in the tradition of Schleiermacher. Douglas Robinson states that:

> these later theorists typically dualise translation and assign overtly moral charges to the two choices: either you domesticate the [source language] text, cravenly assimilate it ... or you foreignise it ... and so heroically resist the flattening pressures of commodity capitalism. (Robinson, 1998b: 127)

According to Timothy Wilt (1998: 149, 151–152), Lawrence Venuti has considered dynamic equivalence from this background, identified it with the domestication that he deprecates, and rejected it. But Venuti's dualistic approach has prevented him from appreciating how dynamic equivalence, as formulated by Nida, finds a valid middle way by rejecting domestication of the cultural background while encouraging domestication of linguistic structures.

More recent refinements of the dynamic equivalence approach may be seen as clarification of this distinction, as

> an attempt to prevent overly domesticating the Scriptures, as occurs, for example, in the inappropriate use of cultural or theological substitutes, and at the same time to maintain the concern to not overly foreignise the text so as to alienate readers or perpetuate stereotypes about biblical language. (Wilt 1998: 152)

By 'overly foreignise the text', Wilt refers to preservation of source-language linguistic structures. For example, de Waard and Nida (1986: 41) explicitly distinguish translations based on functional equivalence (which may be understood as linguistic domestication), from 'cultural reinterpretations' (which involve cultural domestication), such as Clarence Jordan's (1968–1973) *Cotton Patch Version* of the New Testament. Beekman and Callow (1974: 35) had earlier judged this kind of cultural reinterpretation as inaccurate because of its lack of fidelity to historical references. Charles Kraft has promoted such 'transculturations' while distinguishing them from translations (see Carson, 1985: 5–7). Contextual adaptation, as first described by Ernst-August Gutt and discussed below, can be considered as a third distinct type of domestication.

Another reason why contemporary audiences and translators, especially for lesser-known languages, might not want Bible translations to sound foreign involves the legacy of colonialism. Nineteenth-century missionary endeavours, and some more recent ones, have been widely and generally justly criticised for their close links with colonial expansionism, and for seeking more to impose Western cultural and religious forms than to present the core Christian message. There were, however, some significant exceptions even in the 19th century: James Hudson Taylor adopted local dress and left the missionary compounds in Shanghai for the interior of China (see Steer, 1996: online). Henry Venn and Rufus Anderson taught as early as the 1850s that churches should be 'self-supporting, self-governing and self-propagating' (Mathews, 1990: online). Over the past fifty years, as colonialism has been an important issue, Christian workers in developing countries have sought, with varying success, to dissociate themselves from the old paternalistic missionary methods and show themselves to be servants of the indigenous peoples and churches. They have attempted to present the Christian message and to translate the Bible within the cultural expectations of the peoples they work with, as far as this is possible. Very often, though not always, this domestication approach has been well accepted by the indigenous peoples. Quoted counter-examples (e.g. Gutt 2000a: 182–184, 193–194) often refer to situations where church members are already using a formal correspondence translation in a national language and expect a new translation in their mother tongue to match it. But these bilingual church members are rarely typical of their community. However, as indigenous peoples cannot generally properly distinguish the foreignness of the ancient Near East from that of modern Europe and North America, they are likely to associate a foreignising translation with colonialism and reject it.

Relevance Theory and Translation

Another important criticism of dynamic equivalence has come from relevance theory, developed by Dan Sperber and Deirdre Wilson, which emphasises the inferential nature of communication (see Gutt 2000a: Chapter 2). It has important implications for translation, and has been studied by many within the Bible translation community. One major issue is that relevance theory has seriously undermined the code model of communication underlying the source–message–receptor model of translation, which is important in Nida's detailed formulation (1964: 120–144) of dynamic equivalence. This shows that some reformulation of these details is required in the light of advances in linguistics; but the general principle of dynamic equivalence is strengthened rather than threatened by such improvements.

A more fundamental challenge has come from Ernst-August Gutt, who, after working in Bible translation in Ethiopia, applied relevance theory to translation and published his PhD thesis in 1991 as *Translation and Relevance: Cognition and Context* (Gutt, 2000a is the expanded second edition of this book). Working within the categories of relevance theory, Gutt characterises translation as 'interlingual interpretive use' and as the interlingual analogue of quotation (Gutt, 2000a: 105–107, 132–136). He makes a clear distinction between 'the all too familiar *language barrier*... [and] the distinct second barrier of *contextual differences* ... the primary responsibility of the translator is the mastery of the first barrier' (Gutt, 2000a: 231, italics as in the original).

Gutt (2000a) then goes on to describe the translator's responsibility to the second, contextual barrier. He accepts that translators may choose to adapt the text to overcome it, and he calls the result an 'indirect translation'. In practice this contextual adaptation consists largely of taking background information that is implicit in the original because it is part of the cognitive context of the original audience, and, if this background information is not known to the target audience, making it explicit in the translation. This adaptation may also include some explanatory renderings of difficult theological and other concepts. Such adaptation is explicitly permitted in the dynamic equivalence approach (Nida & Taber, 1969: 109–112; Beekman & Callow, 1974: 45–48), and needs to be distinguished from cultural adaptation or cultural translation (e.g. of historical references, as for example in the *Cotton Patch Version* of the New Testament), which is explicitly not permitted in dynamic equivalence because it changes the meaning and compromises accuracy (Nida & Taber, 1969 13 as quoted above; Beekman & Callow, 1974: 35–36). Gutt claims (2000a: 228, 231) that even the former, contextual adaptation, although permissible in a translation, compromises its authenticity: if a translation is to claim authenticity, it must be a 'direct translation' in which contextual adaptation is disallowed.

Gutt (2000a) associates his approach with Schleiermacher's foreignising strategy, claiming that they share 'the requirement that the readers of the translation should familiarise themselves with the historical and cultural setting of the original'. Gutt adds that 'Schleiermacher does not stress that this may mean considerable work on the part of the receptor language audience' (Gutt, 2000a: 174–175, note 4).

It should be noted that Gutt (2000b: 52–53) fully accepts the need to overcome the language barrier by adaptation of linguistic forms; he insists that he is not calling for a return to literal or formal correspondence translation. But his analogy between direct translation and direct quotation, whose essential feature is correspondence in form to an original utterance, has proved highly confusing. Thus even a scholar such as Ernst Wendland (1996: 130–131), noting that 'the relatively literal RSV [Bible translation] is promoted as "an instance of direct translation"', has misunderstood Gutt's concept of direct translation as equivalent to formal correspondence.

Concerning controversy over translation methods Gutt writes:

> This problem of clashes of expectations shows itself with particular clarity in the case of Bible translation, because here the urge to communicate as clearly as possible is equally strong as the need to give the receptor language audience access to the authentic meaning of the original. Since the differences in cognitive environment between the source language and the receptor language audiences are generally great, these two objectives are bound to clash. (Gutt, 2000a: 186)

So the translator has to adopt one of two strategies (Gutt, 2000a: 187): either 'the translator wants to make the translation clear to the receptors' and produces an indirect translation; or 'the translator aims at authenticity' and produces a direct translation. In *Translation and Relevance* Gutt is careful to avoid explicitly choosing between these two. But elsewhere, in papers intended for fellow Bible translators and so in a context where he can appeal to shared theological presuppositions, he makes clear his preference for direct translation. He writes (Gutt, 1988: 36), 'translation is bound by its commitment to keep the content of the original Scripture unchanged', and, concerning insertion of background information for contextual adaptation (Gutt, 2000b: 52), 'Our reverence for the integrity of the biblical texts and our concern for the authenticity of Bible translations require us to abandon this practice as quickly as possible and to solve the problems by other, more acceptable means'. In his book written for Bible translators, Gutt's general preference for direct translation seems clear in the latter part, but at the very end he seems to retract, concluding, uncontroversially, that 'the freer translation and the stricter one serve two different audiences' (Gutt, 1992: 75).

But the direct translation approach of putting authenticity, as Gutt understands it, before communicative clarity leads to a serious theoretical and practical problem. The central claim of *Relevance Theory* is that human communication is based on a simple principle of relevance. Gutt himself summarises the theory: 'To be consistent with the principle of relevance, an utterance must achieve adequate contextual effects and *put the hearer to no unjustifiable effort in achieving them*' (Gutt, 2000a: 35, see also 31–32; italics as in the original, but I would choose to emphasise the same words). This must apply equally to an utterance that is a translation; 'If translations are not perceived as being relevant by the receptors, they will not be used' (Goerling, 1996: 53). Gutt offers a model of an ideal authentic direct translation without contextual adaptation, but, because the contextual barriers to communication are not overcome within the text, the translation will initially be neither understood nor perceived as relevant. Therefore 'the deployment of translation may require *additional* measures which lie outside of but are *complementary to the translation effort* itself and which are designed to adjust the target audience's context as necessary' (Gutt, 2000a: 231, italics as in the original). In the context of Bible translation, typically 'the contextual differences are great, requiring the provision of extensive information about the socio-cultural and historical setting in which the original was written' (Gutt, 2000a: 231). But the target audience needs to accept these additional measures. If they need to study to assimilate this 'extensive information' before they can start to read and correctly understand the text, they are likely to see this as 'unjustifiable effort', and so, as relevance theory teaches, they will perceive the translation as not relevant and will not read it. This is a situation that Gutt himself describes: 'Translations ... that prove to be inconsistent with the principle of relevance for the receptors, run a great risk of remaining unread' (Gutt, 1992: 68).

Even if some of the target audience can be persuaded, as perhaps in a church context, to accept the additional measures, communication is still likely to fail, for as Farrell and Hoyle (1997: 25) explain, 'Relevance theory predicts that the audience will misunderstand a passage where it seems more relevant to them to do so'. Information about a different culture may be learned well, but, as soon as the learners return to their everyday life, their knowledge of their own culture becomes more easily accessible than the learned information. So, when they read or hear a translated text that can be understood differently in their own culture than in the learned culture, they will prefer the understanding in their own culture because it requires less processing effort and so is more relevant. Unfortunately this is not the way that the text is intended to be read. Wendland (1996: 132–133) argues in a similar fashion about footnotes; the same principles apply to learned external measures.

Conclusions

This chapter has examined several different attempts to make a bipolar classification of translation strategies: the ancient distinction *literal* vs. *free*, Schleiermacher's *foreignising* vs. *domestication*, Nida's *formal correspondence* vs. *dynamic equivalence*, and Gutt's *direct translation* vs. *indirect translation*. Although these distinctions differ from one another in several significant respects, as their proponents are careful to point out, there seems to be a common factor underlying each of them. According to the first of each pair of strategies, the translator's priority is to preserve the 'authenticity', in the sense of the word used by Gutt, of the original message; according to the second of each pair, the priority is to communicate the message to the target audience. Each distinction is based on a realisation that in general full authenticity and communicative clarity cannot both be achieved, especially when, as with the Bible, the source and target cultures are very different. A choice must therefore be made.

The first option is to give authenticity priority over clarity. It is sometimes suggested that only literal or formal correspondence translations are authentic. Gutt, however, links authenticity to the relevance theory concept of interpretive resemblance, which is resemblance not in form but in meaning. So, although his direct translation is not literal but includes linguistic adaptation, he concludes that 'the target audience can expect to gain from direct translation *as authentic an understanding of the original as it ever could across language boundaries*' (Gutt, 2000a: 228, italics as in the original). But '*as authentic ... as it ever could*' implies that some authenticity is necessarily lost in translation and, as discussed above, a direct translation of the Bible can be understood only after extensive background study. One is left feeling that, if authenticity is all-important to certain readers, they should take the additional step of learning the biblical languages, as well as the biblical background, so that they can access the fully authentic original language text as established through proper textual criticism. For, as Iver Larsen concludes from a different approach, 'a translation neither can nor should be authentic in the *primary* sense of that word, because translation is different from original authorship' (Larsen, 2001: 42, italics as in the original). This accords with Christian understandings of the 'authority', 'inspiration' and 'infallibility' of the Bible, which generally apply such terms only to the original language texts. Gutt appears to miss this distinction between original texts and translations when he argues from the importance of preserving the source texts that 'the integrity of the historically attested biblical text is violated by the insertion of extraneous background information' (Gutt, 2000b: 52). In other words, if his kind of authenticity is the controlling criterion, the Bible is untranslatable.

But if the second option is chosen and clarity is given priority over authenticity, a completely different set of parameters comes into play. The priority becomes clear communication of the message. Contextual adaptation becomes an acceptable and necessary strategy, but the amount of it required depends on the audience's needs. The dynamic equivalence approach, as refined over more than 40 years, seems to be, at least in general terms, the best way currently available to achieve communicative clarity. It is important to remember that dynamic equivalence continues to demand accuracy as well as clarity and naturalness. But its definition of accuracy, or faithfulness, is not the same as Gutt's definition of authenticity; rather it is that the translation 'communicates the exact meaning of the original message' (Barnwell, 1987: 40). While dynamic equivalence demands faithfulness to historical and didactic references as well as to 'the dynamics of the original', it accepts contextual adaptation and allows that some parts of the meaning that are implicit in the original text may be made explicit in the translation (Beekman & Callow, 1974: 33–66). This is one of the areas in which the theory needs continuing improvement and clarification, perhaps even reformulation, in the light of relevance theory and other theoretical advances, as well as of ongoing experience.

But what of the argument that a translation, especially of the Bible, should be authentic? According to Gutt's definition of authenticity, a translation with contextual adaptation is not authentic. But, as he recognises (Gutt, 2000a: 229, 2000b: 52–53), it is not always possible to make even a direct translation that perfectly resembles the original and so is fully authentic, because of linguistic differences between source and target languages. Linguistic adaptation, for example, may require that some ambiguities are resolved and some implicit information is made explicit. Since no translation is fully authentic, readers whose primary concern is this kind of authenticity (such as pastors and theological students) should be encouraged to learn the original languages and read the original language texts, or to refer to technical commentaries. Larsen (2001: 43) argues that a translation can have authenticity, but only in a secondary sense of trustworthiness certified by a suitable authority, such as an accredited translation consultant. Authenticity in this sense depends on communicative accuracy, for the authority must certify that 'the translated text communicates the same message as the original text' (Larsen, 2001: 43).

Is there in fact a middle way? Theoreticians tend to suggest that there is not; but a look at real translations suggests that there is. Beekman and Callow (1974: 21) comment, 'Even though there are few, if any, translations that are completely literal or completely idiomatic, each has been produced with one or the other approach in mind'. For, as David Andersen (1998: 12) writes, 'Making a good translation always requires creative compromise in the face of conflicting demands', which include acceptability to the audience. According to Larsen (2001: 40), 'the expectations of the intended audience are of crucial importance for the success of every Bible translation project'. The principles are simple: first define the audience, and then help them to make an informed decision about what kind of translation will meet their needs. If they are academics or well-educated church members, they may choose a formal correspondence translation or a direct translation. When the issues are properly explained, a less-well-educated audience is likely to choose a dynamic equivalence or indirect translation approach. As indirect translation does not necessarily exclude cultural adaptation, the audience might need encouragement to specify historical faithfulness as a further requirement. In this case continuing consultation will be necessary concerning how much contextual adaptation is required for clear communication; if rather little is necessary, the translation may appear to embody a middle way, but its theoretical background and orientation towards communication rather than authenticity should be clear.

Part 2

Specific Studies

Chapter 9

Settling Hoti's Business: The Impossible Necessity of Biblical Translation

DAVID JASPER

The Victorian poet Robert Browning dates the event described in his poem 'A Grammarian's Funeral' to a time 'shortly after the revival of learning in Europe'. Yet the poem is a sad lament on philological pedantry:

> So, with the throttling hands of Death at strife,
> Ground he at grammar;
> Still, thro' the rattle, parts of speech were rife:
> While he could stammer
> He settled *Hoti's* business – let it be!
> Properly based *Oun* –
> Gave us the doctrine of the enclitic *De*,
> Dead from the waist down.
>
> Browning, 1913 (lines 125–132)

(*Hoti* (ὁτι) means 'so that'; *Oun* expresses 'then', 'therefore' or 'thereupon'; *De* is often untranslatable – perhaps 'and' or 'but'.)

Browning's lines come as a dire warning to all who still think it worthwhile to teach Greek grammar. They alone, perhaps, will recognise what a stroke of genius it takes to settle *Hoti's* business. How is this so?

The reference is to one of the most puzzling passages in the Gospels, Mark chapter 4, which is concerned with Jesus's teaching about the parables and in particular refers to verse 12, which refers back to the Greek Septuagint version of Isaiah 6:9. Here Jesus seems to be saying to his disciples that parables are told 'so that (ἱνα) they may look and look but see nothing, and listen and listen, but hear nothing, lest (μηποτε) they shall turn again and be forgiven.' The implication appears to be that parables are told to *prevent* these people from understanding! The writer of Matthew's Gospel, who was almost certainly working from the text of Mark, appears to be trying to overcome the problem of Jesus's deliberate mystification of the people by replacing ἱνα ('in order that') with ὁτι ('because'), and with this small change, the whole sense is turned around. Parables in the Matthean version are told precisely *because* people try to look but fail to see. In actual fact the matter is not quite so simple since, according to Charles F.D. Moule in his *Idiom-Book of New Testament Greek*, Semitic influences behind the word ἵνα with the subjunctive suggest an unwillingness to divide sharply between purpose and consequence. Matthew's emendation may still remain essentially true to Mark's sense (Moule, 1959: 143). Nevertheless, the revision, it would seem, is an attempt to draw the sting out of a difficult text rather than an approach to the difficulty itself.

Surely the author of Mark cannot mean that the parables were told to *prevent* understanding that leads to salvation? Moule thought not: it was, he says, simply 'too incongruous with any part of the NT period to be plausible.' Most of his colleagues in the world of New Testament scholarship more or less agree. In his standard commentary *The Gospel of St Mark*, Vincent Taylor suggests unconvincingly that 'the original form of the saying may only be conjectured. Probably it had nothing to do with parables at all' (Taylor, 1966: 257). C.H. Dodd speculates on the lost literature of the early Church, blaming the problem on a now-forgotten early Christian theologian, and thus letting Jesus himself off the hook (Dodd, 1961: 4). A.M. Hunter believes that Mark was mysteriously 'misled' by someone and that the use of the Septuagint Isaiah text was inappropriate for parables 'as it affords no criterion for their interpretation' (Hunter, 1960: 13). Finally (and there are many more such comments elsewhere) Joachim Jeremias simply avoids the problem of the translation and goes behind the Greek of the Septuagint to the Aramaic of the Targum of Isaiah 6:10. The word then becomes more like 'unless' rather than 'lest' making it read 'unless they turn again and be forgiven'. The whole passage becomes thus a reference to God's promise of forgiveness (Jeremias, 1972: 15). The problem with this suggestion is, however, that the Septuagint was probably a rendering of the Hebrew and not the Aramaic Targum – and Jeremias's ingenious solution to the problem is thus itself rendered irrelevant.

It seems that the scandal will not go away. In spite of different suggestions, the translation still stands firm and the settling of *Hoti's* business remains apparently beyond our grasp. Yet there may be help from another quarter, outside the field of New Testament scholarship itself. The literary critic Professor Frank Kermode suggests sticking with the problem of the text, rather than trying to argue around it, although he does not relish the prospect. I have always found his book *The Genesis of Secrecy* (1979) a valuable but depressing read. Kermode writes:

Matthew took the first step toward reducing the bleak mystery of Mark's proposals, and later a rational, scientific scholarship spirited away the enigma by detecting behind the text of Mark a version more to its liking. (Kermode, 1979: 33)

If for Robert Browning's defunct Grammarian there is no conclusion to scholarship as he endlessly settles the business of grammar's intractable problems, for Kermode there is only the bleak mystery of the insoluble; at best, in his own words, with a glance back to the Parable of the Doorkeeper in Franz Kafka's *The Trial*, 'a momentary radiance before the door of disappointment is finally shut on us' (Kermode, 1979: 145). Each scholar, in his own way, inhabits the endless corridors of Kafka's godless nightmare.

What, then, if this text finally resists translation – or, at least, resists the interpretation we want to give to it? What begins as a problem of translation ends as a problem of understanding and interpretation, for, as George Steiner has remarked 'translation *between* languages is, formally and substantively, a special case of translation within the *same* language. To attempt understanding is to attempt translation.' (Steiner, 1993: xi). And, we might say, vice versa. The Bible has always been a translated text, and, indeed, within its own pages there are already translations. In Mark 15:34, Jesus's last words from the Cross, 'My God, My God, why hast Thou forsaken me?' are translated into Greek from Aramaic with an explanatory phrase (ὁ ἐστιν μεθερμηνευομενον), and the verb here in Greek means either to translate or to interpret. Texts or parts of texts of Scripture have been themselves translated from earlier languages, some of which now are lost. The Hebrew text wends it way into the Greek Septuagint and is no less a text for that. The rough cadences of the common or *koine* Greek of the New Testament become the majestic Latin of Jerome's Vulgate Bible; and from English there spring the geniuses of Tyndale and Coverdale, and so on *ad infinitum*. What is the Bible – the original Bible? In one sense there is no answer for it is all endless translation. If we speak of reading Mark's Gospel 'in the original' (meaning his rather idiosyncratic Greek), that is only true in a limited and rather pedantic sense. Linguistically there is no original – which is what I take to be the point of Pentecost as recounted in Acts 2:6 ' ... they were bewildered, because each one heard them speaking in his own language ... how is it that we hear, each, of us in his own native language ... we hear them telling in our own tongues the mighty works of God' (Revised Standard Version).

Now I am beginning to stray from the point. and this is almost becoming like a sermon. And the point is well taken. For at the heart of the impossible necessity of Biblical translation there is a religious imperative and mystery.

Let me return for a moment to Mark 4: 'And he said to them: "To you has been given the secret (το μυστηριον) of the Kingdom of God, but for those outside everything is in parables"'. All the disciples can hope for is a 'mystery', while those outside are damned to remain interpreters for eternity. They are left battling with texts and, like Browning's Grammarian, they are doomed to be people who have opted not to live but to know, and finally realise that they know only that they know nothing.

I will come back to the privileged if rather dim disciples of Mark's Gospel in a moment. For now, what can we say of the spirit of the great translators of the Bible; those who have joyfully embraced its impossible necessity? A constant, indeed commonplace, theme in the early literature of the Church in the West is the importance of the Vulgate Bible, on the grounds that no one should be kept from salvation by mere barriers of language (Steiner, 1992: 257). Translation is a theological necessity, central to spiritual progress and salvation. In the same spirit, William Tyndale translates Erasmus's *Exhortations to the Diligent Study of Scripture* (1516) – two great translators speaking to us in one voice.

> I would desire that all women should reade the Gospell and Paule's epistles, and I wold to god they were translated in to the tongues of all men. So that they might not only be read and knowne of the scotes and yryshmen, But also of the Turkes and Saracenes. Truly it is one degre to good livinge, yee the first (I had almost sayde the cheffe) to have a little sight in the scripture, though it be but a grosse knowledge ... I wold to god the plowman wolde singe a texte of the scripture at his plowbeme, and that the wever at his lowme with this wold drive away the tediousness of the tyme. (Steiner, 1992: 258; Erasmus: online)

In 'Unto the Reader', his preface to his 1534 translation of the New Testament – a rendering from the Greek fully conscious of the Hebraisms and grammatical oddities of the *koine* – Tyndale is well aware of his scholarly and religious duty to be clear and plain so that readers would not be led astray 'unto greater damnation'. Thus, he earnestly affirms, 'if I shall perceive either by myself or by the information of other that ought be escaped me, or might be more plainly translated, I will shortly after, cause it to be mended.' (Daniell, 1995: 3). Six years later the point was again emphasised by Archbishop Thomas Cranmer in his preface to the 1540 revision of the Great Bible, largely the work of Miles Coverdale. Cranmer added that translations of the Bible in English should be used only as long as their idiom is readily understood by the people. The Saxons, Cranmer pointed out, had their Bibles in their 'mother's tongue', but 'when this language waxed old and out of common usage, because folk should not lack the fruit of reading, it was again translated in the new language' (Frost, 1973: 6; Cranmer, 1549: online).

Translation, like hermeneutics, as Schleiermacher reminded us, is never finished. But in the preservation of this theological necessity, which is the true text of Scripture – the Hebrew, Aramaic, Septuagint Greek, *koine* Greek, Latin Vulgate, the King James Version, the Revised Version, in French, German or Swedish? The answer is all and none. There is an imprecise but telling analogy to my point with Torah – the text and blueprint of creation itself. For the words of the written text are but the garments of scripture, and yet, as Susan Handelman has said of Torah:

> the written text is not only the enclothing of the fiery pre-existent letters in which are contained the secrets of creation, but with the proper methods of interpretation, one can unlock the mysteries of all being. Every crownlet of every letter is filled with significance, and even the forms of letters are hints to profound meanings. (Handelman, 1982: 38)

William Tyndale, too, believed his English text to be the very word of God, yet the words are but garments adorning the pre-existent word, and in the end there is nothing outside the text.

Ah, there's the rub, as Hamlet might have said. For there is nothing new under the sun, and Jacques Derrida's (1967) celebrated aphorism '*il n'y a pas de hors texte*' (rendered in English more precisely as 'there is no outside-text') nicely acknowledges the nature of Mark's Gospel and is also indeed celebrated, albeit unconsciously, by Tyndale, Coverdale and Cranmer. For what is there beside the word of God? But before we fall into sermonising again, we need to take a few steps back and come at the point by another route, that is, through the text itself. Kevin Hart comments succinctly on Derrida's aphorism:

> The doctrine that there is nothing outside the text is neither esoteric nor difficult: it is merely that there is no knowledge of which we can speak, which is unmediated. What Derrida adds to this familiar epistemological thesis is the contention that this knowledge is always in a state of being constituted and never arrives at a state of final constitution: there is no immediacy, even in mediation; no self-identity, even in difference. (Hart, 1989: 26)

Oddly, or perhaps not so oddly, you would find something not so far from this in Tyndale's celebrated book *The Obedience of a Christian Man*, published in 1528, two years after the first edition of his English New Testament. As a translator Tyndale knows very well that, as spiritual sustenance comes only from Scripture (for there is nothing outside the text), the translator's task is never finished, for it bears the responsibility of the mediation of that which is 'always in a state of being constituted.' Indeed, in a sense, this is an acknowledgement of the Bible's living nature as an always and inherently translated book. There is no absolute text, and so to 'settle its business' is nothing less than to decide not to live. Translators always open up the transgressive boundaries of discourse in the recognition of the impossibility of their task, thus verging on the very limits of language. And there is the challenge.

Here are some examples from the Bible of what I mean. No one has ever finally translated the words describing the 'still small voice' of I Kings 19:12. Or, in Mark 1: 15 there is that impossible verb ἤγγικεν. Tyndale translates this startling cry of Jesus as 'the Kingdom of God is at hand', and he is followed in this by the King James Version and the Revised Standard Version. The New English Bible suggests the phrase 'is upon you'. The Jerusalem Bible offers 'is close at hand'. The New International Version and the Good News Bible try 'is near'. Yet none of them is quite right, though all nestle within the ambiguity of the Greek perfect tense of the verb, which is both temporal and spatial. The Kingdom is at once here and yet is still arriving; the verb is dynamic and active in time and space; it can never be translated and so it must be translated again and again.

'In translating', Goethe once wrote, 'we must go to the brink of the Untranslatable' (see Steiner, 1992: 270ff). In translating and struggling to speak with clarity of this intractable text of Mark's Gospel, we come to have some sympathy with those confused disciples. They are the insiders who are given the secret, but it is a secret that is not explained. The word μυστηριον remains on the page, a mystery in its very nature. At least those on the outside might have a go at understanding the parables. So why is the mystery better? Here I am reminded of Roland Barthes's descent into writing:

> The closer I come to the work, the deeper I descend into Writing; I approach its unendurable depth; a desert is revealed; there occurs – fatal, lacerating – a kind of *loss of sympathy*: I no longer feel myself to be *sympathetic* (to others, to myself). It is at this point of contact between the writing and the work that the hard truth appears to me: *I am no longer a child*. (Barthes, 1977: 137)

As I write I am sitting here surrounded by books of Greek grammar, lexicons, commentaries, and still I do not understand. I remain like the disciples in Mark, who are continually challenged by Jesus, 'οὔπω νοειτε οὐδεσυνετε ('Do you not yet see or understand?') (Mark 8:17). I am no longer a child. To whom do I turn for help?

And yet, perhaps, Jesus's most faithful disciples, so unwilling to grow up, have always disappointed him the most. Readers try to understand by reducing the text into what they can define or absorb – parables, analogies, doctrines that harden into dogma. One can learn and observe the rules of grammar. Yet Jesus himself does not write for us to read his words, except very rarely. Once, in the Fourth Gospel, he writes with his finger on the ground (εἰς την γην) (John 8:8). But writing in the dust is not very sensible or enduring, and no manuscript has survived of his inscription. Returning then to the translating of Mark, as I translate, what do I see? I see the disciples stumbling at each word and Jesus the mystery-man (μυστηριον). The postmodern New Testament scholar Stephen Moore, who is nothing if not a witty translator, writes of what he sees:

> Here is what I saw:
> Writ(h)ing in pain on his cross, Jesus can at least be read: 'Truly this man was a Son of God!' exclaims Mark's centurion, his reading glasses reflecting the harsh glare of the afternoon sun. Jesus is in the process of becoming a book. (Moore, 2001: 91)

But as always there is nothing new under the sun. The 14th century mystic Richard Rolle said the same thing when he wrote in *The Fire of Love*: 'More yet, sweet Jesus, thy body is like a book written all with red ink; so is thy body all written with red wounds' (Rolle, quoted in Finaldi, 2000: 148). The 18th-century hymn writer Isaac Watts pursued the same theme in his Passiontide hymn 'When I survey the wondrous Cross' in the verse about Christ's 'dying crimson', which almost all hymnbooks omit as too visually stark and overwhelming.

> His dying crimson like a robe
> Spread o'er his body on the Tree,
> Then am I dead to all the globe,
> And all the globe is dead to Me.
>
> Isaac Watts, 'Crucifixion to the World by the Cross of Christ' (verse 4)

Ironically, all too often the very part of the text that makes sense is left out. In the same way, as Moore suggests:

> As writing, Jesus is censored by his disciples. 'Words, whole clauses and sentences are blocked out so that what is left becomes unintelligible' (Freud, *Origins of Psychoanalysis*). Faced with a script that they have rendered illegible, the disciples flee the set when Jesus is arrested. (Moore, 1992: 16)

Endless translations and endless attempts to pierce the unreadable text hold before translators the mysterious stranger, a Jesus who 'drifts from misunderstanding to misunderstanding across the surface of Mark's page', a writing subject to endless misreadings. I am reminded here of Socrates's warning to Phaedrus of the helplessness of writing, when words written down become subject to abuse and misunderstanding and are in need of a father's support, of a parent who may come to the rescue:

> When once it has been written down, every discourse rolls about everywhere, reaching indiscriminately those with understanding no less than those who have no business with it, and it doesn't know to whom it should speak and to whom it should not. And when it is faulted and attacked unfairly, it always needs its father's support; alone it can neither defend itself nor come to its own support. (Cooper, 1997: 81)

Perhaps all a translator can do is remind us that we do not understand, so that, like blind watchers we can only say, with Derrida at the end of *Memoirs of the Blind*, 'I don't know, one has to believe' (Derrida, 1993: 129).

Without the translator there is no salvation, for only the translator acknowledges that there is nothing outside the text. There is no easy solution, and the business always remains unsettled. For this chapter, there remains one last visit to the Gospel of Mark. Scholars and grammarians insist that the Gospel properly concludes 16:8. The remaining verses, we are told by the scholars, with their reassuring words about Jesus's post-resurrection appearances, were added by a later scribe or editor. We then are left with the famous mystery of the women rushing out of the empty tomb, the tomb in which there is *nothing*, speechless: 'και οὐδενι οὐδεν εἰπαν ἐφοβουντο' ('and they said nothing to any one, for they were afraid'). This does not seem to be a very propitious beginning to Christianity – saying nothing to no one (Greek is tolerant of double negatives) out of fear and bewilderment. At this point the commentaries tend to break down, stop reading the text, and break the golden rule. They suggest that there must be an answer to this problem *outside* the text. At the very least it is a problem arising out of bad grammar, for no one finishes a sentence, let alone a book with the word γαρ (for). I suggest, though it would border on bad manners, that New Testament scholars are very busy people, and clearly they have not taken the time to read James Joyce, who would be perfectly happy with such an ending. Here is one example from a standard commentary by Vincent Taylor, still used by students of Mark's Gospel: 'The view that ἐφοβουντο γαρ is not the intended ending stands.' (Taylor then refers us to a galaxy of scholars including Hort, Swete, Moffatt, Burkitt, Bultmann, Turner, Streeter, Branscomb and Schniewind.)

> How the Gospel ended we do not know. The natural sequence to ἐφοβουντο γαρ would be a μη clause ('lest') referring to the Jews or to the charge of madness, followed by appearances to Peter and to all the disciples. How the original ending disappeared is equally obscure. The mutilation of the original papyrus MS, Mark's premature death, and deliberate suppression have been conjectured. (Taylor, 1966: 609–10)

An interpreter, like Browning's Grammarian, dead from the waist down! Rather should one not read the text as received, with all its impossible necessity? The best translators such as Tyndale and Coverdale are more than grammarians. They are of the company of poets – individual talents within the traditions of textuality, with all its echoes and resonances. Such people, if time had allowed, would have read James Joyce and would have loved *Finnegans Wake,* which in some ways is perhaps the closest that modern literature approaches to Scripture. The clue to the puzzle of Mark 16:8 perhaps lies in the simple, or not so simple, act of *reading*. I may be wrong, but this is what I mean. I love to read the stories of Genesis, and especially the story of Joseph and his brothers (as did Thomas Mann). I have even read them in the Greek Septuagint translation. And in my reading I came across another sentence that ends with the word γαρ. In Genesis 45:3, the brothers realise who Joseph actually is, and that he is, against all reason, still alive. The description concludes with the words, 'and they were dismayed', ending with the word γαρ. I have no idea whether I am right, but an echo is sounded in my head. Mark knew his Septuagint. Is there a connection here? If this is so, then it makes Mark 16:8 what literature since Aristotle has known as a *recognition scene*. These women are not just terrified, but they are astounded. Yet this still does not answer the question, why does the text finish on what my lexicon calls a 'coordinating particle'? What is it coordinating with? The link is there in the text, but it is at the beginning rather than at the end. There is no time to finish the sentence in this most breathless and hasty of all the gospels, with its repeated εὐθυς ('immediately') and its warnings in chapter 13 about being alert and ready. Now the alert and ready reader, like the women, should immediately go back to the very beginning of the mystery, the first sentence of chapter I that reads, 'The beginning of the Gospel of Jesus Christ, the Son of God', and realise that this is now validated by the empty tomb. In the ending lies the clue to the beginning and all that follows from it. Do you not now see, as Jesus might have said to his disciples? We have all been looking in the wrong place, too busy settling *Hoti's* business, when the answer is there in the text all the time, in the glorious empty space of the tomb. We might say that reading the Gospel alone makes it possible to read the Gospel and its mystery. The text is its own best interpreter. Joyce did the same in *Finnegans Wake,* whose ending is an opening to its beginning. Joyce and Mark are, after all, both poets and, despite the age difference, know a thing or two about writing.

Robert Browning's poem, with which we began, is a biting satire on learning and its ivory towers. The Grammarian's funeral procession is as stately as any ceremony on Graduation Day:

> Leave we the unlettered plain its herd and crop;
>   Seek we sepulture
> On a tall mountain, citied to the top,
>   Crowded with culture!

Browning, 1913 (lines 13–16)

In the business of texts and their translation, translators need to know when to leave their cities of learning behind and just stop and look, admitting the impossible necessity with Tyndale's 'boy that driveth the plough'. After all, the writer of Mark's Gospel was no fool, and Tyndale, perhaps, was more right than he knew in his belief that Mark was schooled by the apostles Paul and Peter:

> Whereof ye see, of whom he learned his gospel, even of the very apostles, with whom he had his continual conversation, and also of what authority his writing is, and how worthy of credence. (Tyndale in Daniell, 1995: 1)

Chapter 10

Guardian of the Translated Dharma: Sakya Paṇḍita on the Role of the Tibetan Scholar

JONATHAN GOLD

Early in the 13th century, when the Tibetan philosopher and translator Sakya Paṇḍita Kunga Gyaltsen (Sa-paṇ) was writing his *Entryway Into Scholarship* (*Mkhas 'jug*), thousands of Buddhist scriptures were available in Tibetan, many newly translated from Sanskrit. By Sa-paṇ's time, the so-called 'second diffusion' of Buddhism in Tibet had been running at full throttle for more than two centuries (see Kapstein, 2000; Ruegg, 1992; Tucci, 1980). Hundreds of Indian and Tibetan scholars had been carrying the Buddha's teachings, the dharma, from India to Tibet and translating it from Sanskrit into the Tibetan language. At the same time, Muslim invasions had recently devastated the monastic universities of Northern India, leaving Indian Buddhism on its deathbed and eventually ending the flow of texts and teachers into Tibet (Dutt, 1988: 359ff). While translation would continue in Tibet for quite some time, the bulk of the great Tibetan translation project was complete. In this context, Sa-paṇ's writing takes up the issue of intellectual practice: What is the role of the Tibetan Buddhist scholar, for whom nearly all of the properly authoritative texts are translations?

Sa-paṇ argues that this situation requires the scholar to be a special kind of guardian of the Buddha's teachings, a breakwater against the dharma's inevitable decay. In the sections of the *Entryway* that I review in this chapter, Sa-paṇ explains how readers of Tibetan translations of Sanskrit Buddhism can keep the dharma from diminishing in its shift into Tibetan language. Throughout, I distinguish between two scholarly roles: the translator who produces a translation, and the expositor, who reads and teaches the translated text. Most translation issues are, for Sa-paṇ, issues of scriptural interpretation – proper interpretation of translated texts. For this reason, I often use the term 'interpreters' where Sa-paṇ would say 'expositors' or 'teachers'.

By examining what Sa-paṇ takes to be the necessary qualifications for being an interpreter and teacher of Buddhism in translation, we can see why Sa-paṇ believes the dharma to be in peril, and why he claims that its only protectors are elite scholars with a particular kind of intellectual training. The hazards to valid interpretation are many, and to avoid them an interpreter must have a vast range of experience not only with texts in translation, but with aspects of the Sanskrit language and Indian literary norms as well. Two points, which come up repeatedly, should be made clear from the outset. First, these interpretive difficulties are not to be blamed on the translators. As I will show, Sa-paṇ appears to be in agreement with the translators about their translation strategies, regardless of the resultant potential for misunderstanding. In fact, the only time that Sa-paṇ criticises the translators as a whole is when, based on ignorance, they sacrifice the Sanskrit meaning in order to make Tibetan comprehension easier. Sa-paṇ believes that the translators have done their job in preserving the original meaning of the dharma in its movement from Sanskrit to Tibetan. It is now the job of the properly-trained interpreter to perceive and pass on an authentic teaching.

Second, Sa-paṇ makes no claim that Tibetan teachers must know the texts in the original Sanskrit versions. Although some interpretive difficulties seem virtually insurmountable without such knowledge, Sa-paṇ never suggests that the translations are unreadable in Tibetan. Instead, I assume that Sa-paṇ believes that even interpreters who cannot read Sanskrit could be trained to identify and avoid all the difficulties he describes.

Below I analyse two sections from the *Entryway*: one where Sa-paṇ is troubled, and one where he seems optimistic about the dharma in translation. His worries, however, take up far more space. He is extremely concerned that the differences between Sanskrit originals and their Tibetan translations are misleading to inexperienced Tibetan teachers. This falls in line with a major theme of Sa-paṇ's writings, wherein he often dedicates space to correcting mistakes of other Tibetan scholars and establishing what he sees to be the standard interpretation of the Indian masters (Sa-paṇ, 2002). In fact, Sa-paṇ believes most Tibetan scholars to be badly educated at best. As he writes:

> Here in Tibet, I have seen that some people who claim to be scholars are unpractised in studies ... that are easy to understand and pleasant, and so [they] are, for the most part, mistaken. This *Entryway into Scholarship* is related for their benefit. (Sa-paṇ, 1992: 370.7–19)

Sa-paṇ believes that such ignorance is causing a widespread corrosion of the dharma in Tibet. When the ignorant give teachings, he says:

> 'That dharma is a [mere] reflection of the dharma, or a dharma-like fabrication', as [the Buddha] says. Teachings of this kind, on top of being of no benefit, bring about the destruction of the dharma. (Sa-paṇ, 1992: 443.16–19)

Destruction of the dharma is, of course, the Buddhist scholar's greatest enemy.

For the sake of this discussion, I have divided Sa-paṇ's numerous concerns about difficulties in interpretation into four broad categories. The interpreter, according to Sa-paṇ, must be familiar with:

(1) difficult words;
(2) the techniques of translation used by Tibetan translators;
(3) the common mistakes in translation from Sanskrit to Tibetan;
(4) elements with an unintelligible or invalid context.

These categories follow Sa-paṇ's organisation of these issues fairly closely, though I have changed the order to indicate increasing difficulties for the interpreter, and I have created and named the last category. Also, Sa-paṇ spends many pages on these topics, while I summarise and include only select representative examples.

Obscure Vocabulary

In the first category, for those unfamiliar with difficult Tibetan translation terms, Sa-paṇ suggests studying a good word list. As he says, 'A good knowledge of synonyms such as [those in] the *Amarakośa* and the *Viśaprakāśa*, etc. settles doubts about all word meanings' (Sa-paṇ, 1992: 446.8–10). He also suggests that, as an introduction, the beginning scholar might study Sa-paṇ's own lexicographic work, the *Word Treasury* (*tshig gi gter*) (Sa-paṇ, 1992: 446.10–11). This kind of study helps prevent four types of errors. (Sa-paṇ in fact gives *five* divisions of reasons that an interpretation might go wrong due to misunderstanding translation terms. I have moved the missing one – terms translated as derivatives from a different root – into my category of unintelligible context.)

Firstly, the uneducated interpreter is often unfamiliar with 'the differences between new and old conventions [employed] by translators of the early and later traditions' (Sa-paṇ, 1992: 446.15–16). Thus:

> For example, when 'bye ma ka ra' [is used] for 'hwags'; 'go yu' for 'gla gor zho sha'; 'rin chen dbal' for 'rin chen tog'; 'gzhar yang' for 'nam yang', and so forth – such are old Tibetan conventions that are difficult to understand today. (Sa-paṇ, 1992: 446.21–447.3)

These are instances of old and new translation terms for Sanskrit words. The uneducated reader, encountering *hwags* and *bye ma ka ra* (both words for sugar), might be familiar with one but not the other and imagine that they translate different Sanskrit terms. Similarly, *rin chen tog* and *rin chen dbal* are two translations for the same Sanskrit term *ratnaketu*. As Sa-paṇ explains in detail in his *Clear Differentiation of the Three Codes*, the problem is that, while in the newer translations *dbal* has been replaced by *tog*, some interpreters look at the old translations and read *dpal* (radiance) for *dbal*, and take it to mean not 'jewel pinnacle' but 'jewel radiance' (Sa-paṇ, 2002: 169–170, 197, n.190). These are problems best solved by memorising a list of translation terms.

Next, Sa-paṇ points out that:

> By virtue of being translated into regional dialects (*rang rang gi yul gyi skad*), [for instance, translating] 'arrow' (*mda'*) as 'nyag phra'; 'bow' (*gzhu*) as 'gnam ru'... and so on – since they are translated [into words] not well known one place to another, they are difficult to understand. (Sa-paṇ, 1992: 447.12–17)

Here again the issue is clear: A scholar who knows the rare Tibetan words used to translate from Sanskrit is able to avoid confusion when faced with obscure words.

Thirdly, Sa-paṇ mentions that sometimes proper names are translated into Tibetan, and sometimes they are left untranslated. For instance, sometimes 'Magadhā' is translated into 'bearing all people' (*byings 'dzin*); 'Vāraṇasī ...' into 'destroyer of attendants and family' (*'khor mo 'jig*) (Sa-paṇ, 1992: 447.3–6). The interpreter who is unfamiliar with translation terms has no way of knowing that an expression like 'bearing all people' is the name of a place, not an abstract quality.

Fourth, and finally, Sanskrit terms are sometimes translated into Tibetan with special translation meaning, or with a change of meaning, for instance with a kind of description instead of a translation. Looking at the expression 'the one that changes everything' there is no way that an uneducated reader could know that it means 'prayer', or that 'the one that turns evil away' means 'merit' (Sa-paṇ, 1992: 447.6–8).

Thus, to read the dharma, the scholar must have a sure grasp of the often obscure vocabulary used to translate Sanskrit terminology into Tibetan. Sa-paṇ is not complaining about the translation practice that burdens the reader with the requirement for an unusually large and obscure vocabulary. It is to be expected that such unusual and obscure terms appear, since 'When beauty appears (*mdzes pa byung na*) in the Sanskrit language, Sanskrit [words] are used that are not, for the most part, well known in the world' (Sa-paṇ, 1992, 446.6). 'Well known in the world' is traditionally contrasted with 'well known in treatises', the latter being knowledge that many scholars, but only scholars, possess. Sa-paṇ recognises that, in order to translate the elevated style of Sanskrit texts, translators have imposed a new, elevated vocabulary on the Tibetan language. The Tibetan translation terms are designed to reflect the unique beauty and character of the Sanskrit.

The Techniques of Translators

In the second category, interpretive errors are the result of the techniques of translation used by the Tibetan translators. These are all mistakes of excessive glossing – ignorant scholars giving expositions on expressions that in fact do not exist in the original Sanskrit. According to Sa-paṇ they fall into five basic types. The first two occasions for error are similar: they are terms that present, in Tibetan, a word that is merely a clarification and not a direct substitution for a Sanskrit term. When an Indian flower or jewel is named, even though the terms 'flower' and 'jewel' do not appear in the Sanskrit, they are often translated:

> Though the Sanskrit language does not have it, a small part is added and [put in the] translation. Even [where] the Sanskrit has no expression ['jewel', the Tibetan shows] 'Vadūrya jewel', and 'Padmarāga jewel', and so on. And though the Sanskrit has no expression 'flower', [the Tibetan] extends it to 'Utpala flower', and 'padma flower', and 'Saugandhika flower', and so on. (Sa-paṇ, 1992: 450.10–15)

Also, Sa-paṇ writes:

> with terms such as 'divine flower' and 'divine incense', etc., some [translators] have added the expression 'property' (*rdzas*), translating [them thus, more clearly,] as 'flower offering' (lit. 'divine property flower') and 'incense offering' (lit. 'divine property incense') (Sa-paṇ, 1992: 451.11–14)

These are terms that are unclear when translated word for word, and so the translators have strategically inserted an extra word to clarify the meaning. Then, when an expositor comes along and comments on the great significance of terms like 'jewel' or 'property', neither of which is present in the original Sanskrit, he is misrepresenting the dharma.

The third translation strategy noted is similar to these, but involves compound words that represent uncompounded, simple terms in Sanskrit. In terms such as *ye shes* (*jñāna*, wisdom) and *phyag rgya* (*mudrā*, seal), the first syllables *ye* and *phyag* represent no proper part of the Sanskrit. The translators have inserted these in order to identify them as translation terms in Tibetan (Sa-paṇ, 1992: 451.3–6). Sa-paṇ chastises interpreters who gloss *ye shes* as 'primordial wisdom' even though there is no word corresponding to 'primordial' in the Sanskrit source. Thus, whenever a pseudo-scholar gives a commentary on a Tibetan syllable that fails directly to reflect a Sanksrit original, Sa-paṇ levels the charge of innovation – 'fabricated dharma'.

Sometimes, merely to reflect the Sanskrit wording, the translators have added extra words that are redundant in Tibetan. As an example, Sa-paṇ cites the *Eight Thousand Line Perfection of Wisdom Sutra* as having the Sanskrit term *pakṣi*, 'winged one' together with the term *śakuna*, 'bird'. Both terms are translated into Tibetan so that the translated term reads, essentially, 'winged one bird' (*'dab chags bya*). A Tibetan interpreter who comments on these words may be tempted to read the verse as 'the winged one and the bird', reasoning that there is no justification for the redundancy unless two creatures are meant. But Sa-paṇ explains that in Sanskrit the terms *pakṣi* and *śakuna* are each ambiguous on their own, and only together mean, exclusively, 'bird':

> For example, the *Eight Thousand* says, 'winged one bird'. If someone should understand the meaning to be 'the winged one and the bird', and think that there is no reason [other than this] that the two should be repeated, it is not so. 'Winged one' in Sanskrit is '*pakṣi*', and since this expression is used [to mean] many things, such as 'side', etc., [the expression] 'bird' is said to eliminate these. Also, 'bird' in Sanskrit is '*śakuna*', and since this [expression] is used [to mean] other [things] as well, such as 'fortune' (*bkra shis*) and 'lucky omen' (*dge mtshan*), [the expression] 'winged one' is said to eliminate these. There is no fault of redundancy. (Sa-paṇ, 1992: 452.5–12)

If this is correct, it would seem that the translator has sacrificed ease of comprehension in Tibetan to a very close adherence to the Sanskrit. That is, there may have been no fault of redundancy in the Sanskrit original, but there does appear to be one in the Tibetan translation. Yet Sa-paṇ takes the translation strategy for granted whereby an understanding of the Sanskrit background accounts for and justifies the apparent redundancy. Instances like this suggest that Sa-paṇ expects that the interpreter will either know something of the Sanskrit terms reflected in the Tibetan, or have the advantage of being forewarned by a teacher of the significance of this specific translation. Perhaps this is why it is in this context that Sa-paṇ points out that, realistically:

> If you desire to understand well the meaning of such words, you need to practice everything in the five sciences. In particular, you should be familiar with grammar, metrics, poetics, and lexicography, etc. (Sa-paṇ, 1992: 453.4–7)

Errors of exposition will continue to arise until the interpreter masters the full complement of linguistic sciences.

As the last aspect of this category, according to Sa-paṇ the interpreter must be aware that translators of Sanskrit into Tibetan have adopted the use of honorific and non-honorific language in accordance with proper Tibetan usage. He writes:

> Although Sanskrit expressions rarely differentiate the honorific from the non-honorific, [the Tibetan] translation uses [the expression] 'he bestows the gift of speech' for the Buddha addressing someone else, [the expression] 'he beseeches [him]' for someone else speaking to the Buddha, and 'he speaks' for a reciprocal inquiry among equals. Likewise, all words are either honorific or non-honorific. As the new language determination (*skad gsar bcad*) [of Khri-lde-srong-btsan] says, 'In relation to the honorific level of Tibetan expressions, translate so as to [achieve] ease of understanding'. (Sa-paṇ, 1992: 451.6–11)

A Tibetan interpreter who does not know the differences noted between Sanskrit and Tibetan honorifics, and who is unfamiliar with the official ruling that guided the translators' choices, might place too strong an emphasis on the use of a particular honorific or non-honorific form.

Translation Mistakes

In the third category, errors arise because the interpreter is unfamiliar with common mistakes in translation from Sanskrit to Tibetan. These are of three types, but all are mistakes that occur in decoding the Sanskrit, as opposed to re-coding the meaning into Tibetan. In fact, it is fair to say that Sa-paṇ criticises translators only when they have performed errors of decoding (Sa-paṇ does not consider it an error of translation when the translators place the word 'bird' twice in succession in Tibetan). This section is particularly interesting for what it suggests about Sa-paṇ's approach to his readers: the passages are remarkably opaque to a reader who is ignorant of Sanskrit. For instance, for the first type of error, where Sanskrit words are mistaken for their synonyms, he writes:

> Words with [errors of] Sanskrit reckoning [include] a translation of 'rhino' as 'sword' or 'sword' as 'rhino'; a translation based on a reversal

of the expressions 'after' (*rjes*) and 'foot' (*rkang pa*); a translation that respectively mixes up 'child', 'sand', and 'hair', and so on. (Sa-paṇ, 1992: 447.20–448.2)

If readers do not know that the Sanskrit word *khaḍga* can mean either 'sword' or 'rhino', and that *bāla* can mean 'child', 'sand', or 'hair', they cannot follow these examples; what they do understand is that in Sa-paṇ's estimation they are under-qualified for explicating the dharma.

Second, sometimes translators simply mistake a word for a similar word:

> Some do not know the expressions, and so, without understanding, translate in ignorance. [For instance], 'essence' (*snying po*) is translated as 'arrow' (*mda'* – that is, the Sanskrit word *sāra* has been mistaken for *śāra*); 'green'(*ljang gu*) as 'rob' (*'phrog pa* – that is, the Sanskrit adjective *harita* has been mistaken for a form derived from the verb root *hṛt*); and 'sense organ' (*'byung po'i dbang po*, i.e. *bhūtendriya*) as [the proper name] Indrabodhi – by force of such erroneous translations we see a failure to comprehend the intended meaning just as it is. (Sa-paṇ, 1992: 448.7–11)

And third, since until very recently Sanskrit was always written without word breaks, sometimes translators have divided words incorrectly, for instance taking the *na* of the instrumental case ending and misreading it as a separate word, the negative particle:

> Some mistakes of word division [include] either mistakenly construing the sound 'na' of the third case ending as an expression of negation of a succeeding word or construing the 'na' that is an expression of negation of a succeeding word as the sound 'na' of the third case ending of a preceding word. [Either] translate into an incorrect expression. (Sa-paṇ, 1992: 448.2–5)

It hardly needs to be emphasised how important it is to divide words correctly when decoding a Sanskrit manuscript. Errors of this kind, Sa-paṇ argues can be fatal: for instance if one were to read *mahāyānena vidyate,* meaning 'the Great Vehicle knows [it],' as *mahāyāne na vidyate,* meaning '[it] is unknown in the Great Vehicle'. For Sa-paṇ such translators' errors are of course frustrating, but here he points them out primarily to place interpreters on their guard, saying that, for the ignorant, 'wrong translations are difficult to *understand*' (Sa-paṇ, 1992: 447.17–18). How could an interpreter without access to the original and not knowing Sanskrit correct this kind of translation error? Probably Sa-paṇ believes it possible to become familiar with the common errors in translation – perhaps he hoped that other scholars would add to the *Entryway*'s compilation of translation mistakes. Still, even to understand the errors, the interpreter must know at least the basics of Sanskrit.

Unintelligible Context

In the fourth and final category of hazards for interpreters, the problems arise from a lack of familiarity with contexts that the translators have left unexplained: methods of commentary and literary characters or places. Sa-paṇ explains many methods of commentary that are 'well known in treatises' but not 'well known in the world' (Sa-paṇ, 1992: 437.21–441.7). For instance, it is a common practice to gloss a word through appeal to its morphological root. Sa-paṇ says that if the word *kāya* is given a straight gloss, it means 'body'; but if it is glossed as a derivative from the root *kai* (to shout), then it is perfectly legitimate to explain 'the body' as 'a shout' (Sa-paṇ, 1992: 438.21–441.7). Yet a passage that claims that the body is a shout is, on the face of it, incomprehensible to anyone unfamiliar with the Sanskrit terminology that lies beneath the word-for-word Tibetan translation. Many other examples of glossing are listed that require some knowledge of the original linguistic context. I offer two more examples. As Sa-paṇ writes, one commentator glosses the term 'body' as 'god'. For 'body' the Sanskrit had *deha*, but the commentator replaced one letter and came up with *deva*, 'god' (Sa-paṇ, 1992: 441.2–4). In another instance, Sa-paṇ writes that the tantric text *Chanting the Names of Mañjuśrī ... (Mañjuśrī-nāma-saṃgīti)* contains the expression 'Thousand bindu-ed, hundred-syllabled,' but when this passage is glossed in the *Kālacakratantra*, the 100 is changed to 6 when the commentator replaces the *śa* and *ṭa* of *śatāksara* (hundred-syllabled) with the retroflex consonants *ṣa* and *ta* to make *ṣaṭākṣara* (six-syllabled) (Sa-paṇ, 1992: 440.20–441.2).

The interpreter who reads these glosses in Tibetan translation must first be familiar with the protocols of such commentary – to know the general principles of glossing that might make it legitimate to call the 'body' a 'shout'. This knowledge consists in a set of culturally-specific expectations for what satisfies a particular type of text. The commentarial style of the Sanskrit would thus seem to contain a set of peculiarly clear instances of what Lefevere (Bassnett & Lefevere, 1998: 5) following Bourdieu, calls textual grids, 'the collection of acceptable ways in which things can be said'. More importantly, it is difficult to imagine how an interpreter who knows no Sanskrit could come to understand the *particular* gloss, unless an explanation of the Sanskrit comes down in a separate commentary – oral or written. Without an additional explanatory tradition accompanying these translations, these elements are left completely unexplained – and, I would submit, are in fact made more obscure – when the Sanskrit words have been changed into Tibetan.

Another case of what I am calling unexplained context consists in proper names that assume knowledge of Indian literature. Sa-paṇ mentions these as mistakes in translation – names that are mistranslated. But I count them as unexplained context because, whether or not the names are correctly translated, they mean nothing without a knowledge of the context. Sa-paṇ notes that what appears in Sanskrit as Dāmodara ('Dha mo da ra'), a name for Kṛṣṇa, is ordinarily translated into Tibetan as *khyab 'jug*, the standard translation term for Viṣṇu. Dāmodara, which means 'rope-belly', is an epithet for Kṛṣṇa because when he was a child Yaśodā tied a rope around his belly. Mani summarises the story:

> When Kṛṣṇa was a small boy, Yaśodā tied him to a mortar stone. The boy ran about, dragging the heavy stone with him and the rope snapped. Part of the rope remained around his abdomen. From that he got the name Dāmodara. Dama means rope and Udara means abdomen. (Mani, 1975: 199)

The Tibetan translators did not know the story, and so mistranslated the name. Sa-paṇ suggests *tha gu lto* (rope-belly) as a better translation (Sa-paṇ, 1992: 449.17–19). The Tibetan name for the goddess Sarasvatī is *dbyangs can ma*, which means basically 'She of the Melodious Voice' or 'She of the Melody'. But, as Sa-paṇ points out, Sarasvatī only becomes 'She of the Melody' if the expression is altered to make 'Svarasvatī'. A more correct translation, according to Sa-paṇ, is *mtsho las byung ba*, 'The Ocean-Born One,' which preserves not only the Sanskrit name, but also the story behind the name (Sarasvatī was born from the ancient churning of the cosmic ocean). But, Sa-paṇ writes 'not having seen the story, and for the sake of making it easier for Tibetans to understand, it is translated "She of the Melody"' (Sa-paṇ, 1992: 448.17–449.1). Ease of Tibetan comprehension is insufficient to justify fabricating a name that fails to resemble the Sanskrit name.

Here Sa-paṇ is finally criticising translators as a group, including even the best of translators (who can avoid the howlers). He writes:

> As for the [standard] words for different names of living beings and places in the non-Buddhists' ancient lore and the various *avadānas* in the *sūtras* (that is, the stories of great deeds from the Buddha's teachings), one sees that even expert translators have translated them incorrectly because of not knowing the ancient tales. (Sa-paṇ, 1992: 448.14–17)

The fact that this is the only place where Sa-paṇ points out a general problem in the translations (a problem for 'even expert translators') makes it the exception that proves the rule: the translations are made for a community of expert interpreters. It is the only case where even the educated interpretation ends in a Tibetan interpolation, and not a Sanskrit original. In every other instance, complex and potentially misleading translation – in the form of obscure vocabulary and phrasing, redundancy, concepts left unexplained, even predictable mistranslation – is tolerable because it is easily countered by scholars who have mastered the structures of Indian texts and the standard practices of the translators. I do not suggest that Sa-paṇ is satisfied with substandard translations. My point is that only here does he find serious fault with the general practice of the translators and thus in the overall transmission of the dharma. Here the translators' ignorance has led to a systematic fabrication of the dharma. By changing the term, the translations represent a shift in meaning that is unrecoverable from the translated record. This makes it clear that Sa-paṇ takes the translators' main task to be the preservation in Tibetan of as much of the Sanskrit as possible, notwithstanding the interpretive difficulties this causes. Once the translators have done their part, then it is the responsibility of the community of interpretation to maintain familiarity with the necessary conventions, in order to compensate for all the problems in shifting from one cultural/linguistic setting to another. So the translations presume, and therefore require, a specialised scholarly community in Tibet to mediate their interpretation.

Untranslatability Denied

From what I have shown so far, then, it is clear that Sa-paṇ views the Tibetan translations of Buddhism to be a minefield of interpretive difficulties. Western discussions of translation with emphasis on mistakes and loss have often fallen into scepticism about the very value and utility – even the possibility – of translation (see Quine, 1960; Whorf, 1956). The passage I now discuss, however, from chapter 1 of the *Entryway*, shows that Sa-paṇ stands by the viability of translation. In this section Sa-paṇ recognises that shifts in phonetic qualities, grammatical relations and etymological implications are the inevitable result of the translation process. However, rather than taking this to show a decay in the dharma, Sa-paṇ uses the occasion to argue that linguistic meaning operates not through the words themselves, but through the speaker's intention. As long as that intention is preserved, the linguistic changes are insignificant.

The argument I describe is framed by a brief study of the two main categories of Sanskrit words: nouns and verbs. Sa-paṇ lists and defines the categories of case, number, and gender for nouns, and person, number, and tense for verbs, but he stops short before detailing the specifics of Sanskrit morphology, saying:

> These are completely necessary for Sanskrit terms, but inflection does not exist in Tibetan language, and moreover, because there is understanding [in Tibetan] owing to the force of established convention (lit. 'well-known to the ancients'). (Sa-paṇ, 1992: 390.14–16)

Since Tibetan words do not undergo inflection – at least not in the same way as Sanskrit words do – the translations cannot replicate Sanskrit morphology and syntax in Tibetan. Thus, instead of learning Sanskrit grammar, interpreters should familiarise themselves with Tibetan scholarly conventions.

Then Sa-paṇ entertains an objection: 'If the morphological constructions are not made in this way [i.e. according to Sanskrit rules], how is one to understand the meaning of a Sanskrit expression from a translation into Tibetan?' (Sa-paṇ, 1992: 387.13–14). This question asks, essentially, how can one language's meaning be understood in another's syntax? In answer to this question, Sa-paṇ first gives several examples of loss in translation between Sanskrit and Tibetan that he sees as both inevitable and unproblematic, and then he argues that, in fact, strong theories of untranslatability are non-Buddhist.

The examples are of three kinds. Sa-paṇ's first, simple point is that the length and strength of a word's sound – phonetic qualities that are important in metrics – are different in Sanskrit and Tibetan terms. Second, he notes that sometimes a grammatical particle, even when it represents the same Sanskrit case ending, might be written in several different ways in Tibetan – for instance the genitive case particle might be written as *yi*, *kyi* or *'i*, depending on the suffix letter of the word it follows:

> Furthermore, through a person's expressive intention and the meaning's context, and the strength of the word, there come about in Tibetan expressions a single meaning in different words, which arises predominantly because of suffix letters. For instance, in the sixth case [i.e. the genitive], even though there is no difference [in the meaning], the [relation to the term 'heap'] in the expressions 'form heap', 'heap of feeling', and 'compositional factor's heap' come in different words. (Sa-paṇ, 1992: 388.2–6)

Finally, he points out, sometimes in order to prevent mistakes, or to conform to the patterns of Tibetan understanding, the cases or the arrangement of Sanskrit words have been changed. For instance, while in Sanskrit the 'reason' (*hetu*) of a logical syllogism is placed in the fifth case, in Tibetan it is always translated into the fourth case:

> And as in, 'There being smoke, there is fire here', all reasons (*gtan tshigs, hetu*), while [originally] in the fifth case, are translated 'Because of their being smoke', or 'Because of performing a function' [which is the fourth case]. (Sa-paṇ, 1992: 388.19–21)

As much as these changes resemble the kinds of hazards of which interpreters are warned in the section already discussed, in this section they are said to be free of fault:

> Even in cases like this, these very [expressions] are consistent even though they are constructed differently. There is no such thing as an essential relation. Therefore they are made only as a speech intention (*brjod 'dod*). Since there is no substance to the connection between a sound and a meaning, its [linguistic] application (*'jug*) relies on the power of a speech intention. For this reason, no matter how it is applied there is no contradiction. (Sa-paṇ, 1992: 389.3–7)

Since this is not the place to elaborate upon Sa-paṇ's philosophy of language, I conclude by suggesting how this argument relates to what we have already discussed. Sa-paṇ is distinguishing between a purported 'essential relation' between words and meaning and the accepted Buddhist view that language is constructed based upon the speaker's intention or supposition. Linguistic use is a pragmatic activity, and linguistic meaning is constructed in dependence upon convention alone.

It is this relative nature of language that Sa-paṇ calls upon to justify the stability of meaning as it moves through the transforming processes of translation. Translation changes only the contextual, linguistic conventions. Since it is the intention, and not the word, that determines meaning, certain kinds of loss in translation are acceptable – as long as the translations preserve the 'speech intention' (*brjod 'dod*) of the original in conventions comprehensible to the interpreter.

But how can this intention be preserved, especially given that Sa-paṇ believes so many things to have been altered in the translation process? We have already seen the beginnings of Sa-paṇ's answer: through an intellectual community that preserves the intentions in conventions called 'well known in the world' or 'well known in treatises'. Translation difficulties, it would seem, are overcome in the same way as all Buddhist knowledges are preserved: namely, through a valid lineage. The translations were made to preserve the dharma, but only in partnership with a continuous Buddhist community – the *sangha* – to teach it and guide its reception. The translations, according to Sa-paṇ can be properly read, therefore, only by a direct inheritor of the authoritative tradition of interpretation. The ideal scholar ought to have inherited the true interpretation of the translated texts at the feet of his teacher, his guru.

Conclusion

Both passages, then, suggest a similar conclusion. If Tibetan interpreters train in the full complement of intellectual skills, as Indian scholars do, the dharma can be protected against the corrosive tendencies of the change in linguistic and cultural context. Sa-paṇ's analyses thus enclose the Buddhist scriptures within a particular set of social practices – primarily educational – that describe the range of both valid interpretations and authoritative interpreters. This is surely a political act, yet Sa-paṇ's transparent method is simply to analyse translation choices. To a significant degree, then, the implicit interpretive context would have to have been encoded in the Tibetan scriptures by the translators themselves. It makes it reasonable to ask, then, to what degree Tibetan attitudes about religious authority (and authority in general) can be traced to translation choices made by the early translators of the dharma. Matthew Kapstein (2000: 11) has recently noted that literacy in Tibet most likely persisted during the so-called 'dark age' between the collapse of the old Tibetan empire and the period of renewed translation activity a century later, but only the form of literate usage characteristic of the Buddhist translations. As he writes, the standardisation of Buddhist usage 'would have contributed to the iconising of Buddhism and its originally Indian context as the paradigms of learned (that is, literate) and prestigious culture'. After the above discussion, I might add that the prestige of Buddhist culture would seem also to have been embedded in the character of the translations themselves, which for various reasons require an elite community of interpretation to stand guard over the true Indian dharma – and perhaps, over literacy itself.

Chapter 11

The Translation of the Hebrew Word 'ish in Genesis: A Brief Historical Comparison

DAVID BURKE

In the spring of 1997, the International Bible Society (IBS), the USA publisher of the New International Version (NIV), released in Great Britain a newly revised, gender-inclusive edition of the NIV, initially called the NIVI. It did not take long for ultra-conservative groups in the United States to become aware of this development and raise an uproar (LeBlanc, 1997: 52–55; Olasky, 1997: 1–7). Within a very short time the publisher gave in to the highly vocal and vehement pressure by agreeing not to so revise the NIV for distribution in the USA.

James Dobson of *Focus on the Family* wrote an editorial in the 3–10 May 1997 issue of *World*, urging readers, 'Don't give in to feminist pressure to rewrite the Scriptures'. On the same day that IBS announced its decision to suppress the NIVI, Dobson convened a meeting at *Focus on the Family* magazine headquarters, to set some guidelines. Representatives attending this entirely male meeting came from *Focus*, IBS and the Council on Biblical Manhood and Womanhood (Spencer, 1997). This hastily convened meeting resulted in the issue of a brief set of 13 highly publicised 'Guidelines for Translation of Gender-related Language in Scripture'. A one-page *Focus on the Family* facsimile of June 3, 1997 lists the 13 guidelines, the fourth of which is given as follows: 'Hebrew *'ish* should ordinarily be translated 'man' and 'men' and Greek *aner* should almost always be so translated' (Figure 1).

As these were announced by *Focus*, the tone of the press release was that these were now new mandates, agreed to by all the participants of the meeting. But it quickly became apparent that much of what had been agreed upon was for the most part based on ideology rather than translation theory, and would not hold up under closer scrutiny. Indeed, the

Statement on Gender-Related Language in Scripture

Guidelines for Translation of Gender-Related Language in Scripture

(A) Gender-related renderings of Biblical language which we affirm:

(1) The generic use of 'he, him, his, himself' should be employed to translate generic 3rd person masculine singular pronouns in Hebrew, Aramaic and Greek. However, substantival participles such as *ho pisteuon* can often be rendered in inclusive ways, such as 'the one who believes' rather than 'he who believes'.
(2) Person and number should be retained in translation so that singulars are not changed to plurals and third-person statements are not changed to second-person or first person statements, with only rare exceptions required in unusual cases.
(3) 'Man' should ordinarily be used to designate the human race or human beings in general, for example in Genesis 1:26–27, 5:2; Ezekiel 29:11; and John 2:25.
(4) Hebrew *'ish* should ordinarily be translated 'man' and 'men' and Greek *aner* should almost always be so translated.
(5) In many cases, *anthropoi* refers to people in general, and can be translated 'people' rather than 'men'. The singular *anthropos* should ordinarily be translated 'man' when it refers to a male human being.
(6) Indefinite pronouns such as *tis* can be translated 'anyone' rather than 'any man'.
(7) In many cases, pronouns such as *oudeis* can be translated 'no one' rather than 'no man'.
(8) When *pas* is used as a substantive, it can be translated with terms such as 'all people' or 'everyone'.
(9) The phrase 'son of man' should ordinarily be preserved to retain intracanonical connections.
(10) Masculine references to God should be retained.

(B) Gender-related renderings which we will generally avoid, though there may be unusual exceptions in certain contexts:

(11) 'Brother' (*adelphos*) and 'brothers' (*adelphoi*) should not be changed to 'brother(s) and sister(s)'.
(12) 'Son' (*huios, ben*) should not be changed to 'child,' or 'sons' (*huioi*) to 'children' or 'sons and daughters'. (However, Hebrew *banim* often means 'children.')
(13) 'Father' (*pater, ab*) should not be changed to 'parent,' or 'fathers' to 'parents,' or 'ancestors'.

(C) We understand these guidelines to be representative and not exhaustive.

Figure 1 *Focus on the Family* fax, 3 June 1997

precise nature of the 'agreement' quickly needed to be qualified and questioned (LeBlanc & Rabey, 1997; 62–64).

These 'Guidelines' were intended as mandates for Scripture translation that would be expected to secure the desideratum of gender-specific consistency in translation. When I saw them, I was immediately intrigued enough to want to explore to what extent the ancient Bible translations, and some much more modern English Versions as well, have actually practised or manifested such desired consistency. For the purposes of this chapter, I limited the scope of the exploration to the fourth of the guidelines. That is, I investigated how Bible translators from the earliest period to the present have actually handled the Hebrew word *'ish*, which the fourth guideline declares should ordinarily be translated 'man' and 'men'.

The study includes in the comparison the two most significant ancient Scripture translations, at least for the Western Church and the English Bible traditions – the Greek Septuagint (LXX) and the Latin Vulgate. The Septuagint is the first-ever Scripture translation, bringing the texts of the Hebrew Scriptures into Greek during the 3rd and 2nd centuries BCE. The tradition is that 70 Hebrew scholars, adept in both Hebrew and Greek, completed the translation for the Greek-speaking Jewish community in Alexandria, Egypt. The Latin Vulgate was prepared by the biblical scholar of the patristic era, Jerome, in the late 4th century CE. Jerome's mandate was to translate as far as possible from the Hebrew, and at the same time bring together a standard Latin text of the Scriptures that would bring textual unity to widely disparate editions.

The English Bible translations compared in this chapter start with the Authorised Version or King James Version (KJV), as it is more commonly called. The KJV was first published in 1611, and has had a subsequent history of orthographic and textual revision at various points since. Next in the comparison is the Revised Standard Version (RSV), published in 1952 as an updating of the venerable KJV text tradition. The revision was on the basis of both English language change and new manuscript evidence for the biblical texts, such as rediscovered ancient Greek codices and papyrus manuscripts, as well as the recently discovered Dead Sea Scrolls in ancient Hebrew. The New International Version (NIV), first published in 1978 by IBS, is also compared (and it should be noted that this is the original NIV edition, and not the NIVI or TNIV, which introduce gender-inclusive revisions). Also compared is the Tanakh (TNK), the 1985 publication by the Jewish Publication Society of the Hebrew Bible in English translation, and, lastly, the Contemporary English Version (CEV), the most recent of the selection, published by the American Bible Society in 1995.

The first step for this study was to organise a comparison of Bible translations involving a representative sampling of texts. The 105 examples of Hebrew *'ish* in the book of Genesis were selected as a broad slice into the textual evidence of how this word was used in ancient Hebrew. The aim was to see what sort of patterns would emerge in a part of the Hebrew Bible where one might at least expect to find a fairly regular consistency for locutions using 'man/men' in translation. It is evident, both from the table of comparative samples (Table 1) and from the statistical proportions given below, that the translation of the Hebrew word *'ish* has by no means been strait-jacketed by concern for some sort of literalist, word-for-word consistency, especially one that seeks to guarantee gender-specific uniformity.

This study makes clear that the Guidelines, hurriedly assembled from a reactionary and ideological perspective, were formulated without any consultation with actual translators or any reference to actual Bible translations ancient or modern. The formulators of the Guidelines shared a perception that the English language is being undermined by gender-

Table 1 How *'ish* is translated: Comparative text samples

Genesis	*LXX*	*Vulgate*	*KJV*	*RSV*	*NIV*	*Tanakh*	*CEV*
2:04	anthropos	homo	a man	a man	a man	a man	a man
10:05	hekastos	unusquique	everyone	each	each	each	their own
23:06	oudeis	nullusque	none	none	none	none	none
29:19	andri hetero	viro altere	another man	any other man	some other man	an outsider	someone else
30:20	aner	maritus	husband	husband	husband	husband	husband
31:49	heteros	inter nos	one	each	each	between you and me	each
37:19	hekastos	mutuo	one	each (other)	each (other)	(to) one (another)	one
41:11	amphoteroi	uterque	each man	each	each	each of us	both
41:38	anthropon	virum	a man	anyone	anyone	a man	no one
42:28	allelous	mutuo	one (to another)	each (other)	each (other)	to one another	one (another)
43:19	tou anthropou		the steward	the steward	the steward	Joseph's house steward	the servant in charge
45:01 (twice)	pantas/ oudeis	cuncti/ nullus	everyman /no man	everyone /no one	everyone /no one	everyone/ no one	them/ alone

inclusive language locutions. However, as this study of the Hebrew word *'ish* shows, they ignored the numerous ways, historically, in which gender-inclusive translation has already been employed from the very beginnings of Scripture translation practice.

Hebrew '*ish* in Genesis and English 'Man/men'

Hebrew *'ish*, like Greek *anthropos*, is a multiple-reference word. It is used in the Hebrew Bible in referring to humans of each gender, as well as to males, whether human or not (for example in Genesis 7:2 it is used to refer to animals). Hebrew *'ish*, like Greek *anthropos*, is capable of being gender-specific or gender-inclusive in meaning. This is true also for the masculine pronouns that refer to it.

Strikingly, the closest correspondent English word, 'man', has historically been used in quite the same way – as both a gender-specific and gender-inclusive term. 'Man' is capable, grammatically and traditionally, of referring to a human being in general, to all humankind collectively, to any particular male person or, in the most specific sense, to an adult male. At this date, in the United States at least, it is in this last sense that the English word 'man' is heard by most users of spoken English. The masculine pronouns – he, him, his – are clearly not heard today as being gender-inclusive (though, of course, they have been, both grammatically and traditionally).

Indeed, the changing character of English as a living language today can be strikingly illustrated by the way the usage of this word 'man/men' has shifted in common speech over the past half-century. When the former Secretary of State of the United States, Madeline K. Albright, gave the commencement address at Harvard University on 5 June 1997, she opened her remarks on the current global responsibilities of the USA with a reflection on the post-World War II Marshall Plan, whose 50th anniversary was being observed that year. She began with these words:

> British Foreign Secretary Ernest Bevin called the Marshall Plan 'A lifeline to sinking men', and it was – although I expect that some women in Europe were equally appreciative. (Erlanger, 1997)

The brief aside that Dr Albright felt compelled to append to the Bevin quote is very revealing about one of the central ways in which English language use has changed over the last several decades. As American English, at least, is spoken and heard today in ordinary speech, a large segment of people would now perceive Mr Bevin's use of 'men' as archaic and obtuse (even though intended in its historic sense to include both genders). It would also be perceived as excluding from its intended audience those who were not male. The fact that Dr Albright felt that this quote from 50 years ago could no longer stand by itself without clarification for her audience is a clear signal of how English usage has changed. It shows why it has become so important, both for translation and for communication in general, to recognise that not keeping up to date with actual English usage can result in significant numbers of people within a translation's intended audience feeling excluded from the scriptural messages intended for them.

A Comparative Look at the Texts

This chapter addresses guideline four, which mandates that Hebrew *'ish* should ordinarily be translated 'man' and 'men'. It focuses on the range of examples presented by this word as it is handled in the various translations compared for the 105 occurrences of the word in the book of Genesis. For the LXX, the first and oldest Bible translation, it is significant that in almost one-third (about 32%) of the occurrences of *'ish* in Genesis the LXX translators opted for a gender-inclusive approach, using words other than those literally meaning 'man'. For the Latin Vulgate the proportionate use of options other than words for 'man/men' runs at an even higher rate of 45%. And a comparable profile shows up in the KJV (20%), RSV (29%), NIV (31%), and TNK (52%). The CEV, being the most recent of the English Versions, and intended to present the scriptural message in the form and style of contemporary spoken (American) English, presents a profile that is even more pronounced (65%), reflecting its close attention to contemporary American English speech patterns. Nevertheless, it is clear from comparing the LXX and Vulgate handling of *'ish* that it would not do justice to the multiple-reference capabilities of this Hebrew word, or to the range of meaning it had in the literature of the Hebrew Bible, if the translators were to try to force it into a gender-specific strait-jacket in every occurrence in translation.

In the LXX book of Genesis, it is clear that these ancient translators understood *'ish* as a multiple-reference word. In approximately one-third of the cases LXX translators, in translating the 105 Genesis passages with Hebrew *'ish*, use Greek words other than *anthropos* or *aner* ('man'). This small sampling from the earliest Bible translations (Table 1) already makes it amply clear that the LXX translators did not operate with a need to maintain a highly consistent gender-specific translation pattern with this word. In all, LXX Genesis employs eight gender-inclusive terms to convey the meaning of Hebrew *'ish* in its various contexts, most frequently the distributive *hekastos*, 'each, every' (15 times) and *oudeis*, 'no one' (5 times). In several instances LXX Genesis is able to convey the meaning from the Hebrew without using any direct equivalent of *'ish* (3 times). In Genesis 7:2 the Hebrew text, referring to the various pairs of animals being herded into the ark of Noah, has *'ish we'ishto* which literally would translate as 'a man and his woman'. The translators of LXX and all the other versions understand Hebrew well enough to know that this phrase cannot be translated literally since the reference is to animals, and they translate accordingly.

For the Latin Vulgate, completed by St Jerome in the late 4th century CE, the data from this probe is even more striking. It makes clear that this ancient translator knew his Hebrew very well and knew that the word *'ish* was not used in Hebrew in any narrow gender-specific sense. Indeed, the sampling reveals that for the 105 Vulgate Genesis passages almost half of the examples (45%) are translated with words other than *vir* 'man' vis-à-vis woman (40 times) or *homo* 'man' or 'human' vis-à-vis animals (16 times).

The Vulgate Genesis uses a wide variety of terms to convey the sense of Hebrew *'ish*. There are distributive terms such as *alter* 'one (of two), the other' (once); *alterutrum* 'one (of two), either' (once); *nullusque* 'nobody, none' (once); *nullus* 'no one' (twice); *unusquisque* 'each one' (twice); *utrasque* 'both parts, each part' (once); *mutuo* 'mutually, reciprocally' (3 times); *ambo* 'both' (once); *quisquam* 'any one' (once); *invicem* (in turn, one after the other' (once); *singuli* 'singly' (4 times); *singulorum* 'individually' (twice); *singulisque* 'to each' (once); *cuncti* 'all' (once).

Where Hebrew *'ish* has the sense of 'husband' or 'spouse' the Vulgate uses *maritus* 'husband' (3 times). In the Joseph narrative, where the Hebrew text continually repeats *ha'ish* 'the man', as his brothers call Joseph (because they have not yet recognised that he is their brother Joseph), the Vulgate uses *vir*, but also simply pronominal substitutes: *eum* 'him' (twice). Joseph's house steward, who in Hebrew is also often *ha'ish* 'the man' is regularly handled in the Vulgate with *ille* 'that one' or simply by means of inflecting the verb. In Genesis 42:30, Joseph is described in Hebrew as 'the man [*ha'ish*] who is lord of the land'. Here the Vulgate simply translates *dominus terrae* 'the lord of the land', not requiring the redundant 'the man'. In addition to this there are 11 other examples in which the Latin handles *'ish* simply through verb inflection. In Genesis 19:09 the Hebrew has *be'ish belot* 'against the man, Lot'. Here the Latin simply has 'against Lot', not requiring the redundant 'man'. NIV and CEV do the same, and TNK has 'against the person of Lot'. Where the Hebrew uses *'ish* in a distributive reference to the pairs or groups of animals in the ark of Noah, the Vulgate uses *masculum* 'male', clearly recognising that *'ish* is not to be taken literally here as 'man'.

In the KJV, a similar number of English words other than 'man' are used for *'ish* (20 times): distributives such as 'one' (10 times), 'each' (twice), 'everyone' (once), 'none' (once), and ethnic or occupational terms such as 'Canaanite' (Genesis 38:02), 'Adullamite' (Genesis 38:01), 'Egyptian' (Genesis 39:01), 'Hebrew' (Genesis 39:14), 'steward' (Genesis 43:19), and 'husbandman' (Genesis 9:20). Distributives are sometimes used in combination with 'man' in other instances (21 times): 'every man' (10 times), 'each man' (6 times), 'any man' (once). The KJV translators, who in many ways tend to be literalistic in their approach to the Hebrew, are nevertheless demonstrably free to use multiple options for bringing the meaning of Hebrew *'ish* in its various contexts faithfully into English. This is significant at a point in the history of English language use when the word 'man' was broadly in use for gender-inclusive purposes.

It is instructive to note that the KJV translators made the deliberate choice to render the Hebrew phrase *bene-yisra'el*, as 'children of Israel' instead of what it literally means, 'sons of Israel', because they knew that that phrase was inclusively used in Hebrew to mean the 'people of Israel'. Even though the word 'children' was not literal at all, and somewhat odd sounding, it served to keep readers from taking too narrow a meaning had they used 'sons'. Also, in eight instances KJV uses 'husband' as the appropriate term contextually for *'ish*. As might be expected, the KJV percentage for instances in which it employs terms other than the literal 'man/men' is the lowest (20%) among the versions compared. All others, ancient or modern, range from about one-third to two-thirds of instances.

As would be expected, RSV shows a similar pattern for using a range of options other than 'man' (30 times); 'one' (10 times), 'each' (7 times), 'all' (once), 'tiller' (once), 'Hebrew' (once), etc. Similarly, the NIV also opts for a wide range of gender-inclusive options (32 times); 'each/each other' (15 times), 'one' (twice), 'no one' (3 times), 'anyone' (twice), 'steward' (3 times), 'Lot' (Genesis 19:09), 'prospered' (Genesis 39:02).

For the Tanakh (TNK) the proportionate use of terms other than the literal 'man' for Hebrew *'ish* is much more striking than for the RSV – 54 instances out of the 105 occurrences. That is, in more than half of the occurrences in Genesis (about 52%) the translation choice of the TNK translators has been for terms other than 'man/men'. While 'man' is used 51 times in the Tanakh, the distributives 'each (one)' and 'one (another)' are also used frequently (17 and 7 times). Elsewhere the Tanakh uses 'husband' (8 times), 'no one/none' (4 times), 'every/everyone' (twice), 'he' (once), 'they' (once), 'tiller of the soil' (once) for Hebrew 'man of the soil'. And similar expressions are also employed without 'man': 'skilful hunter' (once), 'smooth-skinned' (once), Egyptian (once); Hebrew (once), house steward (once), Canaanite (once); as well as combinations like 'between you and me' (once). What is significant here is not only that this English translation registers less than 50% literal use of the word 'man' for Hebrew *'ish* but that this is a translation by Jewish biblical scholars. These are translators who clearly have a very thorough and intimate knowledge of the Hebrew language and Bible.

The CEV from its inception has viewed a 'gender-faithful' translation approach as integral. Consequently it displays a significantly broader range of possibilities for conveying the meaning of *'ish* across the barriers of language, culture and time in ways that endeavour always to be translationally and contextually valid as well as clear and easily understandable for the reader/hearer. CEV Genesis reveals the use of multiple appropriate meanings for *'ish*. In contrast to the other English Versions compared, CEV had gender-specific words in only about one-third of the occurrences. This means that in almost two-thirds (70) of the *'ish* passages, CEV uses words or phrases that are not gender-specific. The numerous examples include: 'each' (8 times), 'one' (4 times), 'they/them' (4 times), 'their (own)' (3 times), 'person' (twice), 'never married/unmarried' (twice), 'Isaac' (twice), 'servant' (10 times) and 'governor' (6 times). In the long Rebekkah narrative of Genesis 24, where the Hebrew Bible consistently describes the servant sent by Abraham to find a bride for Isaac as *ha'ish*, 'the man', the LXX consistently provides *ho anthropos*. The KJV, RSV and NIV are similarly consistent with 'the man', whereas the CEV (drawing out the information implicit in the text in order to help to the reader) consistently uses the much less ambiguous descriptor, 'Abraham's servant' or 'the servant'. In Genesis 25:27 the LXX has *anthropos* in the construction that KJV translates as 'a cunning hunter, a man of the field' for Esau and 'a plain man, dwelling in tents' for Jacob. The CEV has 'hunter' and 'shepherd' as the key identifiers in the sentence: 'Esau liked the outdoors and became a good hunter, while Jacob settled down and became a shepherd'.

In the Joseph story (Genesis 42), Joseph is frequently referred to by his brothers as 'the man' (43:05 LXX, *ho anthropos*) in the more titular designation, 'the man who is the lord of the land' (KJV 42:30). KJV, RSV, and NIV consistently continue with 'the man', whereas CEV is consistent in using the functional equivalent for this phrase, 'the governor'. In Genesis 39:02, where KJV translates (of Joseph): 'he was a prosperous man' (LXX, *aner*), NIV has 'he prospered' and CEV has 'to be successful in everything he did'. Numerous other examples may be found.

In addition, while one cannot extrapolate from the evidence on how Hebrew *'ish* has been handled in historic and recent Bible translations to general conclusions about terms for 'man' in the Greek New Testament, there are some things that can be observed. The most common Greek word for 'man' in the New Testament is *anthropos*. But its essential meaning is 'human being'. This can be seen in passages such as John 16:21, which describes how a woman, after the pain and anguish of giving birth, rejoices 'that a human being is born' (in Greek *hoti egennethe anthropos*). The joy is not at all about bearing a male child, but about bringing a new human being to life. Similarly, in Paul to the Phillipians 2:07 (part of the great hymn of Christ's incarnation), Jesus is described as 'coming in human likeness' (New American Bible). In Greek this is *en homoiomati anthropon genomenos*; cf. CEV, 'when he became like one of us'. Similarly, the derivative adjective, *anthropinos* means 'human' and not 'manly' as, for example, in Corinthians I, 2:13, where Paul speaks of his message as being imparted 'in words not taught by human wisdom' (RSV; *anthropines sophias*). In both its singular and plural forms *anthropos* is often used to mean 'people', in other words not simply 'male' persons but any or all persons regardless of gender. In Matthew 4:4, for example, the Greek text has the singular *ho anthropos* in the familiar saying of Jesus: 'Man shall not live by bread alone...' (KJV). More recent translations have recognised the generic and distributive nature of this singular: 'One does not live by bread alone...' (New Revised Standard Version, NAB); 'Human beings live not on bread alone...' (NJB); 'People need more than bread... '(NLT).

Similarly, the plural form (*pasin anthropois*) appears in Titus 2:11, in the familiar line, 'For the grace of God has appeared for the salvation of all men' (RSV). But, again, recognising that the Greek does not only mean 'all males', some recent translations have been more sensitive to the fact that some receptors are not hearing themselves addressed by the phrase 'all men'. And, since the Greek did not intend *anthropois* to refer to males only, neither should an English translation convey gender exclusion. The NRSV thus makes the adjustment to RSV: 'the grace of God has appeared, bringing salvation to all' (compare NAB '... saving all'; NLT ... 'bring salvation to all people'; CEV '...to save all people').

The use of *anthropos* in the Creed of Nicea (composed 325 CE) may also be compared instructively, particularly the line traditionally translated: 'who for us men and for our salvation came down and was incarnate, becoming human'. In the first instance, 'for us men', the Greek *anthropos* intends to convey 'for us human beings' (vis-à-vis God), indicating that God's action in Jesus Christ was graciously directed to all humankind in its common need for God's grace, and not at all directed only to males. Indeed, for many persons reciting the creed in liturgy today, the appearance of this word 'men' seems superfluous, but its intent was to convey our status before God as humans. And, precisely because this word 'men' today conveys 'males', it has indeed been excised from many English texts of the

Creed of Nicea (and the Constantinopolitan of 381). The reading 'for us and for our salvation' has become the common alternative translation. It has the virtue of not giving the erroneous impression that God's grace is directed only to men, but it may be that it should more properly (albeit more verbosely) be 'For us human beings...'

In the second instance, 'becoming human', the Greek here is a combined verb, *enanthropeo*, literally 'to take on human form'. It should be clear from both the form and the context that it cannot be about 'taking on male form'. The centrality of incarnation is becoming human, not becoming male.

The Greek word *aner* 'man' (as noted above) generally designates a man in contrast to a woman, and yet it is also used in the NT in an inclusive sense. It is used a number of times, for example in the letter of James, to mean more than just males; cf. 1:12, 'Blessed is anyone (Greek *aner*) who endures temptation', where NRSV has reflected its distributive sense.

Greek practice was to use the plural of *adelphos*, 'brother' to address persons of both genders, since it had no common plural. To address or refer to a group as 'brothers', as Paul often does in the NT, thus cannot be taken to mean he was addressing only males. Although English has the same problem of not having a common plural, any English translation that chooses to render '*adelphoi*' simply as 'brothers' must be aware that some parts of the intended audience will not feel addressed or included. Clearly a few generations ago, a speaker or writer could have expected the word 'brothers' to be heard by those in the Christian community as addressed to all people, but that is no longer the case. Like the words, 'man/men' it is heard as addressing males and no longer communicates what the Greek *adelphoi* intended (Strauss, 2002). Thus, some translations have chosen to translate *adelphoi* as 'brothers and sisters', since that was intended in the Greek (NRSV, 2 Corinthians 13:11; Romans 10:l).

A final example from the NT – Matthew 16:24 – may illustrate how translation committees have approached this issue where it is simply a matter of masculine pronouns in a text (not terms for 'man') that are not intended by Greek usage to refer only to males. The passage in the traditional KJV is: 'If any man [Greek, *tis*] will come after me, let him deny himself and take up his cross, and follow me'. While this Greek pronoun *tis* 'one, someone, anyone' is masculine in form, it is generic in its intent and does not intend that only males are meant here. But in traditional English renderings it does appear that only males are invited. One recent approach, that exemplified in NRSV, recognising the distributive sense of *tis*, uses plural equivalents to convey the message here as addressing all people: 'If any want to become my followers, let them deny themselves and take up their cross and follow me'. Another approach is exemplified by CEV, which also recognises that direct address in 'you' language is a much more natural and familiar equivalent for English speakers today to Jesus' indirect third-person form of address: 'If any of you want to be my followers, you must forget about yourself. You must take up your cross and follow me'.

Conclusion

In conclusion, the aim was to examine a modest but representative scan of one small slice of the textual data to see how this Hebrew word *'ish*, has been translated in Bibles from the time of the LXX to today. Even from this small sample it has become clear that ideologically conditioned notions of controlled consistency in regard to gender-specific words was never a factor in Scripture translation in earlier times. This brief look at the evidence in the book of Genesis reveals that there have always been both gender-specific and gender-inclusive translation capabilities for such key terms as Hebrew *'ish*. Conclusions can be made on the basis of this evidence. Rigidly consistent patterns that would limit translation of such key words to gender-specific terms only could actually hinder, rather than help, the transfer of meaning for present-day users of English. In contrast, the more balanced approach evident throughout the history of actual Bible translation practice is less in conflict with obvious audience realities. When restrictive injunctions are issued about Bible translation, without weighing either audience needs or historical evidence of how translation has actually been carried out from the earliest times, the Bible-using public is being misinformed and misled.

Postscript

Interestingly, some five years later in 2002, the International Bible Society issued a news release announcing that it would indeed publish a gender-inclusive edition of the NIV, to be called TNIV – Today's NIV. The announcement also made clear that the TNIV would be published as an alternative to the traditional NIV, which is not to be replaced by the TNIV (Strauss, 2002; Polythress, 2002).

Chapter 12

Translating the Spoken Words of the Saints: Oral Literature and the Sufis of Aurangabad

NILE GREEN

In common with several other branches of Muslim learning, the Islamic mystical tradition known as Sufism has given great emphasis to the importance of the living spoken word (see Goody, 1987). Concerned to maintain the epistemological purity of the original idiom of communication, Muslim scholars have over the centuries regarded acts of translation (of the Qur'an in particular) with some suspicion. Yet at the same time Islam has functioned as one of the great civilisations of translation in human history, pioneering translations of works in classical Greek, Syriac, Sanskrit and Middle Persian (and in recent centuries translation of works in modern European languages) into Arabic, Persian and other languages of Muslim scholarship (Gutas, 1998; al-Nadim, 1970).

In spite of the importance attached to the spoken word by long generations of Sufi masters, Sufism also developed a rich tradition of written knowledge. This tradition was based in large part on branches of learning (particularly metaphysics) and modifications of behaviour (particularly classical rules of etiquette) that may be seen as dependent upon the configurations of expression and recording that are peculiar to written traditions. At the same time, the translation of written religious works, particularly into emergent vernacular languages, has been no less a characteristic of Sufism than the preservation and teaching of such classical languages as Arabic and Persian. In Sufism, therefore, as in Muslim civilisation more generally, competing evaluations of oral and written modes of knowledge along with the uncertain epistemological value of translation have led to the formation of complex and at times opposing criteria for the defining of valid religious knowledge and its transmission.

This chapter focuses on one particular example of these processes, and investigates the question of the translation of the spoken to the written word as perceived through the oral–literary tradition that developed around the Indian Sufi Nizam al-din Aurangabadi, who died in the Deccan city of Aurangabad in 1729. As a means of comparison, I shall also draw reference to the oral–literary tradition of Shah Musafir (d.1715), one of Nizam al-din's fellow Sufi saints in Aurangabad. By looking at some of the processes through which a written saintly tradition was systematically developed from the oral teachings of Aurangabad's 18th-century Sufi masters, some insight may be gained into the ways in which translation was at times implicit in the very creation of religious literature. For, if translation refers in its original sense to the act of handing something over, it is important to bear in mind that such translations have characterised the later history of scriptural traditions at points well advanced in their histories – points at which their 'original' language or message was no longer transparent. Conversely, such translations have also at times been a feature of the earliest stages in the histories of written religious traditions.

In the following pages I examine some of the ways in which premodern Muslims handed over the inspired teachings of their saints to successive generations of their co-religionists in South Asia through the special genre of the *malfuzat*, or recorded conversation. While this genre, with the patent insistence in its formulation upon the role of the spoken word, is in some ways an unusual case, this very (or at least apparent) candour about the role of the spoken word makes it a rewarding genre to examine. For a great many of the written traditions of the world's religions have had at least part of their origin in oral traditions of some kind, and have accordingly undergone acts of translation from the spoken to the written registers over time. It is, then, from this wider perspective that the processes involved in the creation of the oral–literary tradition of Aurangabad's Sufi saints are perhaps most illuminating. It must be made clear, however, that the oral traditions of the Sufi saints of Islam are located within a highly literate culture, albeit a culture that placed a special emphasis on orally-transmitted knowledge within the religious sphere. The most interesting aspect of dealing with the oral tradition of such highly literate cultures as Islam is the perspective it presents on the question of the sacred status of oral tradition vis-à-vis the far better-established claims to the sacred of the culture's primary sacred written texts.

In the first part of this chapter I discuss the sense in which the oral traditions of such saints as Nizam al-din have been conceived by Muslims as part of their own sacred tradition. In the second and main part I address the issues of translation that are highlighted by the specific forms of sacredness that were claimed for oral traditions of the Sufi saints. I am not addressing present-day matters of linguistic translation, but rather the issues of translation faced in the past by those originally responsible for passing on the saints' oral tradition. For in translating the spoken word into written form, the oral tradition surrounding the Aurangabad saints involved its transmitters in the wider problematic assembly that is inherent in the process of translating the sacred spoken word into an appropriate form of sacred literature.

The hagiographical literature of Islam encompasses a vast body of writings not only in the classical languages of Muslim expression in Arabic and Persian (Mojadeddi, 2001), but also in almost all of the regional languages of the Islamic world. While saintly traditions were never granted the same status in Islam as the Qur'an or Hadith (the 'reports' of the Prophet Muhammad's sayings and deeds), in the premodern period they were often granted a status that placed them within a continuum of sacredness. For, insofar as the saints were seen as the successors of the Prophet Muhammad, indubitably secondary to him in status but nevertheless representative of him in his absence, so were their words and deeds regarded as sources of religious inspiration and guidance. Indeed, as inspired utterances (*shath*), the words of the saints were sometimes effectively regarded as a secondary form of revelation in their own right, though this was a matter that long vexed the minds of many Muslim theologians and jurisconsults. In fulfilling these roles, stories of the saints and accounts of their oral teachings came to form what was in some sense a secondary category of written religious authority, not only in India but throughout the Islamic world.

The popularity of such saintly literature is a much more complex matter than the sharply dichotomised model of Great and Little Traditions might suggest in its prescription of zones of literary, political and cultural centres and peripheries (Redfield, 1956). This is partly because the literature (if, as we see below, not always the words) of the saints was often itself composed in the Arabic and Persian languages of elite cultural and religious expression. But it is also because this literature transcended barriers of social and religious class division in a way that is inimical to such models of cultural dichotomy. Nevertheless, in reflection of the constant interaction between (written) tradition and (oral) re-formulation that is a feature of all major religious traditions over time, the success of saintly traditions was irrevocably bound up with the problem of the continuity (the 'handing over' through time) of the teachings of any given religion. That is, it was a reflection of the problem of communication itself. In this sense the saints may themselves be seen as translations, as the embodiments of Islam translated into its many and multifarious linguistic and cultural environments.

Between the 10th and 14th centuries, an Islamic literature of the saints took shape in genres that would in large part last through to the present day. In medieval Delhi, the historian of the period Ziya al-din Barani described how a text entitled *Fawa'id al-Fu'ad* came to form a popular source of religious guidance (Nizam ad-din Awliya, 1992: 43). This text claimed to comprise the collected discourses of the celebrated Sufi Nizam al-din Auliya (d. 1325) of Delhi (Nizam ad-din Awliya, 1992), after whom the later Nizam al-din of Aurangabad was named. The fame that this text achieved during that and successive periods was instrumental in assuring the saint's continuing fame and prestige down to the present day. Yet here is the rub, for this collection of Nizam al-din's sayings claimed to present the literal spoken words of the saint transcribed verbatim into a written document by one of his disciples and later passed back to the master for his approval of their authenticity. In hagiographical terms, this revolutionary text was the first example of an extremely popular genre in Muslim South Asia subsequently known as the *malfuzat*, or recorded conversation (Ernst, 1992). Such collections of *malfuzat* later documented the sayings of a wide variety of Muslim saints, in practice providing one of the classic proofs of saintly status in South Asia. Such texts form what I term the oral–literary tradition of the Sufi saints.

The crucial importance of these texts to their audience lay in the claim that they were the literal *spoken* words of the saint. They functioned not simply as written documents, but as the living words of the saint in written form. This mode of transmission aimed at nothing less than an imitation of the primary sources of scriptural guidance in Islam, the Qur'an and the Hadith. For while both of these exist as written texts, their origins were of an oral nature (Graham, 1985: 23–40). Thus the name Qur'an itself indicates a 'recitation', something 'spoken aloud' – a name reflecting the belief that the Qur'an represented the speech of God. The Archangel Gabriel spoke the words of God to the Prophet and the Prophet in turn spoke them to his followers, who wrote them down. (A similar notion occurs also in Hinduism in the concept of *śruti*, that which has been heard; this form of transmission was regarded as both the origin and nature of the revelation of the Vedas.) As with the Hadith (literally 'reports' of the Prophet's words and deeds handed down orally at first), both the nature of the content and the chain of its transmission was oral. This oral–textual rhetorical mode was also mirrored in the development of the scripture of Shi'ite Islam, most notably in the collection of sermons known as *Nahj al-Balagha* attributed to the Prophet Muhammad's son-in-law, Ali (Ali ibn Abi Taleb, 1984).

The spoken word maintained this level of esteem owing to the context of the predominantly oral culture in which early Islam emerged. Interestingly, this reverence found continuity in the development of other secondary scriptural forms in societies where in almost all other walks of life the spoken word had long yielded its place to the written document or contract. Just the literal spoken word of God via the Prophet was captured in the Qur'an, so the genre of the *malfuzat* sought to present itself as capturing the literal spoken word of the saint, who, many believed, was inspired by a comparable (if non-prophetic) divine impulse. Thus mediation, always a dubious notion in Islam, was in this way minimised, for there was, in theory, no writer whose poor memory or unsuitable flourishes interfered with the authentic and inspired words of the saint. In attempting to avoid the epistemological mediation of writing, the *malfuzat* thus circumvented a more widely acknowledged distrust of the mediation of translation of any kind, a formulation classically expressed in the theological dogma of the untranslatability of the Qur'an. Yet as the formative ideal of the *malfuzat* clearly shows, the intertwined linguistic and epistemic problem of mediation was something rooted as much in the transmission of communication itself as in a specifically theologically-inspired conception of the Qur'an's uniqueness.

In returning to Aurangabad, one can get a glimpse not only of how followers created such *malfuzat*, but also of the ways in which other more straightforward hagiographies functioned in a strictly oral method of transmission. For, of all the many Sufis of Mughal Aurangabad, it was a spiritual descendent of the Nizam al-din Auliya of Delhi (for whose speeches the term *malfuzat* had been invented) who over time achieved fame as the greatest Muslim saint of the city. His name, like that of his predecessor, was Nizam al-din. Having studied first in Delhi, Nizam al-din migrated to Aurangabad and after teaching there for more than two decades died there in 1729. As with his forerunner, one of the later Nizam al-din's followers, Kāmgār Khān, recorded the words of his master in the form of a *malfuzat* (Kāmgār Khān, c. 1739). This lengthy document presents a picture of the religious life of Nizam al-din and his followers in the Sufi hospice that he ran in Aurangabad.

A striking feature of this religious life is the prominent role played by stories of the earlier saints of Nizam al-din's lineage of Sufis, the Chishtiyya. According to the descriptions in Nizam al-din of Aurangabad's *malfuzat*, this role of saintly traditions functioned in two separate ways in which oral *and* written transmission interacted and overlapped. Thus, a large proportion of the words attributed to Nizam al-din himself consisted of exemplary tales of the pious and charismatic deeds of earlier saints; in other words, his speeches formed an oral hagiology. Nevertheless, the students of Nizam al-din also heard the written stories of other saints contained in classic hagiographies of earlier generations. That is, the disciples listened to a written hagiology read out loud, thus bringing the words of the earlier saints to life once more through their verbal expression through the spoken word.

In a somewhat vertiginous prospect, the *malfuzat* of Nizam al-din provided a verbatim written rendition of the words of a saint describing the words (and deeds) of other saints. At the same time, it is an ear- and eyewitness written account of the deeds of the saint's followers. These deeds consisted in large part of reading from and listening to written accounts of the words and deeds of other earlier saints. The fact that the colophon of the document informs us that it was first written down a full decade after the death of Nizam al-din increases this entanglement of claims to oral authenticity and adds a more pragmatic reliance on the written word. Yet rather than disparaging the text as a 'fake' *malfuzat* (with its questionable assumption that there was also a tradition of 'true' *malfuzat*), let us consider the dynamic in which the oral and written word interacted – and claimed to interact – in the creation of a saintly hagiographical tradition. For what the text clearly shows is the important role of oral communication in the transmission of sacred traditions in premodern Islam. It demonstrates also the continuing claims to the greater spiritual authenticity of the spoken word within a highly literate environment, a society dependent upon and collectively valuing writing.

These hagiological formulations of Aurangabad's 18th-century Sufis and their followers show how the axiom of orality as authenticity, of the epistemological prestige of the unmediated spoken word, continued to operate in matters of religious writing. This situation prevailed at a time when written knowledge had long taken precedence over the spoken word as the proof of authenticity in other matters of social and cultural life, as well as in other matters of religious life. For by the time of Aurangabad's Nizam al-din, Indian Sufis had for several centuries proven themselves great seekers of the written certificates (*ijazat*) issued by famous mystics in order to testify to their students' claims to advanced spiritual achievement. This was a highly literate environment. What these hagiographers were doing in borrowing a rhetoric of orality was establishing the sacred credentials of the hagiographies that they were creating by moulding their forms after the uncontested scriptural models of the Qur'an and Hadith. The claim to orality was clearly understood as a means of proving the spiritual authenticity of a religious document, a claim revealing something of the processes of emulation and re-invention implicit within any extensive scriptural tradition.

There is a strong sense in which these movements of the sacred word from oral to written (and then at times back to oral, and again to written) were all movements of translation. For while it may seem churlish to question the aim of capturing the literal words of the saints by many of their followers, their desire to furnish the saints' words with a suitably edifying literary, indeed in some sense scriptural, format is questionable. The medieval Sufi followers of Nizam al-din Auliya of Delhi first extensively adopted the genre of the recorded conversation in a religious context in Muslim South Asia, but it had a much longer history in an Islamic courtly context. In both the Persian and Arabic literary traditions, scribes had for centuries sat recording the *bon mots* of sophisticated sultans and their witty and learned boon companions, the *nadims* of classical Arabic literature. The recorded conversation also has parallels in written material of courtly and administrative provenance in Ottoman Turkish (Veinstein, 1995). The *malfuzat* was, then, not only an attempt at imitating the forms of the Qur'an and the Hadith. It was also an attempt at borrowing a regal and courtly literary form to capture the words of the saints, a gesture pregnant with the suggestion of glorification for the status of the often materially impoverished Sufis. What the writers of the *malfuzat* collections were doing was perhaps not quite so candid and artless as it seemed, not so technologically impoverished by the absence of modern technologies capable of precise and unerring recordings. For, in recreating the spoken words of the saint in a written form, they were translating the spoken word into what sometimes became very polished literary documents belonging to a genre fit for a king. Naturally, after such a translation it became impossible to say how broken the original speeches of the master may have been and how impoverished or ill-attended the setting. Through this semantically rich change of context, through the movement from the oral to the written register, the *malfuzat* writers gave a whole new dimension of meaning to a saint's words. Indeed this very act of relocation, this translation of the saintly speech from an oral to a written context, created a new genre of Muslim religious literature.

This literary dimension to the creation of *malfuzat* collections raises some questions, especially in an environment such as that of 18th-century Aurangabad. Here the Sufis often spoke Persian, in which the *malfuzat* were written, only as a second language, and this was almost certainly the case with Nizam al-din. This raises other issues of translation implicit in the transfer of the spoken word to its written equivalent. The writer of the *malfuzat* of Nizam al-din of Aurangabad, for example, employs elegant and fully grammatical Persian prose. Perhaps this should be a matter of no surprise, since Islamic tradition regards learning itself, especially knowledge of the rich textual heritage of Sufism that in part comprised complex metaphysical poetry full of obscure terminology, as an important saintly attribute. Yet consider the dilemma of a recorder of saintly exhortations faced with a saint whose grasp of the finer points of rhetoric or grammar, of the eloquence that was next to godliness, was rudimentary in the extreme. Should recorders abide by the principles of the *malfuzat* as recorded speech, or quietly improve upon the words of the saint? Should they capture the literal, perhaps unintelligible speech of their rustic master or transform it into something more familiar to the educated reader and listener? Moreover, if they were oral documents, why were such *malfuzat* always written in Persian when it is well known that the Sufis frequently used various Indian vernaculars? In fact, occasional phrases and lines of poetry in early dialects of Hindi have been found in some *malfuzat*, but such rare exceptions further support the general point of widespread use of vernaculars. Indeed, it was precisely in Aurangabad, around such North Indian immigrants to the Deccan as Nizam al-din, that the different early versions of the Urdu vernacular language began to assume their final form. But, despite the undoubted presence of non-classical languages in Sufi circles, the *malfuzat* continued to favour the classical language. The exclusive use of written Persian in such multilingual environments is thus in itself suggestive of more literal acts of translation.

It is impossible to say to what extent Nizam al-din of Aurangabad's spoken Persian corresponded in grammatical, rhetorical or figurative terms to the speeches ascribed to him by the writer of his *malfuzat*, nor to what extent he used the vernacular subsequently known as Urdu in teaching his followers. But the point remains a valid one for, in the transition from the spoken to the written word, much semantic content is lost and much also gained, particularly with regard to pre-modern writing conventions. Intonation, stress, pauses and speed may all be lost, whereas the organisation of material, the setting of the scene, the tidying of word-endings and other points of grammar might be added. But in linguistic terms, spoken and written languages are always different. Whether or not Nizam al-din's Persian phraseology was as adequate as that *ascribed* to him, his speeches had therefore been irrevocably translated, irrevocably altered in their semantic content in their movement to written form.

The next step is to place these slightly arcane matters into a wider sociolinguistic context. In this respect scholars are helped by the presence of another saintly text from Aurangabad claiming to record the words (as well as in this case rather more of the deeds) of one of Nizam al-din's Sufi contemporaries. This document, known as the *Malfuzat-e-Naqshbandiyya*, was written in the mid-1730s, around eight years before the *malfuzat* of Nizam al-din (Mahmud Awrangabadi, 1358/1939–40). It recorded many of the sayings of the Central Asian Naqshbandi Sufi, Shah Musafir, who had died in Aurangabad in 1715. This text again combines oral and written forms of communication, for its author explains that the document forms the remembrances of the saint as recollected by his followers in the years after his death. In other words, it provides a written version of a tradition of oral hagiology concerning Shah Musafir that was already extant a few decades after his death. Once again, closeness to the source of events in an oral chain of transmission forms the rhetoric used to construct the text, a rhetoric again suggestive of the model of the chains of oral transmission presented in the written collections of the Prophetic Hadith.

The entire text is written in the colloquial dialect of Persian spoken by Aurangabad's immigrant Central Asian (Turani) community. So here, if perhaps unwittingly, it seems that the scribe captured more of the nature of the saint's *spoken* words and made a more linguistically accurate translation from the spoken word to the written. Yet this would appear to also reflect the fact that the writer of the text, Shah Mahmud, was himself also a member of this Central Asian community. Shared membership of the same sociolinguistic group could therefore pay a kind of linguistic dividend in the quest for the authentic transmission of a saint's words.

Interestingly the destinies of the two texts from Aurangabad were very different. A significant number of scribes later made copies of the *malfuzat* of Nizam al-din, at times embellishing with gold leaf in plenty. Its success may not have equalled that of the first example of the genre, *Fawa'id al-Fu'ad*, but it did achieve a considerable degree of fame and became known in the sophisticated circles surrounding the last Mughal emperor in Delhi, Bahadur Shah II (r.1837–58). Well known and read in different regions of South Asia over the course of the next century and a half, it became an accepted and treasured part of the sacred literature of the Muslim saints. By contrast, the *malfuzat* of Shah Musafir spent the next two centuries lying within the building in which it was first written, and probably never achieved a readership outside of the shrine of its eponymous saint until its eventual publication in Hyderabad during the 1940s. Thus it never established itself as part of the shared tradition of hagiography into which the *malfuzat* of Aurangabad's Nizam al-din had been accepted.

One factor among the many shaping the distinct fortunes of these two texts written at the same time in the same city may have been this very issue of their translation from spoken to written speech. For, in being quoted perhaps *too* vividly in his colloquial and informal style, Shah Musafir simply did not fit the established norms of saintly etiquette required by many of the readers and listeners of such hagiographies. Nizam al-din on the other hand, the apparent heir to the more learned legacy of his spiritual forefather in Delhi, suited this model rather better through the use of the more refined and literary Persian attributed to him in his *malfuzat*. Amid the broadly literate and often highly sophisticated circles within which such hagiographies were enjoyed, and moreover patronised, as expensive items requiring time-consuming re-copying, Shah Musafir perhaps seemed a little too rustic, a little too far detached from those esteemed saintly qualities of learning and good manners. For, in spite of the rhetoric of the spiritual authenticity of the spoken word, a too-authentic translation of the spoken word into its written form could be of great detriment to a text's chances of achieving recognition as an esteemed source of guidance.

Paradoxically, the most important element in the creation of this sacred literature was the apparent stamp of oral speech placed upon many of the forms and norms of written language (Toury, 1978). In this way, fine and polished speeches could attest to a saint's eloquence, and such eloquence was at times considered as a supernatural attribute in Islam. Once again the classic exemplar here was the Qur'an, with its unmatched metaphors and classical grandiloquence, though the notion of the supernatural wonder of eloquence also had a long history with regard to the secular poetry of the Muslim world. For the learned arbiters of hagiographical prose in Islam, the holy thus required not only a mode of translation of suitable finesse, but was in itself often conversely conceived as the very source of eloquence.

Oral speech possessed a powerful claim to the sacred in Islam, but in practice could often realise this claim only when it had undergone an adequate and appropriate translation into the stylistic norms of written language. While the *malfuzat* of such saints as Nizam al-din presented their own sacred status as due in large part to their orally conceived authenticity, in the highly literate societies in which they emerged the opposite was the case. For the spoken word required translation into written form in order to secure its claims to the sacred and so assume a place in the great tradition of celebrated hagiographies treasured by the great and good of Muslim South Asia over the centuries. Such inconsistencies, such semantic, rhetorical and contextual shifts, are an inevitable part of the *translatio*, the handing over through place and context, involved in any extended diachronic act of communication. Ultimately, however, as the dictum on the fragility of knowledge that was popular among many classical writers reminds us, it is only when written that the spoken word endures: *littera scripta manet*. *Malfuzat* texts are testament to the ideals and compromises that South Asian Sufis attempted to reconcile in confronting this most basic fact of premodern communication.

Chapter 13

From Scriptorium to Internet: The Implication of Audience on the Translation of the Psalms of the St Albans Psalter

SUE NIEBRZYDOWSKI

At some point in the 1120s or 30s, the magnificent and impressively illuminated Psalter, now preserved in St Godehard, Hildesheim, Germany, was produced at St Albans Abbey in the United Kingdom. The evidence of its contents and illustrations indicates that it was ultimately presented to the anchoress Christina of Markyate by Geoffrey Gorron, Abbot of St Albans (1119–46), and was probably made specifically for her (Thompson, 1982: 119–20; Geddes, 2003).

Beautifully illustrated throughout, the Albani manuscript contains computational tables for calculating the date of Easter, a calendar and the following texts: the French *Chanson of Alexis* and in Latin a Psalter, a selection of Canticles, the Lord's Prayer, the Nicene and Athanasian Creeds, a Litany and a further selection of prayers. The Psalms appear on pages 72–372, and comprise nearly three-quarters of the volume. The final page of the canticles became separated from the book and is now in the Schnütgen Museum, Köln, Germany. The version of the Psalms in Albani is one associated with Alcuin of York (ca. 735–804), the teacher, scholar and translator working at the court of Charlemagne who was invited in 782 to aid the Emperor in revising the text of Jerome's Vulgate (Reynolds & Wilson, 1984: 83). It has been known since the 9th century as the Gallican Psalter because of its popularity in France in Alcuin's time. Although Weber (1969: xxi) has described Alcuin's version as a text that 'left much to be desired' the Gallican Psalter was eventually to supersede the Roman version. The scribes at St Albans produced at least two Gallican Psalters in the 12th century: the one contained in Albani and the breviary now in London, British Library (Royal Collection 2 A X; mid-12th century).

The major study on the Psalter, by Pächt, Dodwell and Wormald (1960) produced a detailed description of its illustrations. The book contains reduced, black-and-white photographs of the flyleaf, the computational tables, every month of its calendar and all of the 40 full-page miniatures within the volume. Photographs of Psalm 1, the opening of Psalm 2 and all 211 historiated initials that appear throughout the Psalter section of Albani are included.

Since Pächt's monumental work, computer technology has advanced dramatically and made available new tools to aid research. From spring 2003, the entire codex has been available at www.abdn.ac.uk/stalban psalter as a result of a project run by Jane Geddes at the University of Aberdeen and funded by the Arts and Humanities Research Board. The detail in which these images can be viewed is far in advance of what was technically possible in Pächt's day. The clarity of the jpeg imaging is such that the pricking and ruling of the leaves is clearly visible, whilst in the illustrations the vibrancy of the colours is breathtaking.

Neither a complete translation nor a gloss of the Psalms was considered necessary for Albani's original audience, although Psalters containing vernacular glosses do survive from this, and indeed earlier, periods. The oldest Latin Psalter glossed in Anglo-Saxon is to be found in London, British Library Cotton Vespasian A. I, and contains an 8th-century text glossed ca. 875–900. It is a Roman Psalter from St Augustine's, Canterbury. The *Salisbury Psalter*, now Salisbury Cathedral MS 150, is a Gallican Psalter with an Anglo-Saxon gloss, dates from the later 10th century and has been edited by Sisam and Sisam (1959). The *Eadwine Psalter* dating from between 1155 and 1160 is an extraordinary feat of translation. As Gibson's edition (Gibson *et al.*, 1992) demonstrates, it provides the three different Latin texts of the Psalms current in England (the Gallican, the Roman and the Hebrew), a Latin gloss of the Gallican and two parallel translations of the Roman and Hebrew in Old English and Anglo-Norman respectively. Albani contains neither gloss nor vernacular translation of the Psalms, which might suggest that its audience was Latin literate or, as is indicated by the exemplary condition of its leaves and the brightness of the illustrations, more probably that the codex was intended primarily for private devotion rather than for public use.

In 1960 Pächt offered neither a transcription nor translation of the Psalter text. In setting the parameters for the Aberdeen project, however, it was felt that transcriptions and translations of the whole book into English were desirable to accompany commentaries, explanatory essays and a bibliography. The texts have also been translated into German at the request of the German proprietors. If there is room for discussion concerning precisely how much Latin was understood by the anchoress Christina, a native

Anglo-Saxon speaker whose social milieu was that of the Huntingdonshire elite (Talbot, 1959: 12), there is less debate over the decline, even since Pächt's study, of Latin literacy. In its 21st-century format, the contents of Albani will be available to Internet browsers worldwide since there is no restricted access to the website. It will be of interest to scholars, undergraduates and postgraduates working in a variety of fields, art historians, liturgists, those interested in Christina of Markyate and the casual browser. Those accessing the website will have differing degrees of Latin literacy, ranging from the expert to those with little or no proficiency. The Latin of the Psalms may not be accessible to all and so its translation into English and German was considered to be a necessary and timely addition.

The St Albans Psalter Project online is a medieval art history study. From its inception it was agreed that the translation's purpose was to provide access to the text of the Psalms in order to shed light on how it inspired its 12th-century illustrators. Indeed, the codex itself supports such a decision since palaeographic evidence demonstrates that this is precisely the *modus operandi* followed in Albani's construction. The text was written first and gaps left for the illustrators to fill in the initial as is revealed in an examination of decorated initial 'Q' of the opening of Psalm 41 (Figure 2). Here the

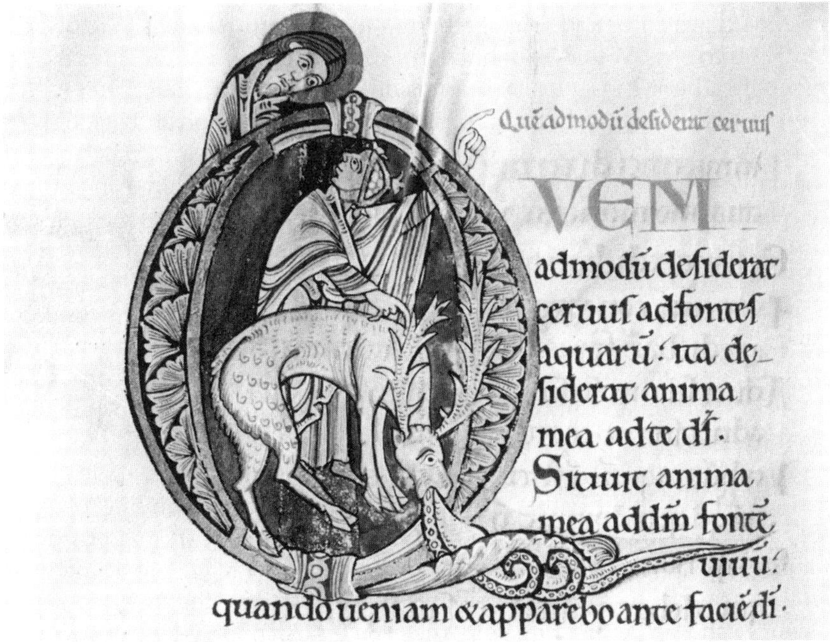

Figure 2 The opening of Psalm 41, St Albans Psalter

illustrator has drawn over the 'c' of *cervus* (stag) and the 'a' of *aquarum* (of water), partially obscuring the first letter of each word.

Several features mark the translational action of the Aberdeen project as *skopos* theory driven (Munday, 2001: 78–81): the definition of the translation's purpose (and by extension what its purpose is not), its audience (or target culture) and the recognition that these considerations affect the translation produced. The translation of the Psalms in Albani is therefore quite specific in its purpose. Neither an exercise in scriptural exegesis nor a critical edition of Albani's Gallican Psalter, the translation is designed to give art historians access to the 12th-century illustrators' working copy of the Psalms that was the source of inspiration for their art. The result is an English translation that retains the infelicities, errata and lacunae of the Albani Psalms and conveys their 12th century interpretation as preserved within the text/image correlation in this section of the codex.

The Gallican Psalter is different in many places from Jerome's Vulgate. This can be seen in their respective versions of Psalm 77:13 in which the Psalmist describes God's parting of the Red Sea to permit the Israelites escape from Egypt. The Vulgate offers *stare fecit aquas quasi acervum* ('he made the waters to stand as if in a vessel') whilst Gallican reads *statuit aquas quasi in utre* ('he contained the waters as in a womb'). Waters standing in a vessel suggests the Red Sea's gathering up and containment to allow the Israelites to pass. Waters contained in a womb conveys not only this movement of gathering up but also the tension of the retained water after which it breaks and floods forth, to the destruction of the Pharaoh and his soldiers as is described in verse 53. A proposal to give a Douai Rheims translation of the Vulgate and merely note the Gallican variants within Albani was rejected since this would not provide the imagery particular to the Gallican text from which the 12th-century illustrators worked and drew inspiration. The English translation provided is that of Albani's Gallican text, 'warts and all,' albeit crosschecked against two Douai Rheims editions (Kellam, 1609; Gildea & Surmont, 1914). The earlier of these translations is very close to the literal Latin, while the later is closer to the English word order. On occasions words and phrases have been inserted in an attempt to make clear the sense of particularly obscure passages.

The Albani translation retains the minimal punctuation of its 12th-century source. In the Latin text, capital letters signal the beginning of a line (but not the names of proper nouns if they do not fall in this position); pauses are shown by an inverted semicolon, and the end of a line by a *punctus* (point). In both transcription and translation, the inverted semicolon is shown as a colon and the *punctus* is followed by a slash in accordance with palaeographic convention. In contrast with modern translations of the Psalms, the Latin orthography of proper nouns is retained as in *israhel* (Psalm 13; modern English Israel), *libanus* (Psalm 28:5; modern English Lebanon), *cades* (Psalm 28:8, modern Kadesh). This decision was made in light of what appears to have been medieval practice: the glossator of the late 10th-century *Salisbury Psalter* either chooses not to or is unable to offer Anglo-Saxon spellings of proper names of people and places (Sisam & Sisam, 1959: 266). The proper nouns are rendered, therefore, as in the source text, that is without capitalisation and in forms unfamiliar today.

Neither the Psalms nor their verses are numbered in the source text. On completion of the translation, however, it was felt necessary to deviate from this feature of the medieval text. The Psalm number (following the Vulgate) was inserted against the *titulus* or running title of each Psalm. In many instances the *titulus*, comprising a selection of words or a complete verse of a Psalm, is the inspiration for the content of the historiated initial, but its location on the page does not always make clear to which Psalm it relates. This difficulty is illustrated on page 246 of the codex. The top of the page contains Psalm 86:5–7. Below this is the red *titulus* that reads *estimatus cum descendentibus in lacum* ('I am counted among those that descend into the deeps'). Nothing to do with Psalm 86, this is in fact Psalm 87:5. The numbering of the *tituli* was considered a necessary and legitimate addition to aid analysis of the connection between the Psalter text, the *titulus* and its interpretation in the accompanying historiated initial.

The translation reproduces Albani's errata and lacunae. Although generally the Albani scribe of the Psalms exhibits a high standard of precision in copying what is an accurate Gallican source text, some errata have occurred that are not explicable merely as Gallican variants. The scribe occasionally provides the wrong word as in Psalm 23:6 where the abbreviation for *deum* is to be found instead of *eum*. The phrase should read *haec est quarentium eum* ('this is the generation of them that seek him') but the scribe gives 'that seek god' in Albani. In Psalm 34:26 the scribe has written *maligna* instead of *magna* in the phrase *qui maligna loquuntur super me* here altering the sense quite significantly from what should be 'those who speak great things against me' to 'those who speak unkind things against me'. There are examples of omissions; sometimes deliberate, as in Psalm 135 where the scribe has consistently abbreviated the refrain, *quoniam in aeternum misericordia* ('because his mercy is forever') to *quoniam*; or sometimes due to forgetfulness, as in Psalm 51:1 where all that has been copied is the letter 'Q' of the phrase *Quid gloriaris* ('why do you glory in') leaving the text to read '*Q* [ ] *in malice*.' In replicating such errata, the translation offered is on occasion incomplete and lacking in coherence, but does reproduce what was before the illustrator.

The aim of producing a translation of the text that lay before the 12th-century illustrators affected the language register employed and the interpretation of certain key terms that appear frequently throughout the Psalms. 'Thee/thou' and the verb ending 'eth', common in many English translations of the Psalms were rejected as reflective of a usage common in translations produced between the Early Modern and early 20th century and not that of the 12th century. The Psalms frequently mention *gentes*, *sanctus* and *infernus*. Douai Rheims offers 'Gentiles' for *gentes*, 'saint' for *sanctus*, and 'Hell' for *infernus*. 'Hell' is retained in the Albani translation since the 'lower world' has been understood to mean Hell from at least the 11th century, but *sanctus* is translated as 'holy one' because in this period 'saint' is usually used as prefix to the proper name of a beatified person (Latham, 1983: 247). 'Gentiles' was rejected as too modern a usage and translated as 'nations' following the example of the Anglo-Saxon gloss of 'þeoda' ('people' or 'nation') for *gentes* in the Salisbury Psalter (Sisam & Sisam, 1959: 77).

In translating the text from which the illustrator worked, the translation needed to be sensitive not only to a general 12th-century interpretation of the source text but also to that particular to the individual artist. As suggested above, his interpretation is to be located preserved in the text/image correlation within the Psalms. For example, the illustrator has chosen to decorate the initial 'Q' of the opening of Psalm 41, with its first verse, *Quem admodum desiderat cervus*. Possible translations for *cervus* are 'deer' and 'hart', but in light of the size of the antlers placed on his creature, the illustrator clearly has a more robust animal in mind. In deference to his interpretation, 'stag' was chosen for the stately creature shown desiring and drinking the waters. Another such example of the illustrator's interpretation can be found within the initial 'L' of Psalm 150 (Figure 3). The accompanying *titulus* reads *laudate eum in sono tubae* ('praise him with the sound of the cornet'). Within the initial the illustrator shows David playing a harp and others playing a selection of instruments: one swinging a handbell, another man holding a bow aloft in one hand and a lozenge-shaped instrument in the other and a final man blowing a horn-shaped wind instrument. Dodwell interprets the latter two instruments as the rebec and cornet (Pächt, 1960: 237). The illustrator has been inspired not only by the *titulus* (Psalm 150:3) but also by the instruments that appear in verses 4 and 5: *Psalterio et cithara... chordis et organo... cymbalis*. The illustrator interprets the source text in terms of early medieval musical instruments, and this is accommodated by translating the Latin in terms common in this period; *tuba* as cornet, *psalterium* as psaltery, *cithara* as harp, *chordis* as rebec and *cymbalum* as bells (Sandon & Page, 1992: 248–9).

Yet another example of the illustrator's own translation of text into image is to be located in the relationship between the aforementioned *titulus* of Psalm 87, *estimatus cum descendentibus in lacum* and its illustration. *Lacum* literally means 'pit' but rather than showing some kind of chasm or abyss, the illustrator appears to have made the Psalmist's end far more

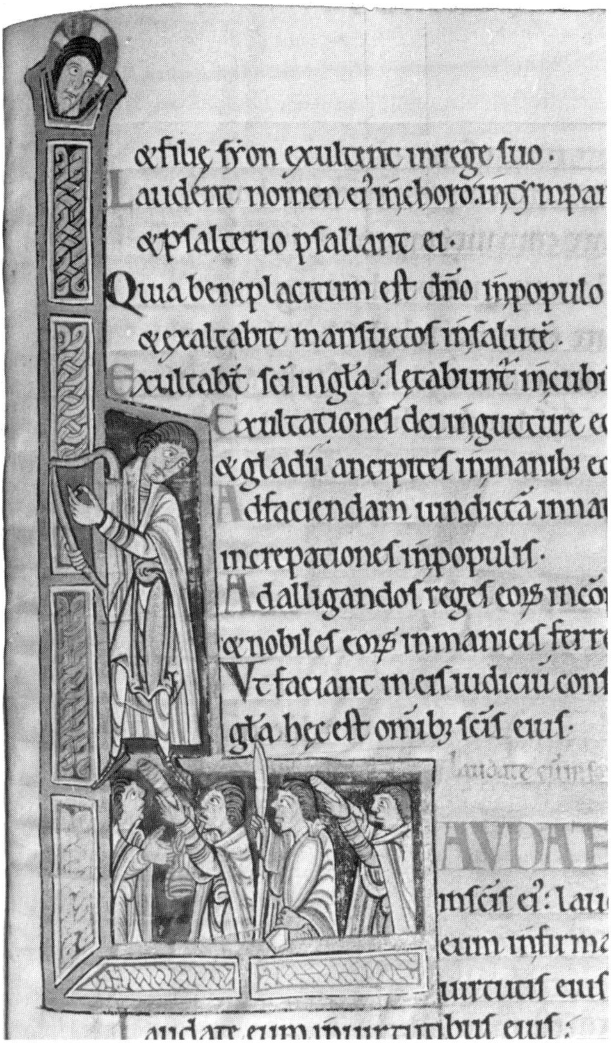

Figure 3 The opening of Psalm 15, St Albans Psalter

watery. Within the initial 'D' of *Domine*, the Psalmist is depicted with a triple leaf emanating from his mouth and drowning in waves full of fishes, whilst Christ listens to his plea in the company of two bystanders. According to Dodwell 'the waters encompassing the Psalmist and the fish in them symbolise the turmoils and tribulations of the world. But the triple leaf flowering from his mouth signifies salvation' (Pächt *et al.*, 1960: 237). It appears that the illustrator has conflated the *titulus* with verse 8 of the Psalm, *et omnes fluctus tuos induxisti super me* ('you have covered me in all your floods'), thus portraying the Psalmist sinking into watery depths.

The translation retains a menagerie of beasts often excised from modern Psalm translations because they are so clearly a part of the illustrator's world view. Psalms 21, 28, 77 and 91 sing of the *unicornus*, Psalm 90 sings of the *basilicus* and Psalms 73, 90 and 148 sing of the *draconus*. The RSV translation removes most if not all trace of these mythical beasts. Instead of unicorns 'wild oxen' is offered (Psalm 21:21, Psalm 29:6). The basilisk is reincarnated as an 'adder' in Psalm 91:13 and dragons are mentioned by name only in Psalm 74:14, disappearing beneath 'Leviathan' in 74:14, 'serpent' in 91:13 and 'sea-monster' in 148:7, terms that for a modern audience might equally evoke images of whales, snakes, and even giant squid. In a lively interpretation of Psalm 57:5, *Furor illis secundum similitudinem serpentis* ('their madness is like a serpent'), the illustrator portrays two men struggling with winged dragons in the initial 'S' that opens the Psalm. In an apparent zeal for dragons, he has chosen to portray the asp that stops the ears of the wicked (*sicut aspidis surdae et opturantis aures suas*), here with its tail, also as a dragon. In his interpretation of Psalm 73:14, *Tu confregisti capita draconis: dedisti eum escam populis aethiopum* ('You have broken the heads of the dragon: you have given him as meat to the people of aethiopia') Christ is portrayed pounding the head of a sea dragon with a mallet. In the 'Q' of Psalm 90 the lion, serpent and horned basilisk are shown being trampled underfoot in an interpretation of verse 13, *Super aspidem et basiliscum ambulabis* ('You shall walk upon the asp and the basilisk').

Texts that detail these monstrous beasts and their Christian significance are not unknown in monastic scriptoria in this period and earlier. *Beowulf* with its trolls and dragons had been copied in this context and Bestiaries cataloguing the properties of dragons, unicorns and basilisks, were produced from as early as the mid-11th century (Baxter, 1998: Chapter one). With the exception of the unicorn that was understood as an allegory of Christ who was slain for the sake of the sinful world (Barber & Riches, 1971: 146), these other creatures were believed to be representative of evil through their physical deformity. The basilisk, part bird, part snake, was thought to kill with a glance of its monstrous eyes (Williams, 1996: 151). The dragon's fiery mouth associates it with Hell, and with Satan in particular (Williams, 1996: 204–5). All are part of the illustrator's image-trove into which he clearly was not afraid to delve in order to illustrate his pictorial translation of the Psalm text.

To those unfamiliar with the Psalms or more used to major orthodox translations, the Albani translation is very compressed in places as it offers none of the help that modern orthography, versification and punctuation provide. Often this compression is a result of the complex literary nature of the source text to which, as Nord notes, *skopos* theory does not pay sufficient attention (quoted in Munday, 2001: 81). A balance had to be struck between satisfying the *skopos* and sensitivity to the stylistic complexity of the source text.

Striking this balance in the translation of metaphor proved challenging, as is exemplified through the struggles with kidneys, horns and fat. Having himself experienced difficulty in satisfactorily rendering 'loins' and 'horns' in his 1949 translation of the Old Testament, Knox advises, 'Words, like iridescent pearls, change colour from one civilisation to another, and from one generation to another' (quoted in Dayras, 1993: 48). Whilst Knox advocates that a literal translation be avoided, this is not the practice of the 12th-century illustrators of Albani who exhibit a penchant for literal interpretation. *Renes* ('kidneys)' appear with startling frequency, usually in a phrase that associates them with the heart, such as in Psalm 7:10 where God is described as *scrutans corda et renes deus* ('god the searcher of hearts and kidneys'). This is clearly metaphorical, conveying the idea that God inquires into all thought and feelings. The decision was taken to translate *renes,* as in many Vulgate translations, by 'reins', an obscure word but one that is found from the Middle Ages onwards and that means kidneys as they were understood as a seat of the emotions (Norri, 1998: Appendix 5). In choosing 'reins' it was felt that the translation replicated the literal meaning of the source text whilst also conveying some sense of its metaphorical significance as understood in the 12th century.

With 'horn' the source text only ever gives *cornus* (horn), but in the context of different Psalms horns convey a variety of meanings: offensive weapons, the altar horns to which fugitives seeking asylum could cling and figuratively in 'lifting one's horn' meaning to be arrogant (Hastings, 1963: 396). This variation is illustrated in Psalm 74:6 and 11, '*Nolite extollere in altum cornu vestrum: nolite loqui adversus deum iniquitatem... Et omnia cornua peccatorum confringam: et exaltabuntur cornua iusti* In each instance a literal translation of *cornus* is given, along with an expansion signalled by square brackets to convey the meaning suggested by the context in which the word appears. For example, in Psalm 74:6 and 11, the translation reads, 'Do not lift high your horn [of arrogance]: do not speak iniquity against god... And I will break the horn [trumpets] of sinners: and the horn [trumpets] of the just shall be exalted'. The same procedure was followed in translating *pinguis* or 'fat', the meaning of which ranges from the literal, fat and particularly the fat of beasts for sacrifice, to the figurative, fertility and abundance. Thus in Psalm 62:6, *Sicut adipe et pinguedine repleatur anima mea* is translated 'let my soul be filled as with marrow and fat'; in Psalm 16:10, *adipem suum concluserant* as 'they have shut up their fat [abundance]' and in Psalm 67: 16–17, *mons dei mons pinguis. Mons coagulatus mons pinguis* as 'the mountain of god is a fat [fertile] mountain. A peaked mountain a fat [fertile] mountain'.

The translation of metaphor posed the greatest challenge, owing to the complexity of providing both a literal and figurative meaning in the translation. Since the purpose of the translation is to provide access to the text that inspired its illustrators, sensitivity was required to the possibilities of meaning that a particular metaphor may have engendered in an historical moment at some significant distance from the present. The illustrators in this instance provide little help, as on no occasion are kidney, horns or fat illustrated within the historiated initials. No blanket solution was found; where a single word existed that signalled both the literal meaning and metaphorical possibilities, such as 'reins', this was used. Where no such word was available, a combination of a literal translation and an expansion as suggested by the context in which it appeared was used.

The road travelled by the St Albans Psalter from the scriptorium to the Internet has been long and includes for the Psalms, in this case, a journey also from sacred text to historical document. The ramifications of this double journey are not insignificant for the translator. That the final destination of the translation is an online publication can prove overwhelming for it inspires in the translator a fearful vision of a vast and virtual audience and the temptation to create the impossible: a translation that serves the needs of all who access the website. The experience of translating for the online Aberdeen St Albans Psalter Project is that a *skopos*-driven translation is an effective method of overcoming the sense of lack of focus that publication on the Internet can incite. Identifying the translation's purpose (and ruling out what it is not) limits the project to the realms of the possible. That the translation was intended neither as scriptural exegesis nor as a free-standing critical edition of the Albani Psalms permits the translator to side-step the problematic of translating what Jasper (1993: 1) terms the 'peculiar difficulty and illusiveness' of a holy text. On-going debate concerning the ethics and impossibilities of translating sacred texts to produce a 'faithful and correct' translation and the wrangles over the updating of language and interpretation for a modern audience are not key matters for concern in this instance. The spiritual edification of the audience, the purpose of so many translations of sacred texts, here gives way to the production of a historical document that is testimony to the interpretation of the Psalms by the early 12th-century illustrators working in the St Alban's scriptorium. The spiritual significance of the Psalms to the modern reader is not the business of The Aberdeen St Alban's Project translation and this makes the translator's job easier. Its primary concern and achievement is to provide art historians access to a particular 12th-century interpretation of the Psalms, frozen in time within the historiated initials of the Psalter. Indeed, in this instance, the dilution and/or distortion of the holy as revealed in the interaction between sacred text and image are wholly desired outcomes.

Chapter 14

Cultural Aspects in Qur'an Translation

HUSSEIN ABDUL-RAOF

Introduction

The Qur'an, for the Muslim, is the word of God; its theological message, therefore, transcends the boundaries of the Arab peninsula and carries a universal message to all mankind regardless of their language or race. Thus, the message of the Qur'an cannot be disseminated without translating its language and culture to other target languages and cultures. For Muslim scholars, the Qur'an is untranslatable since it is a linguistic miracle with transcendental meanings that cannot be captured fully by human faculty. This is why we find titles like *The Meaning of the Qur'an* or *The Message of the Qur'an*, but *The Qur'an* is not used as a title for the translated text. For Muslim scholars, the Latin Qur'an can never be a replacement of the Qur'an because translation, for them, is 'as a traducement, a betrayal, an inferior copy of a prioritised original' (Bassnett & Lefevere, 1998: 25). Their concern, however, is not unjustified.

The Qur'an was revealed in an Arab context of culture that is entirely alien to a target language (TL) audience outside the Arab peninsula. Thus, we encounter Qur'an-specific cultural expressions as well as Qur'an-specific linguistic patterns that cannot be domesticated by the TL linguistic norms; in this case, we are dealing with cases of both cultural and linguistic untranslatability (Catford, 1965: 93). The interrelation between culture and language makes me feel that the occurrence of special linguistic patterns and rhetorical tools in Qur'anic discourse is also culture-bound. The translator needs to be familiar with the micro- and macro-textual features of the source language (SL) which constitute major impediments during the process of translation. Bassnett (1991: 25) recognises this problem of translation, which for her involves far more than replacement of lexical and grammatical items between languages. To put the reader into the picture pertaining to the different cultural settings in both Arabic and English, a brief account of non-Qur'anic cultural expressions is provided below. This is an account of the prototypical sociolinguistic features of Qur'anic discourse. The examples explain how these salient features impose sociolinguistic constraints on the translation of the Qur'an. The aim of the following sections is to set the scene for the translator to appreciate how culture encroaches upon language and how it influences our conceptual and ethical judgements.

Pragmatic, Connotative and Emotive Meanings in Translation

The context of culture, the natural habitat for words, needs to be preserved in order to achieve a successful ethnographic translation. Peoples of different cultures perceive the world and its objects around them differently: words that are functionally identical have different mental and ethical associations. For the Inuit, the lexical item 'home' conjures up a hut or an igloo, for a Bedouin Arab, a tent, for an Arab in a rural area, a hut made of clay and straw, for a city-dwelling Arab and for a European, a house built of bricks. Similarly, the same word (home) triggers a rainbow of associations related to its internal components. For a European (but not for an Inuit or an Arab), the fire, hearth, or heating is one of the semantic field's elements. The word 'bread' also generates various different associations pertaining to shape, taste and method of baking. With the world becoming a small village, semantic associations may change, too. For a European brushing the teeth is associated with the word 'toothbrush'. In the early years of the 20th century, brushing the teeth for an Arab was associated with مسواك *miswaak* (a stick taken from the roots of a special tree), which also has a religious connotation since it is an Islamic tradition to brush the teeth with the *miswaak* during the ablution.

And for an Arab visitor to the United Kingdom, there is still confusion about what tea is. When Arabs asks for tea in a café or from a host family, they expect a black (specially brewed) tea with sugar; to their dismay, they are served with white tea mixed with milk and made from a tea bag and often without sugar. An Arab student once commented that European tea was tasteless and looked like sewage water and as for the bread it was like a sponge. No doubt European visitors to Arab countries are similarly perplexed by differences in what they expect to be familiar foodstuffs.

To take another example, the word 'farm' in British culture refers to a vast piece of land with grass, crops and livestock; this word can at a surface level be easily translated into Arabic as مزرعة *mazra'ah*. However, in Arabic culture the word *mazra'ah* has the denotative meaning of a piece of land with fruit trees, mostly dominated by date palms and livestock.

While some words are taboo or considered improper in one culture, they have neutral connotative meanings in another. In other words, the denotative meaning of some words is identical in the two cultures, but their connotative meanings are completely distinct. Connotative meanings, in House's view (1973: 166), are too elusive to be rendered correctly into translation because of their inherently indefinable nature. Larson (1984: 132) also warns us of the problem of the SL connotative meaning. According to the Arabic culture, words such as كلب *kelb* (dog), حمار himaar (donkey), بومة *boomah* (owl), حذاء *hithaa'* (shoe) have negative significations and designate a great insult: to dub an Arab a dog, donkey, owl, or shoe is a major humiliation. These same words, however, convey neutral or even positive connotative associations in English: the dog is man's best friend (a symbol of loyalty), the Elisabeth Svendsen Trust for Children and Donkeys (EST) has centres based in Leeds, Birmingham and Sidmouth encouraging people to adopt a donkey (an animal with a direct calming influence, according to the EST's brochure), the owl is the logo of the Leeds Metropolitan University and Leeds City Council (a symbol of wisdom), and the shoe is a neutral word with no negative overtone. In Arabic, however, the dog is viewed as a dirty animal. Under Islamic law, you cannot perform your prayers if a dog touches your clothes because they are viewed as unclean; the word *kelb* also appears in the Arabic vulgar expression إبن الكلب *ibn al-kelb* (son of a dog) whose cultural equivalent in English is 'son of a bitch'. Reference to both the donkey and the dog is made in the Qur'an, as in Q62:5 and Q7:176, but their connotative meaning is different from what is explained above. The owl in Arabic has the connotative meaning of stupidity and bad omen, the donkey reflects the connotative meaning of utter stupidity, and the shoes are considered as dirty objects and refer to disrespect. The shoe connotative meaning is also used in the Iraqi Arabic vulgar idiomatic expression إبن القندرة *ibn al-qundarah* (son of a shoe) which is the cultural equivalent in English to 'son of a bitch'. Therefore, sitting on a chair with one of your legs on top of the thigh of the other leg is regarded in Arabic culture as an insult, as in this position your shoe or the sole of your foot is facing someone else. This same act, however, is regarded in the British or European culture as an acceptable practice (Abdul-Raof, 2001b). It is important for the translator and the interpreter to be aware of the connotative associations underpinning the message of these expressions that are denotatively similar but are connotatively distinct from one culture to another.

Emotive words are employed to achieve ideological or moral hegemony. Emotive expressions such as شرف *sharaf* have Arabic culture-bound connotations that are lacking in the TL. Lexically, it can be rendered as honour, but that is not what the Arabic word conjures up in the mind of the

Arab speaker/writer. In English, the words honour and honourable are rather old fashioned, but still valid. In Arabic, however, the word *sharaf* echoes stronger overtones and reflects a rainbow of highly emotive componential features, the most important of which is sexual honour. Thus, an Arab lady with no *sharaf* is dubbed as غير شريفة *ghayr shareefah* (a lady with no sexual honour), has no chance of getting married, and may be a social outcast. Owing to its highly emotive moral influence, the word *sharaf* is frequently used in Arabic political discourse such as political speeches and editorials. Thus, the expression has acquired a new ideological emotive meaning, as in شرف الأمة *sharaf al-ummah* (the honour of the nation) echoing both political and ethical meanings represented by the periphrastic translation (the nation that should not be allowed to be raped by foreign powers). There is, therefore, a conceptual and intertextual relation between the word *sharaf* and the other culture-bound word عذراء *athraa* (virgin). The major mental image which the word عروس *aroos* (bride) conjures up for an Arab in the context of the wedding night ليلة العرس *laylat al-'urs* or the wedding party (which are also culturally different) is that the *aroos* is both *shareefah* and *athraa* (honourable and virgin) (Abdul-Raof, 2001b).

The translation or interpreting strategy one needs to adopt when encountering cultural words like these is to abandon the literal rendering and adopt cultural transposition which allows one to transfer the underlying connotative, cultural or emotive associations of the SL word to the TL culture. In other words, only the connotative meaning needs to be transplanted culturally into the TL without infringing the latter's linguistic norms. Thus, when someone from a Western culture dubs an Arab as an owl, the message should be culturally rendered as 'wise man' and not verbatim.

So-called 'false friends' (Newmark, 1988: 72) are another serious problem that may arise from the literal rendering of a culturally-nuanced word. For example a 'casino' in English echoes negative connotative associations; the transliteration of this word into Arabic as كازينو is an example of false friends; the word *casino* in Arabic is used for and is the cultural equivalent of a cafe, which in Standard Arabic is called مقهى. *maqhaa*.

Qur'anic Discourse

I shall now turn to examples showing how Arabic and English are both linguistically and culturally incongruous languages from the perspective of Qur'anic discourse. Some of the Qur'an-specific cultural and linguistic features are translation-resistant and therefore constitute interesting translation problems idiosyncratic to the Qur'an. These include the following cases.

Theological expressions

Culture exercises tremendous impact on the semantic composition of a given word with conceptual and theological overtones; theological expressions have religious and cultural sensitivities. The SL word is always processed and translated according to our own cultural, socio-political, and ethical perception. Conceptual Qur'anic expressions, for instance, are unique cases that have a specific Islamic culture scenario. Words such as الله *Allah* (God), جنة *jannh* (paradise), نار *naar* (hell-fire) relay distinct messages to different non-Muslim TL readers whose faith provides different theological meanings to these same words. Although there is no translational problem involved in rendering their surface denotative meanings into English, these words and their translations relay different mental images and expectations to both the SL and TL readers; the word الله *Allah*, for instance, has a number of componential features idiosyncratic to Islam. It designates above all the oneness of God, (i.e. monotheism) who has 99 attributes mentioned in the Qur'an, the Lord with whom no one else can be associated, and the Creator of every thing including the Prophets. To highlight the divinity and the notion of oneness of God, the Qur'an employs the word الله unique in its grammatical form: it cannot take the plural form, i.e. the notion of oneness is backed up by the very morphological form of the word itself. This is not the case with the TL. In English, the Arabic word الله is translated as God which (with lower case letters) can be made plural; one can say 'gods' in the TL. Secondly, and most importantly, the Biblical concept of God as Father, Son and Holy Spirit reflects Christianity's semantic componential features that fail to accommodate the Qur'anic notion of absolute monotheism. Although a Christian would argue that the notion of the Trinity refers to three aspects or personae of God and most certainly not three gods; for a Muslim, the Biblical God is associated with polytheism. Thus, while both the Qur'an and the Bible use the same expression God, their adherents have distinct theological perceptions of the same word.

Ritual expressions

Religious vocabulary like 'altar' and 'candle' have no equivalent value in the mosque; however, expressions like بُخور *bukhoor* (incense) and أضحية *udhhiyah* (sacrifice) are shared rituals with similar connotations in both Christianity and Islam. Another shared word with a different context in Arabic is حج *haj* (pilgrimage). Although the Arabic and English words both refer to a religious ritual, the SL and TL words convey different concepts of ritual and also refer to different places where these different rituals are performed; thus, the two expressions are referentially and pragmatically distinct in the two cultures. For a Muslim, performing the ritual of pilgrimage is one of the five pillars of Islam and is obligatory to every physically and financially able individual Muslim. It should be done at least once in a lifetime; it must be performed during the first ten days of a month called thu al-Hijjah ('the month of pilgrimage'); it involves putting on a simple garment of unsewn cloth in two pieces when the pilgrim is still some distance from Mecca. Wearing the pilgrim garb is symbolic of renouncing the vanities of the world. After this and until the end of the pilgrimage, the pilgrims must not wear other clothes or ornaments, anoint hair, use perfumes, hunt or have sexual intercourse. The completion of the pilgrimage is symbolised by the shaving of the head for men and the cutting off of a few locks of the hair of the head for women, the putting off of the pilgrim garb and the resumption of the ordinary dress. Pilgrimage in Islam also involves a number of ritual ceremonies undertaken in Mecca including a sevenfold circumambulation of the *Ka'bah,* a cube-shaped building within the precincts of the Great Mosque of Mecca. It is an ancient sanctuary whose presence is designed to raise man's heart and worship to God. On the ninth day of the month of the al-Hijjah occurs the standing in the Plain of Arafah outside Mecca; without this, the pilgrimage is considered invalid. Prayers are said at Arafah, and pilgrims listen to a sermon. On the tenth day of the same month, pilgrims sacrifice an animal at Mina, imitating the projected sacrifice by Abraham of his son Ishmael, and this day constitutes one of the great feast days of the Muslim calendar (Ali, 1983: 77; Netton, 1997: 92, 139). For a Christian, the rite of pilgrimage is entirely different in both place and ritual ceremonies performed.

Abstract moral concepts

Abstract concepts such as تقوى *taqwaa* (piety, righteousness) exist within the ethical and spiritual code of various faiths; their semantic associations and componential features vary from one faith to another as the prerequisites for piety are specified by the scripture of a given religion. Abstract concepts are faith-specific and, therefore, culture-bound. Just as the notion of righteousness (*dikaios*) caused problems for Bible translators, so the Qur'anic concept of *taqwa* uncovers the enormous difficulty in translating the Qur'an. There seems to be no unanimous agreement amongst the various Qur'an translators as to how to render this abstract notion or its derivative plural form متقون *muttaqoon* (pious, righteous people). Pickthall's (1969: 24) 'those who ward off evil', Asad's (1980: 3) 'God-conscious', and

Ali's (1983: 17) 'those who fear God' are all under-translations since they overlook many of the other significant Islamic characteristics that underpin the notion of *taqwa.* al-Hilali and Khan (1983: 3), however, opt for the transliteration of *taqwa* and then follow it up by a within-the-text note detailing the exegesis of this notion: the pious and righteous persons are those who fear Allah greatly and abstain from all kinds of sins and evil deeds that He has forbidden, who love Allah greatly and perform all kinds of good deeds that He has ordained.

Similarly, the abstract concept of عذاب *'athaab* (wrath of God, punishment) also has different cultural denotative significations; there is a recurrent reference to this notion in the Qur'an, as in:

> ما يفعل اللهُ بعذابكم إنْ شكرتم وآمنتم وكان اللهُ شاكراً عليماً
> What can God gain by your punishment, if you are grateful and you believe? Nay, it is God that recogniseth all good and knoweth all things. (Q4:147) (Ali, 1983: 226)

To highlight the underlying Qur'anic message that there is no pleasure nor advantage to God in punishing His own creatures over whom He watches with loving care (al-Razi, 1990: 11:71), the Qur'an translation needs to achieve cultural equivalence that addresses the TL cultural perceptions of punishment. For example, in the context of a New Guinea audience the TT idiom 'God does not hang up jaw bones' achieves a captivating effect for the above Qur'anic statement. This is what is referred to as dynamic equivalence (Nida, 1964) or as cultural transposition (Dickens *et al.*, 2002).

Delexicalised expressions

Delexicalized expressions are SL black holes that refer to lexical items that are lacking in the TL, in other words lexical voids. Such expressions are usually found in Qur'an translations either transliterated, domesticated, periphrastically translated or transliterated and followed up by an exegetical within-the-text note, or else transliterated and then given a detailed exegetical footnote.

A unique example is the word عمرة *'umrah* which occurs twice in the Qur'an (Q2:158, 196):

> وأتموا الحجَّ والعُمرةَ لله And complete the Hajj or *'umrah* in the service of God. (Q2:196) (Ali, 1983: 77)

The Qur'anic expression *'umrah* means a minor pilgrimage to Mecca that does not count towards the fulfilment of the religious duty and may be made at any time and requires less ceremonial (Netton, 1997: 92).

Although the Islamic cultural expression وضوء *wuthoo'* poses no problem in rendering it into the TL as 'ablution', the Qur'anic expression تيمم *taymmum* represents an example of cultural untranslatability as it is absent from both the lexicon and the culture of the TL. This Qur'anic expression is an interesting case of lexical compression that needs to be paraphrased in the TL to provide an informative meaning; an exegetical translation is, thus, provided: to take resort to pure dust, passing therewith lightly over your face and your hands, as in:

فتيمّموا صعيداً طيّباً
Then, take resort to pure dust, passing therewith lightly over your face and your hands. (Q4:43) (Asad, 1980: 112)

In Islamic culture, ablution is a minor ritual washing of parts of the body before prayer; *tayammum*, however, may be used if water is scarce or unavailable (Netton, 1997: 259); it is also a symbolic ablution that can also be used because of illness. Transliterated or paraphrased, the Qur'anic expression *tayammum* remains culturally obscure and unfamiliar to the TL audience. Similarly, the word عقيقة *'aqeeqah* is also a lexical void that is delexicalised in the TL; it has an Islamic connotative meaning that can be arrived at through a periphrastic translation. The word refers to a party for relatives and friends that is held by the parents of a newly born baby shortly after the baby's birth, and in which a lamb is slaughtered and served with rice.

Material culture

Articles of clothing provide examples of material features that differ from one culture to another and may lead to translation difficulties (Catford, 1965: 100), as in:

وليضربنَ بخُمُرهنَّ على جيُوبهن
Let them [the believing women] draw their head-coverings over their bosoms. (Q24:31) (Asad,1980: 538)

The word خُمُر *khumur* (head-coverings), whose singular is خمار *khimaar* is not found in the TL culture; thus, it represents an interesting example of the limits of cultural translatability in Qur'anic discourse. The Qur'anic statement Q24:31 is an injunction (i.e. an Islamic legal ruling) regarding the head-covering that a Muslim woman is instructed to wear in such a way that it should cover her bosoms. Pickthall (1969: 360), Ali (1983: 905) and al-Hilali and Khan (1983: 471) opt for 'veil' as a means of domestication, but the TL word neither provides comprehensive details nor does it give the TL reader a mental image similar to that conjured up by the SL word. The veil

(الحجاب) in Muslim culture is meant to cover up or hide the lady's hair as well as provide decent covering.

In order to highlight the horror of the day of judgement and how worldly possessions are of no value to the individual, the Qur'an refers in Q81:4 to an expensive Arab property, namely the heavily pregnant she-camel which was most valued and cared for by her owner.

> وإذا العشارُ عُطِّلت
> When the she-camels, ten months with young, are left untended. (Q81:4) (Ali, 1983: 1693)

We are told that on the day of reckoning, even this valuable property, the camel about to give birth, will be left untended. The expression العشار *al-'ishaar* (pregnant she-camels) provides luxuriant imagery in the Qur'an, but the TL culture does not put the same value on the animal and so the impact is lost.

Linguistic voids

Cross-linguistic differences, for Jacobson (1959), centre on obligatory grammatical and lexical forms. I cite one case only of the many Qur'an-specific linguistic patterns that have cultural bearing on the understanding of the TL message. Qur'anic discourse provides numerous examples of linguistic untranslatability because of the different linguistic mechanisms of the SL and TL; in other words, the SL linguistic requirements cannot be accommodated by the TL linguistic norms. Therefore, the intentionality of the SL message is not relayed to the TL reader.

The nominative vs. the accusative case provides an interesting example of a grammatico-cultural translation problem. Arabic is an inflectional language; it has three major inflectional cases, namely, the nominative, accusative, and genitive, one of which accompanies the noun. Culturally, the nominative case enjoys an elevated grammatical status over the other two cases; the nominative case in Arabic is called المرفوع al-marfoo' meaning 'the elevated'; thus, usually, the subject is in the nominative case since it performs the action denoted by the verb. Let us consider the following Qur'anic example:

> إذ دخلوا عليه فقالوا سلاماً قالَ سلامٌ قومٌ منكَرُون
> Behold, they entered his [Abraham's] presence, and said: 'Peace!' He said: 'Peace!' [And thought] 'These seem unusual people.' (Q51:25) (Ali, 1983: 1424)

Here we have two nouns سلاماً *slaaman* (peace), which is in the accusative case, and سلامٌ *slaamun* (peace) which is in the nominative case. It is part of the Arabic culture to greet people with the expression 'peace be upon you' and the other person's reply is 'and peace be upon you, too'. The TL audience has no cultural familiarity with this Arabic expression. The TL word 'peace' echoes cultural foreignness owing to the literal rendering; therefore, I suggest that in cases like this, a cultural transposition (i.e. domestication) approach should be adopted (Dickens *et al.*, 2002: 29). The best TL cultural equivalent for the Arabic expression *salaam* would be 'hello, hey (hi)'. But this proposed solution does not respect the status of the Qur'anic text and violates the register of the SL. The failure of the translation does not lie in the cultural aspect per se; the most important component of the message lies in the grammatical nominative case that is cliticised onto the second noun سلامٌ *salaamun* but which cannot be accommodated by the TL expression (peace). The Qur'an instructs its adherents to be courteous and exchange greetings: when people are greeted, they should answer the greeting with a better and warmer greeting expression or at least should exchange the same greeting expression with the other person. This cordiality in manners is highlighted by Q4:86:

وإذا حُيّيتُم بتحيةٍ فحيُّوا بأحسنِ منها أو ردُّوها

When a (courteous) greeting is offered you, meet it with a greeting still more courteous, or (at least) of equal courtesy. (Q4:86) (Ali, 1983: 206)

Thus, intertextuality plays a significant role here in the interpretation of this linguistic and cultural problem in Qur'anic discourse. Abraham was unfailingly courteous; he met the greeting expression *salaaman* with the same greeting expression *salaamun*; his greeting, however, is more courteous and warmer. This is achieved by the employment of the nominative case (-un) attached to the word *salaam*. Q4:86 is, therefore, intertextually related to Q51:25. Prophetic tradition also reiterates the same matter. It is now clear why we cannot accept the TL first expression (peace) as the linguistic equivalent of the second TL expression (peace). The two SL expressions are different and reflect cultural overtones pertinent to the Muslim culture. (For more details on the linguistic features of Qur'anic discourse, see Abdul-Raof, 2001a.) To achieve the underlying message of high respect of the word 'peace' in the nominative case, one can resort to paraphrase such as 'peace be with you'.

Conclusion

The Arabic and Qur'anic examples provided in this chapter are a testimony to the fact that 'sameness cannot exist between two languages' (Bassnett, 1991: 30). Larson (1984: 180) also admits that terms dealing with the religious aspects of a culture are usually the most difficult, both in analysis of the source vocabulary and in finding the best receptor language equivalents. This is because the TL reader is not conscious of the various aspects of meaning involved. The religious expressions of divinity and pilgrimage, and expressions of moral concepts such as piety, and of the hereafter, among other things, conjure up distinct mental images and meanings in the minds of the SL and TL speakers. Language, in the view of Lefevere (Bassnet & Lefevere, 1990: 26), is not the problem. Ideology and poetics are, as are cultural elements that are not immediately clear, or seen as completely 'misplaced' in what would be the target culture version of the text to be translated. The translator, therefore, needs to be both bilingual and bicultural. To narrow the gap of cultural unfamiliarity, I suggest domestication of the SL expression and exegetical footnotes in order to bring the message home to the TL audience, increase the level of source text informativity, and maintain SL intentionality. For Nida (1995: 130), 'notes about cultural differences are indispensable in many instances'. I believe that such illuminating notes are more effective in preserving the authenticity of the source text than the creative adjustments that Nida calls for in order to accommodate the sociolinguistic sensitivities of the TL audience. The literal rendering of cultural lexical items leads to cultural interference that distorts the message underpinning the SL text, thus impairing the volume of both informativity and intentionality of the SL text producer. One may wonder whether the importation of SL cultural expressions through either transliteration or literal rendering would enrich the TL. In both cases, the translation provides nothing more than a fractured end product. The Qur'anic text is rich with liturgical, emotive and cultural key expressions that are lacking in the TL. It is not easy to find parallel English expressions because the two languages are diverse linguistically and culturally. Audience expectations (Nida, 1995: 134) cannot be met without some kind of distortion. The Qur'an's distinctive sociolinguistic constraints are, therefore, serious impediments to comprehension. The translator's creativity is tied to the SL linguistic and cultural norms. Paraphrase, through domestication, transposition or dynamic equivalence, may be the solution, but it robs the Qur'anic text of its distinctive religious character.

*

Chapter 15

When East meets West via Translation: The Language of Soka Gakkai in Italy

MANUELA FOIERA

The cartoon in Figure 4 is taken from *Il Nuovo Rinascimento*, the official magazine of the Italian chapter of the Soka Gakkai International (SGI), which is the Japanese Buddhist organisation founded upon the teachings of Nichiren Daishonin. The cartoon depicts the setting of a typical Buddhist meeting, or *zadankai*, a Japanese word that roughly means 'to sit together, pray and have a peaceful discussion'. It is also the very same word that Italian practitioners of the Soka Gakkai's form of Buddhism use to describe their meetings in Italy. The apparent impossibility of finding an Italian equivalent of this (and many other foreign words related to the practice of SGI Buddhism) is symptomatic of the difficulties one encounters in Italy when examining the language and practices of a 'foreign' religion. The 'Carmen la Candela' cartoon strip was published monthly in *Il Nuovo Rinascimento* from 1999 to 2001. The magazine's boards of editors, however, decided not to publish this particular cartoon, for fear it would offend the sensibilities of Catholic readers.

The cartoon features Carmen the Candle and Vincense the Incense Stick, two ever-present objects found on every Buddhist's altar, and they are commenting upon the behaviour of Italian practitioners at a *zadankai*. An invisible voice-over begins by urging the attendees to stop employing Japanese religious terminology. 'Italian', it says, 'is a beautiful language, rich in history and tradition. I therefore suggest that we return to our cultural roots and start speaking Italian!'

The assembled practitioners agree and voice their approval by means of the following bursts of enthusiasm:

- 'Holy Virgin, that's a very good idea!'
- 'It's a miracle!'
- 'Ohhh! Thank Heavens!'

- 'Good God, I can't believe my ears!'
- 'Ah, the ways of the Lord ...'
- 'By all the Saints in Heaven!'
- 'Thank God! It's about time!'
- 'Jesus, Joseph and Mary, how true!'

The voice-over then reacts to this outpouring of support: 'Hmmm, maybe we should wait for better times'. To which Vincense the Incense Stick comments: 'Yeah, and God help us!'

Figure 4 'Carmen la Candela' strip cartoon

Reproduced with the author's permission. Copyright 2000 Adriano Giannini. [The layout of this cartoon strip has been changed for this publication.]

Over the past 30 years, Italians have increasingly found themselves interested in a broad range of Oriental religions. This phenomenon is particularly worthy of study in as much as it has taken place in what is generally considered to be the Roman Catholic country par excellence. Indeed, as Italian religious practices have deviated from the standard and homogeneous traits long associated with the official model proffered over the centuries by the Catholic Church, the issue has been widely analysed from sociological as well as from theological points of view (Burglassi, 1968, 1980; Calvaruso & Abbruzzese, 1985; Cipriani, 1989; Marchisio & Pisati, 1999). In this chapter, I propose to investigate this phenomenon with respect to what it tells us about language and translation. Put somewhat differently, I argue that once Roman Catholicism's relations with other foreign religions are examined from a Translation Studies perspective, it then becomes possible to understand more fully the nucleus of what Italians call their 'religious sense'.

In this respect, it is particularly important to emphasise the resistance that the Italian word *religione* offers when applied to a non-Christian belief system. Jacques Derrida suggests two possible etymological derivations of the Latin word *religio*: the first stems from the Ciceronian tradition, *relegere* from *legere* (to harvest, gather), while the other, following Lactantius and Tertullian, is based upon *religare* (to tie, bind) (Derrida & Vattimo, 1995). Those interpretations overlap to build a strong link between men and a supreme deity. This is evident in the Italian definition of the word *religione*: *'Il rapporto, variamente identificabile in sentimenti e manifestazioni di omaggio, venerazione e adorazione, che lega l'uomo a quanto egli ritiene sacro o divino'* (Devoto-Oli, 2002), in which the acts of 'homage, reverence, adoration' are of particular relevance.

The semantic reverberation of this one word, considered both from its etymological origins and from its long-standing use as a synonym for Roman Catholic dogma and for the Roman Catholic Church itself, renders it largely impermeable to any attempt to accommodate references to alien practices and rituals within its meanings.

Two very distinct Buddhist presences flourish on Italian soil today. First, there is the Unione Buddisti Italiani (UBI) an association that represents about 35 groups from different traditions, such as Indian, Tibetan and Zen Buddhism. In the year 2000, the UBI numbered 50,000 members. Second, there is the Italian Soka Gakkai, a Japanese-inspired form of Buddhism founded upon the writings of Nichiren Daishonin, which includes by itself some 30,000 members (*La Repubblica*, 2000).

The teachings of the Soka Gakkai are a blend of several elements. The basic source is the work of Nichiren Daishonin (1222–1282), a Japanese monk who, having studied the teachings of Shakiamuni Buddha via translation from Chinese, came to believe that the Lotus Sutra was the highest, and the only valid, scripture. That is, he associated the creed that the Buddha-nature is immanent in every aspect of reality and intrinsic to every living creature with the Lotus Sutra. Faith in this Sutra, he wrote, is the only effective means of salvation in an age (the Latter Day of the Law, or *Mappo*), in which the authentic teachings of the Buddha have fallen into general decay (Soka Gakkai Translation Committee, 1999).

Nichiren introduced several novel elements into Buddhism. The first is the *Gohonzon*, or object of worship, a *mandala* of symbolic representation of the universal, eternal Buddha, inscribed by Nichiren himself. The second is the *daimoku*, the invocation of *Nam-myoho-renge-kyo*. Nichiren taught that one who takes faith in and chants *Nam-myoho-renge-kyo* to the *Gohonzon* will definitely attain the same life condition of Buddhahood as he himself possessed. But these doctrinal aspects could not alone account for the enormous popularity that this religion achieved worldwide following the conclusion of the Second World War. Until the beginning of the last century, in fact, the doctrine was confined to Japan and restricted to the various temples established by a number of sects that grew after the death of Nichiren. For a strong organisation to be built, it was necessary to wait until a series of three outstanding figures assumed a strong leadership role both in spreading Nichiren's teachings and in gathering around them adepts from all social strata. The turning point occurred in 1930, when the scholar and teacher Tsunesaburo Machiguchi founded the Soka Gyoiku Gakkai (Value-Creation Academic Society).

Dissatisfied with the prevalent educational approaches, Makiguchi elaborated a pedagogical system based on the teachings of Nichiren Daishonin. The religious core of Gakkai ideology was reinterpreted and adapted for the masses by its second president, Josei Toda, who was deeply determined to spread the organisation throughout Japanese society. The third and current president, Daisaku Ikeda (born in 1928) further developed the doctrine into a planetary movement for peace and education. Charismatic and calmly authoritative, Ikeda expanded the organisation outside Japan. He succeeded in the task of simplifying the doctrine, thereby rendering it more palatable and appealing to the Western world. During this process of cultural translation, the international organisation became more and more centred on the cult of Ikeda's personality: Ikeda's writings on guidance are considered equal to the teachings of Nichiren himself and are similarly viewed as official repositories of truth. In the early 1990s, the Gakkai was solidly established in more than 150 nations, ready to sever the knot with the Head Temple and its clergy and to become an entirely lay organisation. When the organisation arrived in Italy, its peculiar features were perfectly suited to elicit curiosity and interest. Its organisation and appearance as a 'religion without priests and clergy' proved to be an irresistible oxymoron, and its protean adaptability fascinated people who were in search of new religious horizons as well as those who were interested in a secular form of spirituality.

Nichiren Daishonin's Buddhism first entered Italy in the early 1970s. At that time, Mitsuhiro Kaneda and his young wife Kimiko left Japan to settle in Rome. Neither of them spoke Italian. With barely any means, they decided to immigrate to Europe for religious reasons, namely, the desire to propagate Buddhism. During the same period, other Japanese followers of the SGI arrived in various European cities to devote themselves to the same task. As we shall see, each nation has had a profoundly linguistic response to the arrival of a hitherto foreign religion. And yet the data suggest that cultures with a religious background that is not Roman Catholic have been able to accommodate via translation a greater number of religious terms within their language, whereas Catholic countries have proved less able to adjust their language to an oriental religion. Italy, in particular, has the highest number of untranslated words and concepts (Table 2). Notwithstanding this fact, the same figures show that the number of people converted to Buddhism across the years is much higher in Catholic countries than in nations with a Protestant or secular religious heritage.

Together with the Kanedas, the only other member to transplant and, in fact, translate in *senso strictu* Soka Gakkai Buddhism in Italy in the 1970s was an Italian woman, Amalia Miglionico, who previously lived in Japan, where she had practised Buddhism for a lengthy period of time. Miglionico became the SGI's first official translator from Japanese, and she still supervises most of the translations published in *Il Nuovo Rinascimento* and *Buddismo e Società* (another magazine published by SGI that examines religious issues in Italy). It is thanks to this three-person nucleus that an interest in the 'exotic' religious practices of the Soka Gakkai first began to grow in Italy. The initial steps may have been painfully slow, but the spread of Nichiren's Buddhism in Italian society has been nothing short of astonishing.

From the 181 SGI members registered in 1975, it had grown to some 30,000 members by 2000. This membership occurs within a highly structured organisation known as Istituto Buddista Italiano (IBIS), which is diffused throughout the entire country and is governed by a tightly woven, hierarchical network of leaders. The organisation was established in 1981. Eight years later the Italian State recognised it as a bona fide legal charity (Ente Morale) entitled to the same privileges as other religious charities. Its charter states that the organisation is 'a secular entity, with no political or financial goals'. Rather, its aim is 'to contribute to peace, culture and education based on the philosophy and ideals of the Buddhism of Nichiren Daishonin' (Charter of Soka Gakkai International, 2000).

Owing to the rapid growth of the IBIS in Italy, the International Soka Gakkai (ISG) made a formal request to the Italian State in late 1999 to be legally recognised as a religious organisation. This decision to seek legal recognition perplexed and discomfited a majority of SGI members who had joined the organisation in its early days when its carefully chosen vocabulary firmly rejected every possible link between philosophy and religion. And yet, no significant number of defections followed, and the

Table 2 How Buddhist words and concepts are represented in four European languages

Japanese	*English*	*Italian*	*French*	*German*
Gojukai	Gojukai	Gojukai	Ceremonie de reception des preceptes	Gohonzon-verlehiung
Juzu	Beads	Juzu	Chapelet Bouddhique	Kette
Jihi	Compassion	Jihi	Bienveillance Bouddhique	—
Zadankai	Discussion meeting	Zadankai	Reunion de discussion	Gruppenversamm lung
Shinrai	Guest	Shinrai	Postulant	Anfaenger
Zaimu	Kosen Rufu Fund	Zaimu	Contribution Financiere	Spende
Butsudan	Shrine	Butsudan	Autel Bouddhique	Butsudan
Onshitzu	Slander	Onshitzu	Faire onshitzu	–
Kaikan	Culture Centre	Kaikan	Centre Culturel	Kulturzentrum
Hombu	Headquarter	Hombu	Centre	Hauptstelle
Taiten	Stop practising	Taiten	Arreter la pratique	Aufhoeren-zu-praktizieren

Source: Cambiaparola, adapted from *Nuovo Rinascimento*, November 1995.
Note: The Italian spellings of Japanese names and religious termionology in this chapter have been taken from the publications of the Soka Gokkai

decision ultimately proved successful. Indeed, the year 2000 marks an historic moment for religious pluralism in Italy. That was the year when, for the very first time, the Italian government officially considered bestowing legal status upon Buddhism, as well as upon the Congregation of the Jehovah's Witnesses, both of which had previously viewed by the government as mere 'sects'. In practical terms, governmental recognition, if forthcoming, means that the Italian State must treat these two newer religions neutrally and on equal terms with older, established 'mainstream' religions such as Roman Catholicism, Protestantism and Judaism. For example, governmental recognition means that Buddhists have the same right as the Catholics to receive religious assistance in hospitals and prisons, to run their own schools, and to have their own special funeral rites observed at public cemeteries.

It is telling, however, that many older Italian converts to Buddhism were troubled by the idea of having their practice recognised as a 'religion'. Indeed, the history of Nichiren's Buddhism's diffusion in Italy is perhaps best examined by considering the problems it encountered in the definition of its statutory identity. When Buddhism was first introduced into Italy, its early pioneers were determined to undertake a massive missionary operation. They formed small discussion groups, usually held in private houses, where friends were often invited under the pretext of a dinner party. During these 'parties', in which there were endless discussions over the mysteries of life, Buddhism was always rigorously defined as a 'philosophy'. People were encouraged to think of Buddhism as a 'way of life' – a broad definition with blurred boundaries, and the perfect umbrella word under which each new convert could hope to find an answer to his or her spiritual needs. Every possible connection between the word Buddhism and the word *religione* – with its rigid, institutional overtones – was strongly discouraged or, if directly confronted, openly denied.

Simply put, a reference to *religione* would have automatically triggered a negative response and generated within the listener an awkward sense of uneasiness. *Religione* was, and remains, a strong synonym for *Chiesa*. *Chiesa* is, of course, not just any church but the Roman Catholic Church, which for 2000 years has routinely proclaimed on the Italian peninsula (and elsewhere) like Cyprian, that *salus extra ecclesiam non est* – 'there is no salvation outside of the Church' (Donna, 1995: letter 73). Thus a standard Italian dictionary definition of the word *Chiesa* refers explicitly to the Catholic Church (Devoto-Oli, 2000).

Catholicism has cast an overwhelming shadow over Italian culture, a dominance that finds expression in an enormous variety of cultural practices. 'The world' Derrida (Derrida & Vattimo, 1995: 32) wrote, 'speaks

Latin'. When religious matters are at stake, we invariably reach an impasse arising from 'global-latinisation' of the language. Terms such as 'religion', 'faith', 'piety' and 'holy' are based upon a vocabulary of dualisms, in which the influence of Western Christianity is undeniable (Derrida & Vattimo, 1995: 39). When Eastern religions are introduced into a world where the religious sense is rooted in the Bible, their vocabularies are doomed to be misunderstood.

From a Translation Studies perspective, the notion of 'religious sense' can be explained in light of what we know as a 'cultural repertoire', i.e. 'the aggregate of options utilised by a group of people, and by the individual members of the group, for the organisation of life' (Even-Zohar, 1997: 355). There is no doubt that Catholic practices constitute an Italian home-repertoire in terms of religious matters, and this appears all the more true if we consider the Roman Catholic Church not only in terms of 'official religiosity', but also in terms of what Cipriani (1989: 32) defines as 'diffused religiosity', that is, the orienting principles that support the surrounding social reality, and condition an individual's response to everyday circumstances of various kinds: moral, political, economic, judicial, or linguistic. In terms of language, an ecclesiastic terminology occupies a central position in the Italian religious system. Buddhism, as well as every other non-Catholic form of spirituality, represents an 'imported-but-not-yet-integrated' set of references that are still struggling to gain a precise status within the dominant Roman Catholic religious system (Cipriani, 1989: 32). The incapacity of the standard Italian religious vocabulary to integrate Buddhist references has its origins in the search for 'perfect equivalencies'.

A central concept in translation theory, equivalence becomes an even more dramatic goal among translators of sacred or religious texts. As well as being a professional concern, it becomes a sort of moral commitment toward texts that are believed to contain, verbatim, the word of God. When Italians have attempted to translate Buddhist words and concepts, their first and spontaneous strategy has been to search empirically for what Nida calls 'the closest natural equivalent' (Nida, 1959: 11). Nida's theories have proven to be effective in spreading the Bible to the most remote regions of our Western-centred universe among 'not only all the major language of the world, but hundreds of "primitive" tongues' (Nida, 1959: 11). But the search for dynamic equivalence has failed to bear fruit in translating Buddhism into the Italian society. Yet, Nida's scientific approach had confronted many problems of communication and provided a wealth of data and background experience. He concluded that, if differences should occur in such areas as behaviours, semantic patterns, grammatical construction or idiomatic descriptions, the translator '[is] obliged to adjust the verbal form of the translation to the requirements of the communicative process' (Nida, 1959: 12). Nida was aware that all types of translation involve 'loss, addition, or skewing of information' and he acknowledged the impossibility of absolute equivalence. In his ethnolinguistic design of communication, he states that the message has to be adjusted in accordance with the background of the receiver. However, the theory of dynamic equivalence has apparently proved incapable of working the other way round, and easing the entrance of a foreign religion into a Bible-based language context. The reason for this failure can be found in the ideology that lies at the basis of this translating approach. Bible translation was essentially a one-way approach, where the Western-Judaic word had to influence not only the religious philosophy of alien cultures, but also the very core of their vocabulary. It was a colonising task that never doubted the supremacy of its message. This is very well expressed in Nida's assumption that:

> [...] the so-called Biblical culture exhibits far more similarities with more other cultures than perhaps any other one culture in the history of civilisation. This is not strange, if one takes into consideration the strategic location of this culture in the Middle East, at the 'crossroads of the world' and at a point from which radiated so many cultural influences. This fact makes the Bible so much more 'translatable' in the many diverse cultures of the world than most books coming out of our own contemporary Western culture. This essential similarity to the cultures of so many peoples helps to explain something of the Bible's wide appeal. (Nida, 1959: 19)

In religious matters, Italy still resents the supremacy of its culture. Its historical connection with the Biblical language is felt to be the first-created original, the yardstick against which to measure all interlingual information transfer. In the search for equivalence, we act as if the agent of *tertium comparationis* was of divine nature, shifting every other religious language into a secondary position.

Before being able to translate a foreign religion successfully, Italy has to reassess the idea of its religious position as the 'crossroad of the world' and to reshape its cultural identity. James Clifford has written that all cultures are travelling cultures, in both a physical and a metaphorical sense, and that every word used to describe them is a 'translation term', a 'word of apparently general application used for comparison in a strategic and contingent way' (Clifford, 1997: 39). Clifford further maintains that all broadly meaningful concepts – fundamental words such as culture, art, society and modernity – are translations, constructed upon an imperfect equivalence. In this sense, comparative concepts are approximations that privilege certain 'originals' and were designed for specific audiences.

I am attempting here to describe the modality through which a culture (Italian culture in this case) constructs a representation of itself and then relies upon this representation to relate to other cultures. Since I am convinced that Italian culture is indivisible from Catholic practices (in both its acceptance or its rejection of them), I would argue that Italian culture's approach to understanding 'foreign' religions has been deeply contaminated and biased by the search for an 'equal' sign. Thus, an Italian approach to Buddhism, which is founded upon the non-existence of a divine essence, but nevertheless requires daily prayer to an Object of Worship (the *Gohonzon*), inevitably generates a cultural short-circuit, as the Italian mind struggles to translate the *Gohonzon* according to its pre-existent semantic category of 'god'. In the same process, such terms as *Sange* (the act of asking forgiveness) and the Daily Prayers, though meant to be self-directed, are perceived to be hetero-directed, i.e. addressed to an external entity. Other specific Buddhist practices, such as 'guidance', are similarly reconfigured to correspond to pre-existing Catholic practices, in this case, confession.

Perhaps it is no accident that Italy is home to the old saying '*traduttore traditore*' ('translator/traitor') It is a sort of cultural taboo to translate the word *religione* in non-Catholic terms, and Italian speakers would consider such an act to be one of betrayal. Buddhism 'cannot' be a religion, as it denies the idea of a supreme being or God. Any translation that incorporates this word would therefore necessarily be unfaithful to the very core of the concept. One of the foundations of Western culture is that it typically makes binary distinction between what is good and what is wrong, an attitude rampant in the field of translation. To Latin eyes, translations are like mistresses: if they are beautiful, they are unfaithful, and vice versa. In the translation of terminology pertaining to religion, the field is even more slippery. In every act of translation, translators postulate the existence of an 'original text', some ideal entity having an absolute, autonomous existence in its own right, against which any given translation can be measured by criteria of adequacy. This is all the more true, I believe, when the very word *religione* is at – involving, as it does, the notion of the unerring word of God. Jacques Derrida was doubtless correct when he provocatively wrote: 'In any case, the history of the word "religion" should in principle forbid every non-Christian from using the name "religion"' (Derrida & Vattimo, 1995: 46). Derrida then undertakes a long excursus on the etymology of the word 'religion' (and the whole subset of specialised languages annexed to its practices) that eventually led to the formation of Christian thought in

Europe, and to the development of a philosophy rooted in a dialectical dualism, an internal duplicity that defines the One and the Other.

We find Derrida's opinions echoed in the words of the Italian philosopher Benedetto Croce who wrote that 'we cannot define ourselves other than as "Christians"' (Croce, 1959:). For no matter how sincerely Italians proclaim themselves to be atheist, libertine, or agnostic, it is most unlikely that they have completely purged themselves of the heritage of 2000 years of Christian culture. Moreover, it is simply not possible for Italian culture, embedded as it is in Classical studies, to rid itself of feelings of inauthenticity when the word *religione* is applied to something other than a philosophical idea based on the existence of an 'almighty God'. Of course, Italians can accept or accommodate the existence of other religions, but these are experienced as something belonging to a foreign (therefore alien) culture, and never as something that 'we' can embrace.

But this is precisely what occurs when 'we' (Italians) decide to convert to the religious practices of the foreigner. The principal reason why people in Italy decide to join a Buddhist organisation rather than one of the dominant religious traditions in Europe lies precisely in those elements of Buddhism that are not found closer to home. Indeed, part of the attraction of a religion that is new to a culture is the opportunity to resolve stresses that are otherwise not relieved by existing cultural mechanisms. This would appear to be particularly true in the case of Nichiren Buddhism, as propagated by the Soka Gakkai, whose doctrine knowingly combines the appeal of traditional, other-worldly Buddhist wisdom with a dynamic approach to the practical and 'this-worldly' aspects of human existence. In short, Soka Gakkai Buddhism offers a powerful alternative to pre-existing forms of belief (Roman Catholicism, in our case) that, having been already absorbed by the cultural texture of society, appear less vital and less able to satisfy the needs of the masses in a period of crisis.

Among all the variations of Japanese Buddhism, the Gakkai is the one that most bears the influence of Japanese culture. While other Buddhist traditions in Japan contain components traceable to their transmission from China, Nichiren Buddhism originated in Japan and is dominated by uniquely Japanese elements. The incorporation of a foreign religion into another society is often accompanied by elements unique to the culture of that religion. This has certainly been the case with respect to the movement spread by the International Soka Gakkai in Italy. When one enters the homes of Italian members, the influence of Japanese culture is immediately apparent. The room where the *Gohonzon* or 'altar' is enshrined is often decorated with objects of Japanese derivation; for example, pictures of Mount Fuji and Japanese ideograms are tastefully displayed. Japanese influence is also evident in the members' social etiquette. At public gatherings, Italian converts display a great amount of courtesy, which is an outgrowth of the honorific vocabulary so deeply embedded in the Japanese language itself. Moreover, portraits of President Ikeda often occupy a central position in the practitioner's room, in homage to the typical Japanese inter-personal relationship pattern that follows a master–child or master–disciple model. President Ikeda is always referred to as *Sensei*, a Japanese word meaning 'master', or 'teacher', which has no translation in Italian. Indeed, the figure of President Ikeda, as perceived in Italy, offers a valuable example of the difficulties one encounters in the translation of an Oriental religion into a Catholic cultural repertoire. For although Soka Gakkai's Buddhism proclaims absolute equality among all human beings, with no clergy or priests to mediate between man and the sacred, the figure of this charismatic leader is often equated to that of the Pope and endowed with the same qualities of holiness and infallibility.

And so, returning to the cartoon mentioned at the beginning of this chapter, the reason – and the consequences – of this domestic case of 'untranslatability' become clearer. (The cartoon remained unpublished for fear of offending Catholic sensibilities.) For the first time since the establishment of the Roman Catholic Church, Italy is confronting the spread of new religious movements that are challenging its cultural foundations and hegemony. This would normally entail a radical reformation of its vocabulary but, for the time being, the Italian language has proven itself unable to translate the core of Buddhism and has been forced to introduce a large number of Japanese words among its speakers. Further, since Buddhism came to Italy via English translations of Nichiren Daishonin's and Ikeda's Japanese texts (from SGI UK and SGI USA), the whole ritual terminology is now expressed using both Japanese and English words and phrases, thus giving rise to a jargon that is comprehensible only to Italian members of the organisation. And, on those few occasions when English words are actually translated into Italian, they have been contaminated by false Anglicisms. Thus, 'piety' is translated as *pietà* (pity), 'to chant' becomes *cantare*, 'dedication' becomes *dedicazione* (a word that does not exist in proper Italian). The cartoon (Figure 4) depicts the tools for the ritual of *zadankai*. It is interesting to note that this act of 'gathering together and praying' is, in unofficial situations, sometimes referred to as *andare a Messa*, no doubt because there is a Buddhist 'altar' enshrining the object of worship. Or, in Italian non-translation, there is a *butsudan* enshrining a *Gohonzon*. Until very recent times, the participants to the ceremony used to leave their shoes outside the room and kneel facing the *Gohonzon*, following the Japanese tradition. This use was understood as an integral part of the ritual, and only elderly people used to sit in chairs. In its early days, Buddhism was learnt through imitation: the first Italian converts considered their Japanese co-religionists as a model for faith and behaviour, and their actions were observed and passed on to new converts in the form of strict rules. Thus, behaviours peculiar to Japanese culture, such as the extreme formality and politeness, the attention to particulars, the act of bowing when speaking to people and the ever-present smile during social interactions, were all part of the training for new adepts. Rigid discipline was considered a sign of strong faith, and new converts were encouraged to chant long hours of *daimoku* while taking particular care to maintain the correct upright position in front of the *Gohonzon*, kneeling in almost absolute immobility in order to reach the necessary mental concentration. This unnecessary and formal rigidity, utterly alien to the teachings of Nichiren Buddhism as propagated by the International Soka Gakkai, was the result of a naive error in the Italian interpretation of Japanese behaviour. It also reveals the profound confusion that existed, and still exists, in Italy regarding foreign religions, and Oriental religions in particular. Although Italy has a long and ancient philological tradition in Oriental studies, the works of Giuseppe Tucci, Eugenio Ghersi and others have always been confined to the academy, and have never reached a wider public (Polezzi, 1998: 321). The popular approach to eastern spirituality was derived from the counter-culture of the early 1970s, largely via the mediation of American literature in translation, as well as cinema, music and various New Age practices. For the large majority of Italians, the figure of Buddha still coincides with the romantic protagonist of Hermann Hesse's *Siddharta* (1922) a novel beloved by generations of Italians (so well beloved that it is commonly acknowledged to be the most stolen book in libraries and bookshops).

Since the 1970s, the Italian conception of Buddhism has also been linked to Zen practices or, more accurately, to stereotypical notions of what Zen was believed to be, with its corollary of individual meditation, silence and self-discipline. It was perhaps inevitable that the first Italian converts to Nichiren Buddhism transposed their idea of Buddhism into their everyday practice. Oddly enough, when the Japanese leaders decided to speak in favour of a more relaxed way of performing the ritual, adjusting it to the more easy-going Italian nature, such a new orientation was difficult to accept, for it did not correspond to the original 'model' of Eastern religious practices that had been deposited within the Italian repertoire of accepted ideas.

The predilection for rigid discipline can also be explained in relation to the dominant religious background of Roman Catholicism, which, as it is understood in Italy, is a religion that emphasises the virtues of suffering and enduring privations. Accordingly, it has filled the popular imagination with a wealth of iconographic representations such as Christ's Calvary and Crucifixion, weeping Madonnas and sanctified Martyrs. Italian Buddhists viewed this pre-existing model of a purgatorial path to salvation as a necessary component of any religion, and thus naturally translated it into their own practices as the 'purgatorial discipline' required to achieve Buddhahood.

When two such different religions meet, they offer a fascinating case study in terms of language and translation strategies. It is too soon to attempt any preview of future developments. An interest in a new religion always entails an interest in a new philosophy and a new culture, and translators and editors are aware of the need to make ethical choices in order to balance the 'function' of their translations and the 'loyalty' to the source culture (Nord, 2001: 185). For the time being, Italian translators have been confronting the primary need to be communicative, and to make Buddhism accessible to an Italian audience. At the same time, they have preserved a significant amount of linguistic and stylistic features of the source culture, thus underlying the foreignness and otherness of Buddhist teachings. In the translation of the written texts (Ikeda's guidance and Nichiren's *Gosho*), the semantic barrier between Japanese and Italian has not been challenged. The key terms of Buddhism are not translated, and are provided with a large number of explanatory footnotes. More notes are required for the explanation of the crucial principles of the philosophy, such as *Itai Doshin* (the importance of unity among the believers) or *Ichinen Sanzen* (3000 worlds contained in a single moment of life). Very often the texts maintain both the highly mannered circumlocutions of Japanese speech and the rich metaphors typical of an Oriental culture. Footnotes are also required when the decoding of such metaphors and allegories is too obscure to Italian eyes. Two periodicals and a publishing house have been established to guarantee the circulation of the texts throughout the national territory. But since religion is something that has to be put into practice, the true force of the Italian Soka Gakkai lies in oral discourse. Italian practitioners perform a tremendous amount of voluntary Buddhist activities. In addition to the *zadankai* (discussion meetings) held every other week, the monthly schedule of a 'standard' practitioner includes one study meeting, where the Gosho is explained, together with other meetings according to the *divisione* he or she belongs to (young or adult, male or female). Even more meetings are scheduled for the *responsabili* (leaders), who are to be prepared to teach the newcomers. In such a hierarchical and capillary organisation, the vocabulary choices play a major role. The basics of Buddhism are often taught by *responsabili* who have barely mastered the philosophy themselves.

Their paraphrases and examples are thus built on the only religious language they are familiar with: the language of Catholicism.

In this first phase of the spreading of Soka Gakkai Buddhism in Italy, then, misunderstanding and false interpretations of the doctrine appear to be inevitable, and it is possible to conclude that for the time being the translation of a Japanese religion into a Catholic background has settled into a blending of religious practices, ideas and elements that have given birth to a hybrid religious practice perhaps better defined as *catto-buddismo*.

Bibliography

Abdul-Raof, H. (2001a) *Qur'an Translation: Discourse, Texture and Exegesis.* Richmond: Curzon.

Abdul-Raof, H. (2001b) *Arabic Stylistics.* Wiesbaden: Harrassowitz Verlag.

Adoremus, Society for the Renewal of the Sacred Liturgy. On WWW at: www.adoremus.org. Accessed 25.10.04.

Ali, A.Y. (1983) *The Holy Qur'an: Text, Translation and Commentary.* Maryland: Amana Corp.

Ali Ibn Abu Taleb (1984) *Nahjul Balagha: Peak of Eloquence.* Elmhurst, NY: Tahrike Tarsile Qur'an.

American Bible Society. On WWW at http://www.americanbible.org/about/. Accessed 25.10.04.

Andersen, D. (1998) Perceived authenticity: The fourth criterion of good translation. *Notes on Translation* (SIL) 12 (3), 1–13.

Asad, M. (1980) *The Message of the Qur'an Translated and Explained.* Gibraltar: Dar al-Andalus.

Baker, M. (ed.) (1998) *The Encyclopedia of Translation Studies.* London and New York: Routledge.

Barber R. and Riches, A. (1971) *A Dictionary of Fabulous Beasts.* Ipswich: The Boydell Press.

Barks, C. (trans.) (1999) *The Glance: Rumi's Songs of Soul-meeting.* New York: Viking.

Barnwell, K. (1975/1986) *Bible Translation: An Introductory Course in Translation Principles* (3rd revised edn). Dallas: SIL.

Barnwell, K. (1987) *Teacher's Manual to Accompany Bible Translation: An Introductory Course in Translation Principles* (3rd edn). Dallas: SIL.

Barthes, R. (1977) *Roland Barthes* (R. Howard, trans.). New York: Hill and Wang.

Bassnett, S. (1980/1991) *Translation Studies.* London and New York: Routledge.

Bassnett, S. and Lefevere, A. (eds) (1990) *Translation, History and Culture.* London: Cassell.

Bassnett, S. and Lefevere, A. (eds) (1998) *Constructing Cultures: Essays on Literary Translation.* Topics in Translation 11. Clevedon: Multilingual Matters.

Bassnett, S. and Trivedi, H. (eds) (1999) *Post-colonial Translation: Theory and Practice.* London: Routledge.

Baxter, R. (1998) *Bestiaries and Their Users in the Middle Ages.* Stroud: Sutton Publishing Limited.

Beekman, J. and Callow, J. (1974) *Translating the Word of God.* Grand Rapids: Zondervan.

Bell, A. (1984) Language style as audience design. *Language in Society* 13 (2), 145–204.

Bell, A. (2001) Back in style: Reworking audience design. In P. Eckert and J.R. Rickford (eds) *Style and Sociolinguistic Variation.* Cambridge: Cambridge University Press.

Benjamin, W. (1968) The task of the translator. In *Illuminations* (H. Zohn, trans.). New York: Suhrkamp. [Also reprinted in Venuti, 2000: 15.]

Bethel, D.M. (1989) *Makiguchi the Value Creator.* New York: Weatherhill.

Beylard-Ozeroff, A., Kralova, J. and Moser-Mercer, B. (eds) (1998) *Translators' Strategies and Creativity.* Amsterdam: John Benjamins.

Bhabha, H. (1994) *The Location of Culture.* London: Routledge.

Bhaktivedanta Swami Prabhupāda, A.C. (trans.) (1968) *Bhagavad Gītā As It Is.* Los Angeles: The Bhaktivedanta Book Trust.

Bible: Revised Standard Version (1974) The British and Foreign Bible Society (19th impression). London: Collins Clear-Type Press.

Billigheimer, S. (1968) On Jewish translations of the Bible in Germany. *Abr-Nahrain* 7, 1–34.

Black, M. (1998) *An Aramaic Approach to the Gospels and Acts* (3rd edn). Introduced by C.A. Evans. Peabody MA: Hendrickson.

Bobrick, B. (2001) *Wide as the Waters: The Story of the English Bible and the Revolution it Inspired.* New York: Simon and Schuster.

Böckler, A. (2001) *Die Tora nach der Übersetzung von Moses Mendelssohn mit den Prophetenlesungen in Amhang.* Berlin: Jüdische Verlagsanstalt.

Brassard, F. (2000) *The Concept of Bodhicitta in Sāntideva's Bodhicaryāvatāra.* New York: State of New York University Press.

Brenneis, D. (1986) Shared territory: Audience, indirection and meaning. *Text* 6 (3), 339–47.

Brockington, J.L. (2001) Sanskrit. In P. France (ed.) *The Oxford Guide to Literature in English Translation.* Oxford: Oxford University Press.

Browning, R. (1913) *Poems.* Oxford: Oxford University Press.

Bruce, F. (1961) *The English Bible: A History of Translations.* London: Lutterworth Press.

Buber, M. and Rosenzweig. F. (1994) *Scripture and Translation* (English translation). Bloomington: Indiana University Press).

Burglassi, S. (1968) *Il Comportamento Religioso degli Italiani.* Firenze: Vallecchi.

Burglassi, S. (1980) *Uno Spiraglio sul Futuro. Interpretazione Sociologica del Cambiamento Sociale in Atto.* Pisa: Giardini Editori.

Buswell, R.E. (ed.) (1990) *Chinese Buddhist Apocrypha.* Honolulu: University of Hawaii Press.

Calvaruso, C. and Abbruzzese, S. (1985) *Indagine sui Valori in Italia. Dai Post-materialismi alla Ricerca del Senso.* Torino: SEI.

Campbell, J. (1996/2000) *Deciphering the Dead Sea Scrolls.* Oxford: Blackwell.

Carson, D. (1985) The limits of dynamic equivalence in Bible translation. *Notes on Translation* (SIL) 121, 1–15. [Reprinted from *Evangelical Review of Theology* 9 (3).]

Carson, D. (1998) *The Inclusive Language Debate: A Plea for Realism.* Grand Rapids: Baker.

Catford, J. (1965) *A Linguistic Theory of Translation: An Essay in Applied Linguistics.* London: Oxford University Press.

Charter of Soka Gakkai International (2000) Printed in every edition of the monthly magazine *Art of Living* available from Taplow Court, Taplow, Maidenhead, Berkshire, SL6 0ER, UK.

Chesterman, A. (ed.) (1989) *Readings in Translation Theory.* Helsinki: Oy Finn Lectura Ob.

Chomsky, N. (1957) *Syntactic Structures.* Gravenhage: Mouton.

Ciobotea, D. (1990) Liturghia ortodoxă: Viziune de via ă atotcuprinzătoare. *Altarul Banatului* 1–2, 25–8.
Cipriani, R. (1989) 'Diffused religion' and new values in Italy. In J. Beckford and T. Luckmann (eds) *The Changing Face of Religion* (pp. 24–49). London: Sage.
Clifford, J. (1997) *Routes: Travel and Translation in the late Twentieth Century.* Cambridge, MA: Harvard University Press.
Cloud, D. (2001) *Dynamic Equivalency: Death Knell of Pure Scripture*. Port Huron: Way of Life Literature. On WWW at www.wayoflife.org.
Conze, E. (1959) *Buddhist Scriptures*. London: Penguin Classics.
Cooper, J. M. (ed.) (1997) *Plato: Complete Works.* Indianapolis: Hackett.
Cranmer, T. (1549) *Prologue to the Great Bible*. On WWW at http://www.gospel com.net/chi/pastwords/chl036.shtml.
Croce, B. (1959) *Perché non Possiamo non Dirci 'Cristiani'*. Bari: Laterza.
Crosby, K. (2000) Tantric Theravada: A bibliographic essay on the writings of François Bizot and other literature on the Yogavacara Tradition. *Journal of Contemporary Buddhism* November (2), 141–198.
Crystal, D. (1995) *The Encyclopedia of the English Language*. Cambridge: Cambridge University Press.
Daiches, D. (1941) *The King James Version of the English Bible: An Account of the Development and Sources of the English Bible of 1611 with Special Reference to the Hebrew Tradition*. Chicago: University of Chicago Press.
Daishonin, N. (2000) *Kumarajiva: Theosophy Library.* On WWW at http://theosophy.org/tlodocs/teachers/Kumarajiva.htm.
Daniell, D. (ed.) (1995) *Tyndale's New Testament 1534.* New Haven: Yale University Press.
Davidson, R.M. (1990) An introduction to the standards of Scriptural authenticity in Indian Buddhism. In R.E. Buswell (ed.) *Chinese Buddhist Apocrypha*. Honolulu: University of Hawaii Press.
Davis, N. and Robinson, R. (1999) Religious cosmologies: Individualism and politics in Italy. *Journal for the Scientific Study of Religion* 38 (3), 339–353.
Dawood, N. (1966 edn) *The Koran*. Harmondsworth: Penguin Books.
Dayras, S. (1993) The Knox version, or the trials of a translator: Translation or transgression? In D. Jasper (ed.) *Translating Religious Texts: Translation, Transgression and Interpretation* (pp. 44–59). London: St Martin's Press.
Delisle, J. and Woodsworth, J. (eds) (1995) *Translators Through History.* Amsterdam: John Benjamins.
Derrida, J. (1981) *Positions* (A. Bass, trans.). London: Athlone Press.
Derrida, J. (1985) Des Tours de Babel. In J. Graham (ed. and trans.) *Difference in Translation*. Ithaca, NY: Cornell University Press. [Also in G. Anidjar (ed.) 2002. *Acts of Religion* (pp. 104–134). London: Routledge.]
Derrida, J. (1987) *De la Grammatologie* (p. 227). Paris: Les Editions de Minuit.
Derrida, J. (1993) *Memoirs of the Blind. The Self-Portrait and Other Ruins* (P. Brault and M. Naas trans). Chicago: Chicago University Press.
Derrida, J. and Vattimo, G. (eds) (1995) *La Religione.* Roma-Bari: Laterza.
Devoto-Oli (2002) *Dizionario della Lingua Italiana*. Firenze: Le Monnier.
Dickens, J., Hervey, S. and Higgins, I. (2002) *Thinking Arabic Translation*. London: Routledge.
Digby, S. (2001) *Sufis and Soldiers in Awrangzeb's Deccan*. Delhi: Oxford University Press.

Diodati, D. (1843) *De Christo Graece Loquente Exercitatio: Qua Ostenditur Graecam Sive Hellenisticam Linguam cum Judaeis Omnibus, Tum ipsi Adeo Christi Domino, et Apostolis Nativam, ac Vernaculam Fuisse* (O.T. Dobbin, ed.). London: John Gladding.

Divine Liturgy of St John Chrysostom (1939) Leighton Buzzard: The Faith Press Ltd.

Dodd, C.H. (1961) *The Parables of the Kingdom.* London: James Nisbet.

Donna, R. (trans.) (1995) *Cyprian, Letters 1–81 The Fathers of the Church* (Vol. 51). Washington, DC: Catholic University of America Press.

Douglas, J.D. (ed.) (1990) *The New Greek–English Interlinear New Testament*. Wheaton, IL: Tyndale House.

Douglas-Klotz, N. (1999) *The Hidden Gospel: Decoding the Spiritual Message of the Aramaic Jesus*. Wheaton, IL: Quest Books.

Dumoulin, H. (ed.) (1976) *Buddhism in the Modern World.* New York: Collier Macmillan Publishers.

Duthie, A. (1995) *How to Choose Your Bible Translation Wisely.* Carlisle: Paternoster Press.

Dutt, S. (1988) *Buddhist Monks and Monasteries of India: Their History and Their Contribution to Indian Culture.* Delhi: Motilal Banaarsidass.

Eliot, T.S. (1979) *The Dry Salvages* (3rd of *Four Quartets*). London: Faber.

ESV (2002) *ESV FAQs* (promotional material for the English Standard Version Bible). Wheaton, IL: Good News Publishers/Crossway Books. On WWW at http://www.gnpcb.org/page/esv_faq.

Edgerton, F. (trans.) (1994) *The Bhagavad Gītā* (two vols. in one). Delhi: Motilal Banarsidass (first published in 1944).

Erasmus, D. (1516) *Exhortations to the Diligent Study of Scripture.* Hanover, IN: Hanover College History Department. On WWW at http://history. hanover.edu/courses/excerpts/346erasmus.html. Accessed 25.10.04.

Erlanger, S. (1997) Albright sees an ambitious world mission for US. *New York Times,* 6 June, A8.

Ernst, C.W. (1992) The textual formation of oral teachings in early Chishtī sufism. In J.R. Trimm (ed.) *Texts in Context: Traditional Hermeneutics in South Asia* (pp. 271–297). New York: State University of New York Press.

Esmail, A. (2002) *A Scent of Sandalwood: Indo-Ismaili Religious Lyrics.* Richmond: Curzon.

Even-Zohar, I. (1997) The making of culture repertoire and the role of transfer. *Target* 9 (2), 355–363.

Even-Zohar, I. (1998) Some replies to Lambert and Pym. *Target* 10 (2), 363–369.

Even-Zohar, I. (1978/1990/2000) The position of translated literature within the polysystem. In L.Venuti (ed.) (2000) *The Translation Studies Reader.* London and New York: Routledge.

Even-Zohar, I. (2001) Laws of cultural interference. Draft in work. On WWW at http://www.tau.ac.il/~itamarez/papers/culture-interference.htm

Farrell, T. and Hoyle, R. (1995) Translating implicit information in the light of Saussurean relevance and cognitive theories. *Notes on Translation* (SIL) 9 (1), 1–15.

Farrell, T. and Hoyle, R. (1997) The application of Relevance Theory: A response. *Notes on Translation* (SIL) 11 (1), 19–26.

Fawcett, P. (1998) Ideology and translation. In M. Baker (ed.) *Routledge Encyclopedia of Translation Studies* (pp. 106–111). London: Routledge.

Fernández Marcos, N. (2000) *The Septuagint in Context: Introduction to the Greek Versions of the Bible*. Leiden: Brill.
Finaldi, G. (2000) *The Image of Christ*. London: National Gallery.
Fisch, H. (1997) *The Jerusalem Bible*. Jerusalem: Koren.
Fitton, P. (1998) Reasons why evangelicals should not use the New International Version of the Bible. On WWW at http://www.ianpaisley.org/article/asp?ArtKey=niv.
Focus on the Family (1997) Guidelines for translation of gender-related language in scripture (facsimile). 3 June. On WWW at http:/www.cbmw.org/resources/nivi/guidelines.php. Accessed 22.10.04.
Ford, B. (ed.) (1992) *Medieval Britain: The Cambridge Cultural History*. Cambridge: Cambridge University Press.
Foucault, M. (1972) *The Archaeology of Knowledge* (M. Sheridan Smith, trans.). London: Tavistock.
Fox, E. (1995) *The Schocken Bible* (Vol. 1): *The Five Books of Moses. A New Translation with Introductions, Commentary, and Notes*. New York: Schocken.
France, P. (ed.) (2000) *The Oxford Guide to Literature in English Translation*. Oxford: Oxford University Press.
Frost, D.L. (1973) *The Language of Series 3*. Grove Booklets No. 12. Bramcote: Grove Books.
Gavigan, J. (trans. and ed.) (1966) On Christian Instruction. In *Fathers of the Church: Saint Augustine* (Vol. 2). Washington: Catholic University of America Press.
Geddes, J. (2003) Commentary on the St Albans Psalter. On WWW at http://www.abdn.ac.uk/diss/historic/stalbanspsalter.
Gibson, M., Heslop, T.A. and Pffaf, R. (eds) (1992) *The Eadwine Psalter: Text, Image and Monastic Culture in Twelfth Century Canterbury* (Vol. 14). London and University Park: MHRA (in conjunction with The Pennsylvania State University Press).
Gildea, G. and Surmont, E. (1914) *The Holy Bible from the Latin Vulgate and Compared with Douai (1609) and Rheims (1582)*. London: Burns Oates and Washbourne Ltd.
Giles, H, Coupland, N. and Coupland, J. (1991) Accommodation theory: Communication, context, and consequence. In H. Giles, J. Coupland, N. Coupland, K. Oatley and A. Manstead (eds) *Contexts of Accommodation*. Cambridge: Cambridge University Press.
Gilman, A.E. (2002) Between religion and culture: Mendelssohn, Buber, Rosenzweig and the enterprise of biblical translation. In F.W. Knobloch (ed.) *Biblical Translation in Context* (pp. 93–114). Bethesda: University of Maryland Press.
Goerling, F. (1996) Relevance and transculturation. *Notes on Translation* (SIL) 10 (3), 49–57.
Goffman, E. (1981) *Forms of Talk*. Oxford: Blackwell.
Gombrich R. (1978) Kosala-bimba-vannana. In H. Bechert (ed.) *Buddhism in Ceylon and Studies on Religious Syncretism in Buddhist Countries*. Göttingen:Vandenhoeck and Ruprecht.
Gombrich, R. (1992) The Buddha's Book of Genesis? *Indo-Iranian Journal* 35, 159–78.
Goodwin, C. (1986) Audience diversity, participation and interpretation. *Text* 6 (3), 283–316.
Goody, J. (1987) *The Interface Between the Oral and the Written*. Cambridge: Cambridge University Press.
Gordon, C. (2004) *The Cotton Patch Gospel*. Macon, GA: Smyth and Helwys.

Graham, W.A. (1985) Qur'an as spoken word: An Islamic contribution to the understanding of scripture. In R.C. Martin (ed.) *Approaches to Islam in Religious Studies* (pp. 23–40). Tucson: University of Arizona Press.
Greenspahn, F.E. (2002) How Jews translate the Bible. In F.W. Knobloch (ed.) *Biblical Translation in Context* (pp. 43–61). Bethesda: University of Maryland Press.
Greenspoon, L. (1987) *Max Leopold Margolis: A Scholar's Scholar*. Atlanta: Scholars Press.
Greenspoon, L. (1988) A book 'without blemish': The Jewish Publication Society's Bible translation of 1917. *Jewish Quarterly Review* 79, 1–21.
Greenspoon, L. (1993) From the Septuagint to the New Revised Standard Version: A brief account of Jewish involvement in Bible translating and translations. In M.I. Gruber (ed.) *The Solomon Goldman Lectures* (Vol. 6, pp. 19–50). Chicago: Spertus College of Judaica Press.
Greenspoon, L. (1999) Traditional text, contemporary contexts: English-language scriptures for Jews and the history of Bible translating. In J. Krasovec (ed.) *Interpretation of the Bible* (pp. 565–576). Sheffield/Ljubljana: Sheffield Academic Press.
Greenspoon, L. (2002a) Jewish Bible translation. In J. Barton (ed.) *The Biblical World* (Vol. 2, pp. 397–412). London: Routledge.
Greenspoon, L. (2002b) Top dollar, bottom line? Marketing English-language Bibles within the Jewish Community. In F.W. Knobloch (ed.) *Biblical Translation in Context* (pp. 115–133). Bethesda: University of Maryland Press.
Greenspoon, L. (2002c) The birth of a Bible. *Norii* (10). Online Romanian journal of culture and ideas. On WWW at http://www.revistanorii.com/Revista_Norii.html.
Greenspoon, L. (2003a) Jewish translations of the Bible. In A. Berlin and M. Brettler (eds) *The Jewish Study Bible*. New York: Oxford University Press.
Greenspoon, L. (2003b) Jewish Bible translation in/and the Enlightenment. *Studia Hebraica* 2.
Greenstein, E. (1989a) *Essays on Biblical Method and Translation*. Atlanta: Scholars Press.
Greenstein, E. (1989b) What might make a Bible translation Jewish? In *Translation and Scripture* (pp. 77–101). Proceedings of a Conference at the Annenberg Research Institute May 14–16. Philadelphia: Annenberg Research Institute.
Greenstein, E. (1990) The scroll of Esther: A new translation. *Fiction* 9 (3), 52–81.
Greenstein, E. (1992) Wordplay, Hebrew. In D.N. Freedman (ed.) *Anchor Bible Dictionary* (Vol. 6, pp. 986–971). New York: Doubleday.
Gregorios of Thyateira (1995) *The Divine Liturgy of Our Father among the Saints John Chrysostom*. Oxford: Oxford University Press.
Grimes, B.F. (ed.) (2000) *Ethnologue: Languages of the World* (14th edn). Dallas: SIL. On WWW at http://www.ethnologue.com/web.asp.
Gutas, D. (1998) *Greek Thought, Arabic Culture: The Graeco-Arabic Translation Movement in Baghdad and Early 'Abbāsid Society (2nd–4th/8th–10th Centuries)*. London: Routledge.
Gutt, E-A. (1988) From translation to effective communication. *Notes on Translation* (SIL) 2 (1), 24–40.
Gutt, E-A. (1992) *Relevance Theory: A Guide to Successful Communication in Translation*. Dallas and New York: SIL and United Bible Societies.
Gutt, E-A. (2000a) *Translation and Relevance: Cognition and Context* (2nd edn). Manchester: St Jerome.

Gutt, E-A. (2000b) Urgent call for academic reorientation. *Notes on Sociolinguistics* (SIL) 5 (2), 47–56.
Hallisey, C. (1995) Roads taken and not taken in the study of Theravada. In D.S. Lopez, Jr. (ed.) *Curators of the Buddha: The Study of Buddhism under Colonialism* (pp. 31–61). Chicago: Chicago University Press.
Handelman, S.A. (1982) *The Slayers of Moses: The Emergence of Rabbinic Interpretation in Modern Literary Theory.* Albany: State University of New York Press.
Hardwick, L. (2000) *Translating Words, Translating Cultures.* London: Duckworth.
Hargreaves, C. (1993) *A Translator's Freedom: Modern English Bibles and Their Language.* Sheffield: JSOT Press.
Hart, K. (1989) *The Trespass of the Sign*. Cambridge: Cambridge University Press.
Hastings, J. (ed.) (1909/1963) *Dictionary of the Bible*. Edinburgh: T. and T. Clark.
Hatim, B. and Mason, I. (1990) *Discourse and the Translator.* London and New York: Longman.
Hatim, B. and Mason, I. (1997) *The Translator as Communicator.* London and New York: Routledge.
Heidegger, M. (1993) Letter on humanism. In D.F. Krell (ed.) *Basic Writings* (pp. 213–265). London: Routledge.
Herbert, A.S. (1968) *Historical Catalogue of Printed Editions of the English Bible 1525–1961*. London and New York: British and Foreign Bible Society and American Bible Society.
Hertz, J.H. (1938) Jewish translations of the Bible in English. In *Sermons, Addresses and Studies* (Vol. 2)*: Addresses*. London: Soncino.
Hertz, J.H. (1961) *The Pentateuch and Haftorahs*. London: Soncino.
Hesse, H. (1922) *Siddharta*. Berlin: S. Fischer. [First Italian edition (1945) Turin: Frassinelli.]
Hickey, L. (ed.) (1989) *The Pragmatics of Style*. London: Routledge.
al-Hilali, M.T. and Khan, M.M. (1983) *Translation of the Noble Qur'an*. Madinah: King Fahad Complex for the Printing of the Holy Qur'an.
Hills, M.T. (1962) *The English Bible in America: A Bibliography of Editions of the Bible and the New Testament Published in America 1777–1957*. New York: American Bible Society and the New York Public Library.
von Hinüber, O. (1996) *A Handbook of Pāli Literature*. New Delhi: Motilal Banarsidass.
Hirshman, M. (1996) *A Rivalry of Genius: Jewish and Christian Biblical Interpretation in Late Antiquity* (B. Stein, trans.). Albany, NY: SUNY Press.
Hooper, J.S.M. (1963) *Bible Translation in India, Pakistan and Ceylon* (W.J. Culshaw, ed.). Bombay: Oxford University Press (original work published 1904).
Horner, I.B. (1938) *Book of the Discipline*. Oxford: Oxford University Press.
House, J. (1973) On the limits of translatability. *BABEL* (19), 166–167.
Hunter, A.M. (1960) *Interpreting the Parables.* London: SCM.
Ingalls, D.H.H. (trans.) (2000) *Sanskrit Poetry from Vidyākāra's 'Treasury'* (4th edn). Cambridge, MA: Harvard University Press.
Jackson, D.P. (1987) *The Entrance Gate for the Wise (Section III): Sa-skya Paṇḍita on Indian and Tibetan Traditions of Pramāṇa and Philosophical Debate* (2 vols). Wiener Studin zur Tibetologie und Buddhismuskunde, Heft 17 (I–II). Wien: Arbeitskreis für Tibetische und Buddhistische Studien.
Jacobson, R. (1959) On linguistic aspects of translation. In R. Brower (ed.) *On Translation.* Cambridge, MA: Harvard University Press.

Jasper, D. (ed.) (1993) *Translating Religious Texts: Translation, Transgression, and Interpretation*. New York: St Martin's Press.
Jeremias, J. (1972) *The Parables of Jesus*. London: SCM.
Jerome (395) *Letter LVII to Pammachius on the Best Method of Translating* (English translation). On WWW at http://www.ccel.org/fathers/NPNF2-06/letters/letter57.htm.
Jobes, K.H. and Silva, M. (2000) *Invitation to the Septuagint*. Grand Rapids: Baker.
Johnson, W.J. (trans.) (1994) *The Bhagavad Gītā*. Oxford: Oxford University Press.
Jordan, C. (1968–1973) On WWW at http://rockhay.tripod.com/cottonpatch/
Kāmgār Khān (c.1739) Malfūzāt-e-Shāh Nizām al-dīn Awliyā Awrangābādī. Unpublished manuscript. Taunsa, Pakistan: Shrine Library of Shah Sulayman.
Kaplan, A. (1981) *The Living Torah: The Five Books of Moses*. New York: Maznaim Publishing.
Kapstein, M. (2000) *The Tibetan Assimilation of Buddhism: Conversion, Contestation and Memory*. Oxford: Oxford University Press.
Kellam, L. (1609) *The Holie Bible Faithfully Translated: Early English Out of the Authentical Latin* (Roman version). Doway.
Kermode, F. (1979) *The Genesis of Secrecy*. Cambridge, MA: Harvard University Press.
Kittel, H. and Poltermann, A. (1998) German tradition. In M. Baker (ed.) *Routledge Encyclopedia of Translation Studies* (pp. 418–428) London: Routledge.
Kokkinakis, A., Archbishop of Thyateira and Great Britain (trans.) (1979) *The Liturgy of the Orthodox Church*. London: Mowbrays.
Kress, G. (1985) *Linguistic Processes in Sociocultural Practice*. Victoria: Deakin University Press.
Ladinsky, D. (1999) (trans.) *The Gift: Poems by Hafiz the Great Sufi Master*. New York: Penguin Arkana.
Lambert. J. (1998) 'Communication societies': Comments on Even-Zohar's 'Making of culture repertoire'. *Target* 10 (2), 353–356.
Larsen, I. (2001) The fourth criterion of a good translation. *Notes on Translation* (SIL) 15 (1), 40–53.
Larson, M.L. (1984) *Meaning-based Translation*. Lanham, MD: University Press of America.
Latham, R.E. (1983) *Revised Medieval Latin Word-List From British and Irish Sources with Supplement*. Oxford: The British Academy with Oxford University Press.
LeBlanc, D. (1997) Hands off my NIV! Bible Society cancels plans for 'gender-accurate' Bible after public outcry. *Christianity Today* 16 June, 52–53, 55.
LeBlanc, D. and Rabey, S. (1997) Bible translators deny gender agenda. *Christianity Today* 14 July, 62–64.
Leenhardt, J. (1980) Towards a sociology of reading. In S. Suleiman and I. Crosman (eds) *The Reader in the Text: Essays on Audience and Interpretation*. Princeton: Princeton University Press.
Lefevere, A. (1992a) *Translation, Rewriting and the Manipulation of Literary Fame*. London: Routledge.
Lefevere, A. (1992b) *Translation, History, Culture*. London: Routledge.
Lewis, F.D. (2000) *Rumi Past and Present, East and West*. Oxford: Oneworld.
Lias, J.J. (ed.) (1886) *Cambridge Greek Testament for Schools and Colleges: The First Epistle to the Corinthians*. Cambridge: Cambridge University Press.
Liddell, H.G. and Scott, R. (1951) *A Greek–English Lexicon*. Oxford: Clarendon Press.

Lieber, D.L., Harlow, J., United Synagogue of Conservative Judaism and The Rabbinical Assembly (2001) *ETZ HAYIM: Torah and Commentary*. Philadelphia: Jewish Publication Society.

Liturgicam Authenticam. On WWW at http://www.vatican.va/roman_curia/congregations/ccdds/documents/rc_con_ccdds_doc_20010507_liturgiam-authenticam_en.html. Accessed 25.10.04.

Lobsang Rampa, T. (1965/1991) *Wisdom of the Ancients*. London: Atlantic Books.

Lobsang Rampa, T. (1956/1995) *The Third Eye*. New York: Ballantine Books.

Lobsang Rampa, T. (1967/1997) *Chapters of Life*. New York: Buccaneer Books.

Long, L. (2001) *Translating the Bible: From the Seventh to the Seventeenth Century*. Aldershot: Ashgate.

Lopez, D.S. (1988) *Prisoners of Shangri-La: Tibetan Buddhism and the West*. Chicago: University of Chicago Press.

Luther, M. (1530/1940) *Ein Sendbrief vom Dolmetschen*. London: Duckworth. On WWW at http://www.german.sbc.edu/sendbrief.html. English translation on WWW at http://www.iclnet.org/pub/resources/text/wittenberg/luther/luther-translate.txt. or at www.bibleresearcher.com/luther01.html.

Macauliffe, M. (1963) *The Sikh Religion* (6 vols). Delhi: S. Chand (original work published 1909).

McGrath, A. (2001) *In the Beginning: The Story of the King James Bible and How It Changed a Nation, a Language, and a Culture*. New York: Doubleday.

Macioti, M.I. (1996) *Il Buddha che è in Noi. Germogli del Sutra del Loto*. Roma: SEAM.

McLeod, W.H. (ed. and trans.) (1984) *Textual Sources for the Study of Sikhism*. Manchester: Manchester University Press.

Mahmud Awrangabadi (2001/1939–40) Malfūzāt-e-Naqshbandiyya: Hālāt-e-Hazrat Bābā Shāh Musāfir Sāhib. Hyderabad: Nizamat-e-'Umur-e-Mazhabi-e-Sarkar-e-'Ali. In S. Digby (trans.) *Sufis and Soldiers in Awrangzeb's Deccan*. Delhi: Oxford University Press (original work published in 1358).

Malalasekera, G.P. (1928/1994) *The Pāli Literature of Ceylon*. Kandy, Sri Lanka: Buddhist Publication Society.

Mani, V. (1975) *Purāṇic Encyclopaedia: A Comprehensive Dictionary with Special Reference to the Epic and Purāṇic Literature* (1st English edn). Delhi: Motilal Banarsidass.

Marchisio, R., and Pisati, M. (1999) Belonging without believing: Catholics in contemporary Italy. *Journal of Modern Italian Studies* 4 (2), 236–255.

Margolis, M.L. (1917) *The Story of Bible Translations*. Philadelphia: Jewish Publication Society of America.

Marlowe, M. (2004) Against the theory of dynamic equivalence. On WWW at http://www.bible-researcher.com/dynamic-equivalence.html.

Mascaró, J. (trans.) (1962) *The Bhagavad Gītā*. Harmondsworth: Penguin Books.

Mason, I. (2000) Audience design in translating. *The Translator* 6 (1), 1–22.

Mathews, E. (1990) History of mission methods: A brief survey. *Journal of Applied Missiology* (Abilene Christian University) 1 (1). On WWW at http://missionsweb.net/ACU/page.asp?ID=297.

Mayer, R. (1996) *A Scripture of the Ancient Tantra Collection: The Phur-pa Bcu-gnyis*. Oxford: Kiscadale Publications.

Métraux, D.A. (1994) *The Soka Gakkai Revolution*. Lanham: University Press of America.

Mojadeddi, J.A. (2001) *The Biographical Tradition in Sufism: The Tabaqat Genre from al-Sulami to Jami*. London: Curzon.

Moore, S.D. (1992) *Mark and Luke in Poststructuralist Perspective: Jesus Begins to Write.* New Haven: Yale University Press.
Moore, S.D. (2001) *God's Beauty Parlour and Other Queer Spaces In and Around the Bible.* Stanford: Stanford University Press.
Moule, C.F.D. (1959) *An Idiom Book of New Testament Greek* (2nd edn). Cambridge: Cambridge University Press.
Munday, J. (2001) *Introducing Translation Studies: Theories and Applications.* London Routledge.
Murata, K. (1971) *Japan's New Buddhism*. New York: Weatherhill.
al-Nadim, Muhammad ibn Ishaq ibn (1970) *The Fihrist of al-Nadim: A Tenth Century Survey of Muslim Culture* (B. Dodge, trans.). New York: Columbia University Press.
Nairne, A. (ed.) (1917) *The Epistle to the Hebrews*. Cambridge: Cambridge University Press.
Navras (2000) *Abida Parween: Songs of the Mystics.* Navras Records NRCD 5505/6.
Netton, I.R. (1997) *A Popular Dictionary of Islam.* Surrey: Curzon.
Newmark, P. (1988) *A Textbook of Translation*. London: Prentice Hall.
Newmark, P. (1991) *About Translation*. Clevedon: Multilingual Matters.
Nicholson, R.A. (ed. and trans.) (1925–40) *The Mathnawi of Jalalu'ddin Rumi* (8 vols). London: Luzac.
Nida, E. (1959) Principles of translation as exemplified by Bible translating. In R. Brower (ed.) *On Translation* (pp. 11–31). Cambridge, MA: Harvard University Press.
Nida, E. (1947/1974) *Bible Translating: An Analysis of Principles and Procedures.* New York: American Bible Society.
Nida, E. (1964) *Towards a Science of Translating*. Leiden: Brill.
Nida, E. (1995) Translators' creativity versus sociolinguistic constraints. In A. Beylard-Ozeroff, J. Kralova and B. Moser-Mercer (eds) *Translators' Strategies and Creativity* (pp. 127–136). Amsterdam: John Benjamins.
Nida, E. (1998) Bible translation. In M. Baker (ed.) *Routledge Encyclopedia of Translation Studies* (pp. 22–28). London: Routledge.
Nida, E.A. and Taber, C.R. (1969) *The Theory and Practice of Translation*. Leiden: United Bible Societies and Brill.
Niranjana, T. (1992) *Siting Translation: History, Post-structuralism, and the Colonial Context*. Berkeley: University of California Press.
Nizam ad-din Awliya (1992) *Morals for the Heart* (B.B. Lawrence, trans.). New York: Paulist Press.
Nord, C. (1997) *Translating as a Purposeful Activity: Functionalist Approaches Explained.* Manchester: St Jerome Publishing.
Nord, C. (2001) Loyalty revisited: Bible translation as a case in point. *The Translator* 72, 185–202.
Norman, K.R. (1983) *Pāli Literature*. Wiesbaden: Otto Harrassowitz.
Norri, J. (1998) *Names of Body Parts in English: 1400–1550*. Academia Scientiarum Fennica.
Noss, P. (2001) UBS Translation Program in 2000: Revisiting the UBS Translation Program: From 'the unfinished task' to 'the cutting edge of the Kingdom of God'. On WWW at http://www.biblesociety.org/transrep2000.htm.

O'Flaherty. W.D. (1987) On translating Sanskrit myths. In W. Radice and B. Reynolds (eds) *The Translator's Art: Essays in Honour of Betty Radice* (pp. 121–128). Harmondsworth: Penguin Books.

Olasky, S. (1997) Bailing out of the stealth Bible. *World* 14/21 June, 1–7.

Orlinsky, H.M. (1969) *Notes on the New Translation of the Torah*. Philadelphia: Jewish Publication Society of America.

Orlinsky, H.M. (1974) *Essays in Biblical Culture and Bible Translation*. New York: KTAV.

Orlinsky, H.M. (1990) The role of theology in the Christian mistranslation of the Hebrew Bible. In *Translation and Scripture,* Proceedings of a Conference at the Annenberg Research Institute May 14–16, 1989 (pp. 117–137). Philadelphia: Annenberg Research Institute.

Orlinsky, H.M. (1992) Versions, Jewish. In *Anchor Bible Dictionary* (Vol. 6, pp. 838–842). Garden City: Doubleday.

Orlinsky, H.M. and Bratcher, R.G. (1991) *A History of Bible Translation and the North American Contribution.* Atlanta: Scholars Press.

Orthodox Liturgy, The (1939/1982) London: The Society for Promoting Christian Knowledge.

Orthodox Liturgy, The (1982) Oxford: Oxford University Press.

Pächt, O., Dodwell, C.R. and Wormald, F. (1960) *The St Albans Psalter* (Albani Psalter). London: The Warburg Institute, The University of London.

Pagels, E. (1979) *The Gnostic Gospels.* London: Penguin Books.

Phillips, J.B. (trans.) (1947/1955) *Letters to Young Churches*. London: Fontana Books.

Pickthall, M. (1969) *The Meaning of the Glorious Koran*. London: George Allen and Unwin.

Pietersma, A. (2002) A new paradigm for addressing old questions: The relevance of the interlinear model for the study of the Septuagint. In J. Cook (ed.) *Bible and Computer.* Leiden: Brill.

Plaut, W.G. (1981) *The Torah: A Modern Commentary.* New York: Union of American Hebrew Congregations.

Plaut, W.G. (1996) *The Haftorah Commentary.* New York: Union of American Hebrew Congregations.

Polezzi, L. (1998) Rewriting Tibet: Italian travellers in English translation. *The Translator* (Special issue: *Translation and Minority*) 4 (2), 321–340.

Pollard, A. (ed.) (1911) *Records of the English Bible.* London: Henry Frowde.

Polythress, V.S (2002) The TNIV debate: No. *Christianity Today* 46/11 (7 October), 37–43.

Polythress, V.S. and Gruden, W. (2000) *The Gender-Neutral Bible Controversy: Muting the Masculinity of God's Words.* Nashville: Broadman and Holman.

Prabhavananda Swāmi and Isherwood, C. (1944) *The Bhagavad Gītā*. Hollywood, CA: The Marcel Rodd Co.

Purohit Swāmi, S. and Yeats, W.B. (trans.) (1937/1970) *The Ten Principal Upanishads*. London: Faber and Faber.

Pym, A. (1998) Note on a repertoire for seeing cultures. *Target* 10 (2), 357–361.

Quiller-Couch, A. (ed.) (1919) *The Oxford Book of English Verse: 1250–1900* Oxford: Clarendon Press.

Quine, W.V. (1960) *Word and Object.* Cambridge, MA: Technology Press of the Massachusetts Institute of Technology.

Ramanujan, A.K. (1999a) Some thoughts on 'non-Western' classics: With Indian examples. In V. Dharwadker, S. Blackburn, J.B. Carmen, E.C. Dimock and W. Doniger (eds) *The Collected Essays of A.K. Ramanujan* (pp. 115–123). Delhi: Oxford University Press.

Ramanujan, A.K. (1999b) Three hundred *Rāmāyanas*: Five examples and three thoughts on translation. In V. Dharwadker, S. Blackburn, J.B. Carmen, E.C. Dimock and W. Doniger (eds) *The Collected Essays of A.K. Ramanujan* (pp. 131–160). Delhi: Oxford University Press.

al-Razi, Fakr al-Din M. (1990) *al-Tafsir al-Kabir* (32 vols). Beirut: Dar al-Kutub al-'Ilmiyyah.

Realms of Faith: *Comparing Bible Translations*. On WWW at wysiwyg://4/http://faith.propadeutic.com/questions.html and also at http://www.cob-net.org/compare.htm. Accessed 25.10.04.

Redfield, R. (1956) *Peasant Society and Culture: An Anthropological Approach to Civilization*. Chicago: University of Chicago Press.

La Repubblica (2000) March 21, p. 29.

Reynolds, L.D. and Wilson, N.G. (1984) *Scribes and Scholars: A Guide to the Transmission of Greek and Latin Literature*. Oxford: Clarendon Press.

Rhodes, E. and Lupas, L. (eds) (1997) *The Translators to the Reader: The Original Preface of the King James Version of 1611 Revisited*. New York: American Bible Society.

Rhys Davids, T.W. (1899/1910/1921) *Dialogues of the Buddha* (3 vols). Oxford: Oxford University Press (reprinted by the Pāli Text Society).

Ricoeur, P. (1995) *Figuring the Sacred*. Minneapolis: Fortress Press.

Robinson, D. (1998a) Free translation. In M. Baker (ed.) *Routledge Encyclopedia of Translation Studies* (pp. 87–90). London: Routledge.

Robinson, D. (1998b) Literal translation. In M. Baker (ed.) *Routledge Encyclopedia of Translation Studies* (pp. 125–127). London: Routledge.

Robinson, H. (ed.) (1940/1954) *The Bible in its Ancient and English Versions*. Oxford: Clarendon Press.

Rouse, W.H.D. (1895) *The Jātaka or Stories of the Buddha's Former Births* (Vol. 2). Cambridge: Cambridge University Press (reprinted by the Pāli Text Society).

Ruegg, D. Seyfort (1992) Some reflections on translating Buddhist philosophical texts from Sanskrit and Tibetan. *Asiatische Studien/Études Asiatiques* 46 (1), 367–391.

Rumi (2002) Bibliographical data. On WWW at htp://ssgdoc.bibliotek.uni-halle.de/vlib/ssgfi/infodata/002384.html. Accessed 25.10.04.

Ryken, L. (2002) *The Word of God in English: Criteria for Excellence in Bible Translation*. Wheaton: Crossway.

Sa-paṇ (Sakya Paṇḍita Kunga Gyaltshen) (1992) *mkhas* pa rnams 'jug pa'i sgo zhes bya ba'i bstan bcos [The treatise called entryway into scholarship]. In *Chab spel tshe brtan phun tshog*, gtsho 'gan dpe sgrig pa (ed.) Sa-paṇ kun dga' rgyal mtshan gyi gsung 'bum, legs bam dang po [Vol. 1]. Gangs can rig mdzod 23 (pp. 367–501). Bod ljongs bod yig dpe rnying dpe skun khang [Tibet: Old Tibetan Text Publishers].

Sa-paṇ (Sakya Paṇḍita Kunga Gyaltshen) (2002) *A Clear Differentiation of the Three Codes: Essential Differentiations Among the Individual Liberation, Great Vehicle, and Tantric Systems* (J. Rhoton, trans., M. Kapstein, ed.) SUNY Series in Buddhist Studies. Albany: State University of New York.

Sale, G. (trans.) [1734] *The Koran Translated into English from the Original Arabic*. London: Frederick Warne.

Samuel, G. (1993) *Civilized Shamans: Buddhism in Tibetan Societies*. Washington: Smithsonian Institute Press.

Sandon, N. and Page, C. (1992) Music. In B. Ford (ed.) *Medieval Britain: The Cambridge Cultural History* (pp. 214–48). Cambridge: Cambridge University Press.

Sarna, J.D. (1989) *JPS: The Americanization of Jewish Culture 1888–1988*. Philadelphia: Jewish Publication Society of America.

Sarna, J.D. and Sarna, N. (1988) Jewish Bible scholarship and translations in the United States. In E.S. Frerichs (ed.) *The Bible and Bibles in America* (pp. 83–116). Atlanta: Scholars Press.

Schaff, P. and Wace, H. (eds) (1979) Letter to Pammachius no. lviii. In *Nicene and Post Nicene Fathers* (Vol. 6). St Jerome, MI: Eerdman.

Schleiermacher, F. (1813) On the different methods of translating. In R. Schulte and J. Biguenet (eds) (1992) *Theories of Translation: An Anthology of Essays from Dryden to Derrida*. Chicago: University of Chicago Press.

Schulte, R. and Biguenet, J. (eds) (1992) *Theories of Translation: An Anthology of Essays from Dryden to Derrida*. Chicago: University of Chicago Press.

Shackle, C. and Awde, N. (eds and trans) (1999) *Treasury of Indian Love Poems and Proverbs from the Indian Sub-continent, in the Languages of India and English*. New York: Hippocrene.

Shackle, C. and Mandair, A.S. (eds and trans) (forthcoming) *Sikh Scriptures: Selected Readings*. London: Routledge.

Shackle, C. and Moir, Z. (eds and trans) (2000) *Ismaili Hymns from South Asia: An Introduction to the Ginans*. Richmond: Curzon.

Shaffer, E.S. (2000) (ed.) East and West: Comparative perspectives. *Comparative Criticism 22*. Cambridge: Cambridge University Press.

al-Shiqiti, Muhammad al-Amin (1996) *Athwa' al-Bayan* (10 vols). Beirut: Dar al-Kutub al-'Ilmiyyah.

Simms, K. (ed.) (1997) *Translating Sensitive Texts: Linguistic Aspects*. Amsterdam: Rodopi.

Simon, S. (1996) *Gender in Translation: Cultural Identity and the Politics of Transmission*. London: Routledge.

Singerman, R. (1990) *Judaica Americana: A Bibliography of Publications to 1900* (2 vols). New York: Greenwood Press.

Singh, G. (trans.) (1960) *Sri Guru-Granth Sahib* (4 vols). Delhi: Gur Das Kapur. [5th edn revised in modern idiom, 1978. New Delhi: World Sikh Centre.]

Singh, M. (trans.) (1962) *Sri Guru Granth Sahib* (8 vols). Amritsar: Shiromani Gurdwara Parbandhak Committee.

Singh, N.G.K. (trans.) (1995) *The Name of my Beloved: Verses of the Sikh Gurus*. San Francisco: Harper Collins.

Singh, S. (trans.) (1982) *Asa di Var: The Ballad of God and Man, by Guru Nanak*. Amritsar: Guru Nanak Dev University.

Sisam, C. and Sisam, K. (eds) (1959) *The Salisbury Psalter*. Early English Text Society, 242. London: Oxford University Press.

Smith, M. (2001) The translators' preface. In A. McGrath (ed.) *Christian Literature: An Anthology* (pp. 356–375) Oxford: Blackwell.

Smith, W. C. (1993) *What is Scripture?* London: SCM Press.

Snell-Hornby, M., Pöchhacker, F. and Kaindl, K. (eds) (1994) *Translation Studies: An Interdiscipline*. Amsterdam: John Benjamins.

Snell-Hornby, M. (1988/1995) *Translation Studies: An Integrated Approach.* Amsterdam: John Benjamins.
Snell-Hornby, M. *et al.* (eds) (1997) *Translation as Intercultural Communication.* Amsterdam: John Benjamins.
Snellgrove, D. (1987) *Indo-Tibetan Buddhism: Indian Buddhists and Their Tibetan Successors* (2 vols). Boston: Shambhala.
Soka Gakkai Translation Committee (eds) (1999) *The Writing of Nichiren Daishonin.* Tokyo: Soka Gakkai.
Spencer, A.B. (1997) Power play: Gender confusion and the NIV. *Christian Century* 2/9 July, 618–619.
Spiro, M. (1971) *Buddhism and Society: A Great Tradition and its Burmese Vicissitudes.* London: George Allen and Unwin.
Stamps, DL. (1993) Interpreting the language of St Paul. In D. Jasper (ed.) *Translating Religious Texts: Translation, Transgression and Interpretation* (pp. 21–43). New York: St Martin's Press.
Steer, R. (1996) Pushing inward. *Christian History.* On WWW at http://www.christianitytoday.com/ch/52h/52h10a.html and also at http://www.christianitytoday.com/ch/52h/52h10b.html.
Steiner, G. (1975/1992/1998) *After Babel.* London: Oxford University Press.
Steiner, G. (1993) Preface to D. Jasper (ed.) *Translating Religious Texts.* London: Macmillan.
Stine, P.C. (2004) *Let the Words be Written.* Atlanta, GA: Society of Biblical Literature.
Strauss, M. (1998) *Distorting Scripture? The Challenge of Bible Accuracy and Gender Accuracy.* Downers Grove, IL: Intervarsity.
Strauss, M. (2002) The TNIV debate: Yes. *Christianity Today* 46/11 (Oct 7), 37–43.
Sussman, L.J. (1985) Another look at Isaac Leeser and the first Jewish translation of the Bible in the United States. *Modern Judaism* 5, 159–190.
Takla, H.N. (1996) *The History of the Coptic Language.* On WWW at http://www.stshenouda.com/coptlang/copthist.htm.
Talbot, C.H. (ed.) (1959) *The Life of Christina of Markyate: A Twelfth Century Recluse.* Oxford: Clarendon Press.
Tanakh (1985) *A New Translation of the Holy Scriptures According to the Traditional Hebrew Text.* Philadelphia: Jewish Publication Society of America.
Tanach, The (1996) *The ArtScroll Series/Stone Edition.* Brooklyn: Mesorah Publications.
Taylor, M.C. (ed.) (1986) *Deconstruction in Context: Literature and Philosophy.* Chicago: Chicago University Press.
Taylor, V. (1966) *The Gospel According to St Mark* (2nd edn). London: Macmillan.
Thackeray, H.St.J. (trans.) (1904) *The Letter of Aristeas.* London: Macmillan.
Thompson, R. (1982) *Manuscripts from St Albans Abbey 1066–1235* (Vol. I): *Text.* Woodbridge: D.S. Brewer.
Tillemans, Tom J.F. (2000) *Dharmakīrti's Pramāṇavārttika.* An annotated translation of the fourth chapter (parārthānumāna) (Vol. 1). Wien: Verlag der Österreichischen Akademie der Wissenschaften.
Today's English Version (1973). New York: American Bible Society.
Toury, G. (1978) The nature and role of norms in literary translation. In J.S Holmes, J. Lambert and R. van den Broeck (eds) *Literature and Translation: New Perspectives in Literary Studies.* Leuven: Acco.
Toury, G. (1995) *Descriptive Translation Studies and Beyond.* Amsterdam: John Benjamins.

Toury, G. (1997) Culture planning and translation. In A. Alvarez *et al.* (eds) Proceedings of the Vigo Conference 'Anovadores de nos, anosadores de vos'. On WWW at http://www.tau.ac.il/~toury/works/gt-plan.htm. Accessed 25.10.04.

Trumpp, E. (trans.) (1877) *The Adi Granth.* London: W.H. Allen.

Tucci, G. (1980) *The Religions of Tibet* (G. Samuel, trans.). Berkeley: University of California Press.

Tymoczko, M. (1999) *Translation in a Postcolonial Context*. Manchester: St Jerome Publishing.

Tyndale, W. (2000) *The New Testament 1526.* London: British Library in association with the Tyndale Society.

Unger, C. (1996) Types of implicit information and their roles in translation. *Notes on Translation* (SIL) 10 (4), 18–30.

United Bible Societies (1999) *Bibla: Dhiata e Vjetër dhe Dhiata e Re.* Albania.

United Bible Societies (2002a) *Incredible Growth in Scripture translation*. On WWW at http://www.biblesociety.org/trans-gr.htm.

United Bible Societies (2002b) *Latest News #185*. On WWW at http://www.bible society.org/latestnews/latest185-slr2001.html.

United Bible Societies (2002c) *2001 Scripture Language Report*. New York: United Bible Societies.

Van Buitenen, J.A.B. (trans.) (1981) *The Bhagavad Gītā in the Mahābhārata*. Chicago: University of Chicago Press.

Vatican online. On WWW at www.vatican.va. Accessed 25.10.04.

Veinstein, G. (1995) L'oralité dans les documents d'archives ottomans: Paroles rapportées ou imaginées? *Revue du Monde Musulman et de la Mediterranée* 75–76 (Special edition: *Oral et écrit dans le monde turco-ottoman), 133–142.*

Venuti, L. (1995) *The Translator's Invisibility: A History of Translation.* London: Routledge.

Venuti, L. (1998a) *The Scandals of Translation: Towards an Ethics of Difference* London: Routledge.

Venuti, L. (1998b) Strategies of translation. In M. Baker (ed.) *Routledge Encyclopedia of Translation Studies* (pp. 240–244). London: Routledge.

Venuti, L. (ed.) (2000) *The Translation Studies Reader.* London: Routledge.

Vermeer, H. (1989) Skopos and commission in translational action. In A. Chesterman (ed.) *Readings in Translation Theory.* Helsinki: Oy Finn Lectura Ob.

Vermeer, H. (1996) *A Skopos Theory of Translation*. Heidelberg: TEXTconTEXT – Verlag.

Waard, J. de and Nida, E. (1986) *From One Language to Another: Functional Equivalence in Bible Translating.* Nashville: Thomas Nelson.

Weber, R. (ed.) (1969) *Biblia Sacra iuxta Vulgatam Versionem* (2 vols): *Tomus I Genesis-Psalmi.* Stuttgart: Wurttembergische Bibelanstalt.

Wendland, E.R. (1996) On the relevance of 'Relevance Theory' for Bible translation. *The Bible Translator* 47 (1), 126–137.

White, J.W. (1970) *The Sokagakkai and Mass Society.* Stanford, CA: Stanford University Press.

Whorf, B.L. (1956) *Language, Thought, and Reality; Selected Writings* (J.B. Carrol, ed.). Cambridge, MA: Technology Press of the Massachusetts Institute of Technology.

Williams, D. (1996) *Deformed Discourse: The Function of the Monster in Medieval Thought and Literature*. Exeter: University of Exeter Press.

Wilson, B. and Cresswell, J. (eds) (1999) *New Religious Movements: Challenge and Response*. London: Routledge.
Winternitz, M. (1933) *A History of Indian Literature* (Vol. 2): *Buddhist and Jaina Literature* (V.S. Sarma, trans. 1983). New Delhi: Motilal Banarsidass.
Wilt, T. (1998) Review of Lawrence Venuti's '*The Translator's Invisibility: A History of Translation*' (1995). *The Bible Translator* 49 (1), 148–152.
Wright, A. (1990) *Studies in Chinese Buddhism*. Newhaven: Yale University Press.

About the Contributors

Hussein Abdul-Raof was born in Baghdad, Iraq, and is a Senior Lecturer in Arabic and Qur'anic Studies at the University of Leeds, UK. He has published widely on Arabic stylistics and Qur'an translation.

David Burke comes from New York and until 2003 was Dean of the Nida Institute for Biblical Scholarship and Director of the Department of Translations and Scripture Resources in the American Bible Society. He has published many articles on aspects of Bible translation and on Jewish/Christian issues.

Kate Crosby lectures in Buddhist Studies in the Department of the Study of Religions in the School of Oriental and African Studies in London, UK. Her main research interests are in the Theravada Buddhism of Sri Lanka and mainland South East Asia, and Pāli literature.

Manuela Foiera divides her time between Italy and the University of Warwick, UK, where she is researching the impact of Italian religious identity on the translation of Japanese Buddhist terms. She has given and published many papers on translation.

Jonathon Gold is a specialist in Indo-Tibetan Buddhism currently teaching in the Department of Religion at the University of Vermont, USA. His research areas are Buddhist intellectual history and Western philosophy of religion.

Nile Green is a Research Fellow in the Theology Faculty at Oxford University, UK. He has published many articles on the literature and social history of Islamic mysticism and has a particular interest in Sufism in the Deccan from the 17th to the 20th centuries, popular Islam and Indo-Persian Sufi literature.

Leonard Greenspoon holds the Klutznick Chair in Jewish Civilization at Creighton University, USA, and is Professor of Classical and Near Eastern Studies and of Theology. His prolific publications on Scripture translation include books, book chapters, articles and conference papers.

David Jasper is Professor of Literature and Theology at the University of Glasgow, UK, and has interests bridging both fields. His many publications include works on the Bible and literature and on translating religious texts.

Will Johnson teaches Hinduism and Jainism in the Department of Religious and Theological Studies at the University of Cardiff, UK. He is also an experienced translator of the Indian epic the *Mahābhārata.*

Peter Kirk was a member of SIL International for ten years and continues to work on Bible translation projects, mainly in Azerbaijan. His articles are informed by his work in the field. He is based in South-East England, but travels extensively.

Lynne Long teaches Translation Studies at the University of Warwick, UK. She has published on the history of translation and on the translation of the Bible into English.

Sue Niebrzydowski is a medievalist whose research interests range from manuscript study through Middle English drama to medieval wedding customs. She teaches in the department of English and Comparative Literature at the University of Warwick, UK, and has published many articles and research papers.

Adriana Şerban teaches at the University of Montpellier, France. She has a background of Translation Studies and Linguistics and particular knowledge of the Orthodox Church. Her publications include articles on literary translation as well as linguistic features.

Christopher Shackle is Professor of Modern Languages of South Asia, in the Department of the Languages and Cultures of South Asia and Professor in the Department of the Study of Religions at the School of Oriental and African Studies, London, UK. His experience and expertise in these areas are demonstrated in his numerous publications and translations.

K. Onur Toker's area of study covers Translation Studies, Philosophy and Comparative Cultural Studies. He teaches and researches in the University of Warwick, UK.

Index